# THE EVILS OF THEODICY

# THE EVILS OF THEODICY

Terrence W. Tilley

*Georgetown University Press*
Washington, D.C.

**Library of Congress Cataloging-in-Publication Data**

Tilley, Terrence W.
    The evils of theodicy / Terrence W. Tilley.
        p.   cm.
    Includes bibliographical reference and index.
    ISBN 0-87840-508-9.  --  ISBN 0-87840-511-9 (pbk.)
    1. Theodicy--Controversial literature.  2. Theodicy--History of
doctrines.  I. Title.
BT160.T55    1991
214--dc20                                                    90-29069
                                                                  CIP


1  2  3  4  5  6  7  8  9  10

For Jack and Audrey Tilley

# CONTENTS

# ACKNOWLEDGMENTS

I have incurred many debts in writing this book. William P. Alston, David Carl Baker, Elizabeth Clark, James Crenshaw, Mary McClintock Fulkerson, Stanley Hauerwas, L. Gregory Jones, Joseph Kroger, James W. McClendon, Jr., Charles Muenchow, William L. Newell, Kate Olgiati, John Priest, David Rainwaters, Kenneth Surin, Peter Tumulty, and James P. M. Walsh have read parts of earlier versions of the text, and saved me from numerous errors; those which remain can be attributed only to my failure to heed their advice. Eleanor Waters, senior editor at Georgetown University Press, has improved the clarity and style of my writing and John Breslin, Director of the Press, has also offered many suggestions for improvement. Working with them has been a delight. Students at St. Michael's College, Vermont, and the Florida State University have challenged me to make my ideas clearer. I am in debt to all of them.

The National Endowment for the Humanities enabled me to participate in a Summer Seminar for College Teachers on "Friendship, the Life of Virtue, and Happiness," directed by Hauerwas at Duke University in 1985. The first early trials of some of the material now in chapters 2, 3, and 8 were developed for that seminar. The great success of that seminar led me to direct a Summer Seminar for Secondary School Teachers on "Job, Boethius, and J.B.," also funded by the NEH, at St. Michael's College, Vermont, in 1987. I deeply appreciate the intensity and enthusiasm my fellow teachers brought to our work; they enabled me to understand the texts treated in chapters 4 and 6 more fully than I ever had before. The NEH also awarded me a Fellowship for College Teachers, enabling me to complete work on the penultimate version of this book and to write a number of other essays during the 1987-88 academic year.

St. Michael's College granted me a sabbatical leave for 1986-87 and graciously extended that leave for 1987-88 so I could accept the NEH Fellowship. The Divinity School of Duke University granted me the status of a visiting scholar from 1986 to 1988 which made the University's excellent libraries available to me. I am grateful to the administrations of both institutions for their support of this work. While at Duke, I participated in the "Theology and Ethics Area Seminar" during the spring of 1988 in the Graduate Religion Program, which gave me an opportunity to develop some of the ideas in chapter 7. The final revisions were completed in the friendly and challenging atmosphere of my new academic home, the religion department of the Florida State University.

An overview of the project was presented as "The Morality of Theodicies" at the Annual Meeting of the American Academy of Religion, Philosophy of Religion Section, Atlanta, Georgia, November 1986, and an earlier version of part of chapter 6 was presented as "A Text for Reinscribing a Self: The Rhetoric of Boethius' *Consolation of Philosophy*" at the Annual Meeting of the American Academy of Religion Rhetoric and Religious Discourse Group, Anaheim, California, November 1989. Earlier versions of some of the material in chapter 4 and most of chapter 7 have appeared, respectively, as essays in *Modern Theology* and *The Journal of the American Academy of Religion*. I am grateful to their editors for permission to use that material here.

Maureen Tilley has given much time to reading and rereading the book at various stages and offering numerous suggestions for improvement, even while she was taking courses, preparing for her own Ph.D. exams, and doing research for her dissertation. Our daughters, Christine (who helped prepare the index) and Elena, have supported us magnificently in our work. We both thank them.

After I had begun the final revisions, I obtained copies of the important new works of Nel Noddings, *Women and Evil* and Rebecca Chopp, *The Power to Speak*. I am most sympathetic with their works. Noddings' unceasing concern with the particularity of evils and her delineation of cultural evils parallels my discussion of social evils. I have not only drawn examples from her work, but learned much from her insights. Chopp's questioning of dominant discourses in Christianity and her valorizing of discourses of emancipatory transformation proceed from a theoretical perspective different from mine, but our investigations are, I believe, generally compatible. Had their works been available when I started my work, my task would have been much easier.

Finally, the book is dedicated to my parents, Audrey and Jack Tilley. What I owe them can never be repaid, but only acknowledged. My deepest thanks go to them.

T.W.T.

March 1990

# INTRODUCTION

This is a book about God and evils. But it is not a theodicy, a 'solution' to the "problem of evil." It is about the problems such solutions create in their attempts to justify God's ways to those who think *the* problem of evil is solved by producing an explanation.

As the predominant modern theological and philosophical discourse practice about God and evil, theodicy misportrays and effaces genuine evils. It warps the way traditional texts are read today. It consigns other discourse about God and evil to philosophical and theological irrelevance. It silences powerful voices of insight and healing. It contributes to the power of the "classical" Humean problem of evil, the alleged incoherence of belief in an all-powerful, all-good, all-knowing God, and that there is genuine evil in the world. These are some of the evils of theodicy. This book seeks to counteract those evils, to overthrow the hegemony of theodicy by making audible the voices theodicists silence and uncovering the insights of the texts theodicists obscure and erase.

An unforgettable incident taught me the power of one of those voices. I had taken many bodies down to the morgue. Over some—many of those I had nursed—I wept. Over all, I prayed. But in my first year as a hospital orderly, I was called to the newborn nursery late one night and told to take to the morgue a baby who had lost her fight for life. She fit comfortably on my left arm like any newborn—placing her on a guerney would have been a silly waste of time. Her receiving blanket covered her face. I expected the elevator to travel nonstop to the basement. But much to my horror, the car stopped and a man and a woman walked in. The door closed. They looked at my starched white uniform, my silent bundle, my frozen face. As we rode down, the man said very simply, "I could never do your job." As the car reached the lobby, he took the woman's arm and they left me alone with my burden. I finished the ride and placed the body in the morgue's storage compartment.

Yet the man's words remain with me, well over two decades later. They were "just the right thing to say." His words were powerful. In those words, he expressed his understanding of a difficult situation, his sadness at the death of the child, and his support for a stranger engaged in a wrenching task. Yet the philosophy I would later study would construe his words as 'merely pastoral,' even irrelevant to the *real* issues of theodicy. That philosophy would rule the wail of the new widow I had held close in the emergency room to be merely "an emotional outburst." That philosophy would declare the powerful impact of my first lecture ever on the problem of evil mere rhetorical manipulation—for at its beginning I had to tell my class that one of their number was hospitalized in a coma after a car accident. That philosophy would recognize as "worthy of serious consideration" and as "central to understanding the problem of evil" scores of articles whose discourse about God and evils is always abstracted so far from concrete issues and particular linguistic uses that the actual issues which people face outside the paper walls built by academic journals disappear from their view. That philosophy would construct the problem of evil as a problem to be solved by a cool and detached explanation, not by a commitment to actions undertaken in order to alleviate the various particular evils, academic and otherwise.

Theodicy proper is a modern undertaking. The theodicy project was initiated in the seventeenth century and received a definitive first version in 1702 with the publication of *De Origine Mali* by the Anglican archbishop of Dublin, William King. Pierre Bayle and G. W. F. Leibniz responded to King's work. His text was translated into English by Edmund Law in 1731 and went through five printings over the next half century. All of these—and their contemporary descendants—center on the project of explaining how there could be evil in God's world.

The term "theodicy" was coined by Leibniz as the title of his 1710 text, which "explains" how the present world is the best of all possible worlds. Yet the term's meaning has been extended to cover numerous other projects. For instance, in his discussion of the problem of integrating anomic forces into the myth that legitimates a social order, Berger sees "theodicy" as a legitimation structure for maintaining the society (1969:59). He claims, "It is not happiness that theodicy primarily provides, but meaning" (58); theodicy is "an attempt to make a pact with death" (80). But theodicy *proper* neither provides meaning (in Berger's sense) to suffering individuals nor does it personify the power of death. In his extended sense, Berger subsumes all discourse on the meaning of suffering—even legitimation of monistic or atheistic cosmoi—under the rubric of "theodicy." However, such extended uses of the term blind one to the unique problems and power of the Enlightenment practice of theodicy proper, a practice which serves to marginalize all other discourse about God and evil.

Indeed, once one stops collapsing all discourse about God and evil into one form, the differences between dry, measured, cool, calm, abstract academic voices and nonacademic voices are obvious. They sound in very different discourse practices. But the contrast between my own academic and nonacademic voices has brought me to see that the relation between concrete and particular discourses, and abstract and general academic discourse, is not one of mere difference. Rather, the usual practice of academic theodicy has marginalized, homogenized, supplanted, 'purified,' and ultimately silenced those expressing grief, cursing God, consoling the sorrowful, and trying practically to understand and counteract evil events, evil actions, and evil practices. I have come to see theodicy as a discourse practice which disguises real evils while those evils continue to afflict people. In short, engaging in the discourse practice of theodicy *creates* evils, not the least of which is the radical disjunction of 'academic' philosophical theology from 'pastoral' counsel.

To counteract the evils of theodicy is, at least in part, an academic task. For theodicy as it is now practiced is an academic discourse, created in the context of Enlightenment theism and developed throughout the modern era. Denunciations of academic theodicy from pulpits or platforms outside academia are not effective because academics find them easy—often justifiably easy—to ignore. To go one's own way and ignore the practice is to leave it unchallenged as the proper way to talk of evil among the philosophical and theological elites in our society. To undermine and counteract the practice of theodicy demands developing arguments inside academia, not abandoning academia.

I have constructed three interrelated analyses for this purpose. First, we must understand the power of the words we use. This requires understanding them as parts of acts performed in particular contexts, that is, acts performed in circumstances, with purposes, and having results. The man who comforted me long ago in an elevator might have used the same words in different contexts, and thus performed different acts with those words, e.g., refusing a job, expressing disgust, etc. The first part of the book develops a pragmatic speech act theory which describes and analyzes the types of linguistic acts performed in religious contexts. Speech act theory shows the actions we perform in speaking and gives a way of understanding their power and moral worth. It provides a grid for showing how we use words to state, to create, to alleviate, to obscure, and to solve problems of sins and sufferings.

Chapter 1 sketches speech act theory, including the constituents of and conditions for engaging in these linguistic practices. The next two chapters analyze linguistic acts in religious discourse. Chapter 2 analyzes actions which one can perform only if one is in specific institutional or social situations, e.g., only an authorized official in a religious institution can *excommunicate* heretics. Chapter 3 analyzes those acts which one can perform without regard to the speaker's institutional or social location, e.g., one doesn't have to be in any specific social, geographical, or institutional place to *pray*.

This pragmatic speech act perspective reveals distinctions and connections philosophers and theologians too often ignore. It shows how bishops, theologians, and ordinary believers, who have different roles in a religious discourse practice, perform crucially different actions with different sense and significance, even though they say "the same thing." It shows how doctrines are properly connected with ritual and ethical practices. For example, I show below why one does not have to believe there is a God to engage in petitionary prayer to God and why dissenting theologians within the Catholic tradition in no way attack the authority of the bishops to teach.[1]

Revealing these important differences in what people do with their words is especially significant for understanding resolutions of the problems of evil. For instance, consider Marx's claim that religion is the opiate of the people. Theologians' and philosophers' debates on the accuracy of that claim have degenerated into little more than shouting matches—when they don't give up and ignore the claim completely. Speech act theory provides a way to preserve Marx's insight and revise his oversight by construing "You will get your reward in heaven" not merely as a proposition which can be true or false, but as a constituent in a communicative action. If her confessor offered Mother Teresa of Calcutta consolation on her deathbed using these words, it is unlikely that he would be administering a verbal opiate—and even if he were, much less likely that his act would be immoral. Yet if a wealthy churchman preached that doctrine to peasants indentured by his most zealous supporter, one action he performs may be administering an opiate—an act that may well be immoral. What is wrong with "you will get your reward in heaven" is not that the proposition is surely false (for it is possibly true) or that the belief is completely unwarranted (for it has some warrants), but that people perform vicious acts in saying it. Speech act theory enables us to show just what is true about the Marxian dictum: such consoling doctrines can be (and too often are) the propositional ingredient in immoral actions of repression and subjugation.

With a speech act theory in place, the second stage is to use it, in the middle five chapters of the book, to analyze classic texts about God and evil. If texts like the biblical Book of Job, Augustine's *Enchiridion*, Boethius's *Consolation of Philosophy*, Hume's *Dialogues Concerning Natural Religion*, and George Eliot's *Adam Bede* merely provide grist for the theodicists' mills, their power is erased, their distinctive voices silenced. The point of these five chapters in Part 2 is that the power of these texts is revealed when they are taken as communicative actions which display or constitute important discourse practices for understanding or counteracting evil without abandoning belief in God.

Part 3 of the book investigates the texts of theodicy as constituting a discourse practice. Chapter 9 shows how theodicy deforms our understanding of classic texts, is concerned only with abstract evils, and declares some real evils not to be evil at all. Having unleashed their power in Part 2, those classic texts reappear in the final chapter to interrupt and counteract theodicy. Finally, theodicy can be unmasked as discourse practice which obscures evils and marginalizes the agents of reconciliation. My conclusion is that theodicy as a discourse practice must be abandoned because the practice of theodicy does not resolve the problems of evil and does create evils.

## NOTE

1.  Unfortunately, most scholars in theology and religious studies tend to ignore the fact that speaking—or writing—is acting. A speech act approach provides a way beyond the impasse between what Lindbeck has categorized as the cultural-linguistic and experiential-expressivist approaches. It accepts the basic cultural-linguistic view that the meanings of speech acts in religion, including those which express doctrines, are shown by their use in the tradition, and that they are neither reducible to nor justified by some common religious experience. It does not presume that *one* linguistic practice, e.g., formulating doctrines or doctrinal rules, determines the significance of *all* religious practices, but that all the practices of a religious tradition mutually determine their significance. But it neither accepts, rejects nor presumes the claim that a single religious experience underlies the diversity of religious traditions.

Like the theological revisionists (or experiential-expressivists, in Lindbeck's terms), a speech act approach presumes that religious practices are comparable. But unlike some revisionists, it does not presume that a basic experience, attitude, or entity is a *foundation* either for all religious traditions or for comparing practices in various traditions. Such a claim could possibly result from, but is not needed as a presupposition for, analyzing religious practices. The present approach presumes that analogous practices (preaching, healing, praying, meditating, speculating, initiating, etc.) can be found in various traditions and may provide a bridge for comparisons (see Tilley 1989).

Hence, a practical speech act approach avoids the theoretical stalemate of whether a common religious experience or particular doctrine is more basic. Neither is assumed as true or presumed as necessary. The present practical theory requires neither for its analysis. Accepting one or another may be a *result* of investigating what people do in religious contexts, but is not a presupposition of the possibility of investigating.

# PART ONE:

## SPEECH ACT THEORY

# Chapter 1

# WORDS ARE DEEDS

*In the Beginning was the Word*
*—John 1*

*In the Beginning was the Deed*
*—Goethe, Faust*

*In the Beginning is the Relation*
*—Martin Buber, I and Thou*

## Introduction: Speech Act Theory

How can people *do* things with words? How can the words we speak have power? How can words be deeds? Publication of John L. Austin's ground-breaking lectures, *How To Do Things with Words* (1962), set the terms for an enduring conversation among philosophers, linguists, and literary critics about how we can and do act as we speak.

Simply put, Austin claimed that (save for some bizarre counter-examples) whenever we say something, we perform a number of actions. We perform a *locutionary* act, saying a sentence. We perform an *illocutionary* act which gives the sentence a certain force. We perform a *perlocutionary* act "*achieving* of certain *effects by* saying something" (Austin 1962:120; emphasis partly in original)—presuming that someone heard it ("uptake"). For example, depending upon the context in which I say, "Oh, God," performing that *locutionary* act may have the *illocutionary* force of praying, expostulating, naming a new-found deity or Hollywood film, blaspheming, concluding an argument, etc. That act may have the *perlocutionary* results, respectively, of ingratiating, upsetting, damning myself, informing, persuading, etc. The acts we perform when we speak depend upon (1) the linguistic conditions that make it possible for us to perform purposeful linguistic acts; (2) the extralinguistic contexts in which we speak, including our abilities, purposes, institutional status, and our relations to those who hear us; (3) the results (intended or unintended) of speaking. Thus, given that the conditions, contexts, intentions, and results can vary, the acts we can perform using the same words can vary. This chapter unpacks these notions.[1]

## Language and Linguistic Acts

One important contribution of speech act theory to the philosophy of language and linguistic theory is its recognition that the language we use can fit the world in different ways. A standard modern view was modeled on the way some third person indicative sentences reflected the world. It pictured the relationship roughly as follows: If one says, "The cat is on the mat," and the cat *is* on the mat, then the sentence is true and saying it is appropriate. If one utters the sentence and the cat *is not* on the mat, then the sentence is false and saying it is inappropriate. In general, the propriety of what one said was determined by whether what one said matched the way things were. In this picture, serious problems arose only when one came across types of sentences whose match to the world wasn't clear. One solved those problems by trying to find or invent ways to show whether that type of sentence could match the world. If one failed, that type of sentence was "meaningless." If one succeeded, then either sentences of that type matched and were true and proper, or they didn't match and were false and improper. The model for all language was the 'standard' utterance of "the cat is on the mat." Debates about the meaningfulness of whole realms of discourse presumed this to be the model for all sentences, from "Juliet is the sun" to "Please open the door" to "Holy Cow!"

Speech act theory offers a more nuanced, postmodern account of language and language use. It recognizes that some utterances don't "match the world" and are nonetheless in perfect order. It accounts for how the standard view went wrong: what the standard view had identified as the sufficient condition for the meaningfulness of all sentences was neither necessary nor sufficient for many sentences to be meaningful (cf. Searle 1979: 117-36). Speech act theory can account for the many ways people actually use, abuse, and misuse language.

Debates about theodicy as a practice or about the reasonableness of specific theodicies presume a modern, rather than a postmodern, approach to language. In seeking to say how God is not culpable for permitting the evils in the world, the theodicist tries to build a verbal system which reflects the world. The antitheodicist tries to pick out inconsistencies in the theodicist's system or to reveal places at which it does not match the world. The issue between them is whether the theodicist's words match the world—an issue which is insoluble. Moreover, the preoccupation with the reasonableness or truth of theodicies also displaces all other talk of God and evil to a realm beyond the frontiers of modern philosophy and theology. By using a more nuanced account of language use, we can discern the importance of other ways of talking of God and evil and replace them in the contemporary discussion.

The key to speech act theory is that it begins with the acts we perform in speaking, the illocutionary acts, rather than with the words we utter. It construes the meaning of what we say as dependent upon the illocutionary point of the speech acts we perform.[2] Searle's descriptive taxonomy of illocutionary points is a useful guide to understanding the general ways in which our linguistic acts fit in the world. He summarized it as follows:

> I say that there are five things you can do with language: you can tell people how things are (assertive); tell them to do things (directives); commit yourself to doings things (commissives); express your feelings and attitudes (expressives); and bring about changes in the world through your utterance (declarations). This is a claim which is subject to possible refutation; thus counter-examples could really bring some progress (1983b:44).

I will use Searle's taxonomy, only noting that each of these five genera of illocutionary *points* includes an indefinite number of specific illocutionary *forces* (cf. Searle and Vanderveken 1985:37-40).[3]

(1) *Assertives* are speech acts whose point is to represent a fact, a state of affairs, or the world. A speaker tries to have what she says fit the way things are. For example, "The cat is on the mat" says something about the way things are in the world. The act the speaker performs is to assert a claim. One can check the claim's truth by finding whether the world is such that the claim fits it.

Assertive illocutionary forces are distinguished by the varying strengths of the speaker's commitment ("hypothesizing," "surmising," "stating apodictically," "opining"), and/or by the ways in which a speaker warrants the assertion ("infer," "deduce," "guess," "estimate," "fantasize"). In some circumstances one cannot perform certain assertive acts, e.g., it is impossible to "surmise" on the witness stand, "predict" a past event, or "guess" a scientific conclusion. In some circumstances one can perform only a limited range of acts, e.g., whatever one asserts on a witness stand one "testifies to."

(2) *Directives* are acts whose point is to get another to do something. "Put the salt near me," for instance, *states* nothing about the way the world is. Rather, it *presumes* that the world is *not* the way the speaker wants it and that the addressee will not do something the speaker wants done (unless the speaker issues the directive). It thus *directs* the hearer to do something to change the world (in this case, to place the salt within the reach of the speaker). Hence, a proper directive and the world fit each other in just the opposite way a proper assertive and the world fit.

Directive illocutionary forces are differentiated by the strength of the directive ("demand," "command," "order," "request," "beg," etc.). One cannot ask whether directives are true or false, for they make no truth claims. However, if the world were already the way the speaker wanted it, it would be inappropriate to issue the directive ("The salt's right by your left elbow, dummy." "Oh, sorry, I didn't see it.") It also may be impossible in some circumstances to issue certain directives, e.g., it is impossible for an army private to "command" an army general to do anything, and only in rare circumstances is it possible for the general to "request" or "beg" anything of the private. Directing someone to do something she cannot do is also inappropriate, e.g., a teacher can direct a student to *recite* the Gettysburg Address, but cannot direct the student to *give* the Gettysburg Address.

(3) *Commissives* have the point of committing the speaker to do something in the future, e.g., "I'll have 100,000 one-eighth-inch ball bearings at your plant by next Tuesday." Promises, offers, or contracts are sample commissives. Commissives *presume* things are not now as they will be if and when the speaker fulfills the commitment, *imply* that the speaker can fulfill the commitment, and are *inconsistent with* any assertives which deny what the commissive commits the speaker to do. Like a directive, a commissive *states* nothing about the way the world is; in issuing it, the speaker commits herself to make the world fit her words. Unlike a directive, which directs its intended hearer to make the world fit the speaker's words, a commissive commits its speaker to a future act.

Commissive illocutionary forces are distinguished by various strengths in ("absolutely," "probably," "until death do us part") and conditions for ("if the rain clears up," "if you'll pay me first") the commitment. If a speaker commits himself to something which would occur without his commitment, the commitment may be empty. If a speaker commits herself to something she cannot do, because of actual limitations or because the event is past, the commitment is hollow. However, if a speaker can fulfill a commitment and fails to do so, that commitment is appropriately made, but is broken because the world does not come to fit his words. In some circumstances, one cannot perform certain commissive speech acts, e.g., I cannot seriously and literally "threaten" to do something you want and need me to do. In other circumstances, only certain commissives are appropriate, e.g., at inauguration the president of the United States can only "swear" or "affirm" to uphold the Constitution, he or she cannot "vow" or "promise to try" to do so. Some commissives such as contracts require an intended audience (other than the speaker) in order to be effective, while others, such as vows or promises made only to oneself, may not require an audience or addressee other than the speaker.

(4) *Declarations* are explicit performatives. Their point is to change the world. They make the world become what they say it is. Here "I baptize you," "I name this ship the *Dobie Gillis*" are paradigms. A person authorized to perform an action (a minister in the first case, a dignitary honored by being invited to crack a bottle of champagne over the prow of a battleship in the second) in speaking performs an action which changes the way things are in the world. The fit of words and worlds is bidirectional, for *declaring* something so ipso facto makes it so.

Declarations are failures if conditions are such that the action cannot be performed, e.g., if a Roman Catholic priest has already consecrated the elements during a Mass, saying "This is my body" a second time doesn't make the bread doubly sacred; or if the dignitary was authorized to name the ship the *Admiral Perry*, his invocation would not "name" the ship the *Dobie Gillis*. Declarations can be deceptive (though possibly still effective) if their speakers take positions to which they are not entitled (under what circumstances does a bogus justice of the peace pronouncing you "man and wife" invalidate your marriage?). Declarations can be defective, but still successful, if relevant presumptions about the way the world is when a person makes a declaration are not true.

There is only one strength for declarations: either they do what they say or they fail. However, there are three types of hybrid declarations, the assertive declaration, e.g., "Out!" as shouted by a line judge in tennis; the commissive declaration, e.g., "You're under arrest," as said by a police officer to a suspect; and the directive declaration, e.g., "I appoint you line judge for this match," as said by an authority to a candidate for a job.[4] These are clearly declarations—they do what they say—but conditions proper to assertives, commissives, and directives, respectively, also apply for them.

For instance, the ball is *out* when the judge "calls" it "out." The judge's assertive declaration presumes that the words she utters fit the world, but even if the declarative "out" were wrong, the ball is still *out*. A tennis player may, of course, protest the call. However, if there is no effective counteraction, then a declaration is successful and can be successful even if it is defective.

But the performance of seriously defective, yet successful, assertive declarations may lead to other events. The "bad call" and the player's protest may lead an umpire to overrule the judge by a supervening declaration that the ball is "in." The umpire's declaration successfully counteracts the judge's defective declaration by overturning it. A tennis official may remove the judge from the privileged position which the declaration requires. Defective declarations can be counteracted, but not all are—as innocent people in jails who were declared guilty when they were innocent can witness.

However, declarations can be defective enough to be failures. If a fleet-footed crook responded to the cop arresting her, "The hell you say," broke out of his grasp, and sprinted to freedom, then the officer's inability to hold the suspect, to make the world fit his words, renders his declaration defective enough to be unsuccessful. The crook may have been momentarily stopped, and later be liable to charges of escape or resisting arrest, but she is no longer "under arrest," the state in which the officer declared her. As with a line judge who could not consistently make correct calls, a police officer who could not consistently hold his prisoners would likely be removed from the position from which he could make such declarations.

In either case, a directive declaration would do the trick: if a superior authority says "I suspend you from your duties" to a police officer or line judge, that declaration also directs the addressee to do something he or she would not otherwise do. Again, the authority has to be in the proper position to make the directive, and other conditions and states of affairs can render this declaration defective in various ways. Generally, hybrid declaratives have the forces of and conditions for both the members of the hybrid.

Declarations ordinarily require that the speaker have a certain institutional position to perform the action. Searle and Vanderveken recognize only two exceptions: the exercise of supernatural power (God said, "Let there be light," and there was light) and those which concern only language, e.g., naming (1985:205). However, some illocutionary denegations, e.g., "I do not state that she was in the car at the time of the murder," in which speakers makes it clear they are *not* performing a specific speech act, may be construed as declarations. Moreover, there are other declarations which do not require institutional status, as chapter 3 will show in exploring autobiographical confession.

(5) *Expressives*, e.g., "congratulate," "thank," "apologize," "condole," etc., have the point of expressing a person's attitudes toward or feelings about states of affairs.[5] Searle claims "that in expressives there is no direction of fit. In performing an expressive, the speaker is neither trying to get the world to match the words, nor the words to match the world, rather the truth of the expressed proposition is presupposed. Thus, for example, when I apologize for having stepped on your toe, it is not my purpose either to claim that your toe was stepped on nor to get it stepped on" (1979:15). Although expressives *imply* no words-world fit, many do *presume* that the world is a certain way, and a hearer can *infer* from those expressives that their speakers *believe* the world is the way their expressives presume. Searle and Vanderveken note that every illocutionary force entails an expressive force because every illocutionary force has some psychological conditions for its successful performance which could be the subject of an expressive (1985:178).

Expressives are at least defective and at most unsuccessful or gratuitous if their presuppositions are false ("You didn't step on my toe." "Oh, well, then I guess I can't be sorry for it.") and can be as appropriate or inappropriate as the feelings they express ("Congratulations!!!" "How can you express *congratulations* for my losing my job!"). Some circumstances preclude successfully performing certain expressives, e.g., I cannot literally and seriously offer you *condolences* for receiving good news. Expressives are deceptive if they express a feeling or an attitude a speaker doesn't have. They are misleading if they have presuppositions which lead a hearer to infer from them something that is false ("Good work!!!" may not *state* that one approves of the hearer's toil, but in certain circumstances, one's hearer will infer that the work she has done is satisfactory). The importance of differentiating religious expressives from other speech acts performed in religious contexts will emerge in the next two chapters. The importance of recognizing that all five types of speech acts are performed in talking of God and evil in various contexts is crucial for the work of the whole book.

## The Social Situation of Speech Acts

The possibility of performing speech acts requires not only that linguistic conditions are met, but that extralinguistic conditions obtain.[6] Indeed, the previous section noted how some nonlinguistic circumstances can constrain the speech acts a person can perform. Other conditions are fairly trivial: a speaker must be able to speak, the appropriate hearer to hear, and they must share a language sufficiently for the utterance to be understood, etc. (cf. Searle 1969:57; McClendon and Smith 1975:59). What nontrivial extralinguistic conditions must obtain for a speech act to be performed, however, has been the subject of much unresolved debate. Two issues are important: whether all speech acts are communicative and whether communicative speech acts require specific institutional or noninstitutional relationships between the speaker and hearer.

(1) Much ink has been spilled over whether all speech acts are communicative. Austin apparently thought they were, as the following implies: "the *circumstances* in which the words are uttered should be in some way, or ways, *appropriate*, and it is very commonly necessary that either the speaker himself or other persons should *also* perform certain *other* actions, whether 'physical' or 'mental' actions or even acts of uttering further words" (1962:8). Habermas (1979:40) also apparently thought all speech acts were communicative, as he equated speech acts with communicative acts, a subset of social acts.

Arguing the other side, Searle has claimed that there can be speech acts which are not essentially communicative. He drew a sharp distinction between the intention to represent and the intention to communicate (1983a:160-79). One can perform an assertive speech act whose point is to represent accurately without intending to communicate. One can simply "talk to oneself" or represent a state of affairs falsely or not care how people respond to what one says. Hence, some speech acts are properly intended to represent things, without being intended to communicate. So not all speech acts are communicative.

However, Searle's point applies only to parasitic cases. One may make a commitment no one else knows of, but one cannot perform that act if one does not understand a social practice which is commissive. One may express one's feelings (e.g., cursing) without anyone hearing, but one cannot perform that act if one has not learned how to be expressive. One may practice giving directives or making declarations in private, but one cannot give actual directives to no one or make effective declarations unknown to anyone else. One may represent something only to oneself, but one has learned from others what can count as a representation and how to represent things. A rare person or group of persons may develop new ways of representing things which reveal facets of things previously hidden: the development of cubism provides an example. One may purposely represent something falsely, but to do so presumes that one knew what would count as a true representation. In short, while an intention to represent may be distinguishable from an intention to communicate (Searle 1983a:166), the ability (and the intention) to represent is dependent on the practice of communication. Learning how to represent is learning a skill as social as vowing, cursing, ordering or declaring. Hence, if there are noncommunicative speech acts, they are parasitic on communicative ones. Speech act theory is essentially a communication theory.[7]

(2) Theorists have also debated the extent to which speech acts are institutionally bound, i.e., "bound" in that they cannot be performed outside of institutional structures. For instance, for me to baptize someone, I must be a minister (or other authorized person) in a church (or other institution, even if I am its founder and presently only member) which practices baptism as an initiation rite. For a teacher to fail a student, both must participate in an institution with a social location (e.g., a college) where there is a practice of grading. The question is whether *all* speech acts are institutionally bound, i.e., whether all require specific institutional relationships to obtain if they are to be performed. Searle develops this point:

> Austin sometimes talks as if he thought all illocutionary acts were [institutionally bound], but plainly they are not. In order to make a statement that it is raining or promise to come and see you, I need only obey the rules of language. No extra-linguistic institutions are required (1979:7).

This claim, plausible on the surface, needs also to be unpacked.

First, institutions need to be differentiated from practices. Habermas, for one, fails to do so. In his theory of universal pragmatics he makes a distinction between institutionally bound and unbound (free) speech acts. People performing the former (e.g., baptism) acquire power to execute the act from the institution in which the act is performed. The latter do not. This plausible view is unfortunately devastated by his failure to distinguish practices (e.g., baptism, betting) from institutions (e.g., church, racetrack), as in the following: "To explain what acts of betting or christening mean, I must refer to the institutions of betting or christening" (1979:39). Some practices, like christening, are institutionally bound and individual acts are also institutionally bound. These acts cannot be performed outside of the institutionally defined requirements, including that the actor have specific institutional status. Other practices, like betting, are at home in many institutional contexts. Individual acts of betting are not institutionally bound—they may be performed in various institutional or social contexts, often without regard to the agent's institutional status. Hence, some acts may require no extralinguistic institutions to be performed, but all require the existence of social practices. Fish has argued (1989:454) that

Habermas has not shown that there are any institutionally unbound speech acts, but Fish's account of institutional boundedness has the same flaw as Habermas's. Hence, Searle is right about institutions, but his point does not also apply to practices.

Second, institutions and practices need to be distinguished from relationships. Searle notes a number of relevant factors here (1979:5-6), but does not develop their significance. For instance, for a teacher to grade a student, it is not sufficient that they both have their relative social locations in an institutional structure and accept the practice of grading. The student must also be registered in that teacher's course. Without this relationship, the teacher cannot grade the student.

Sometimes the relationship requirements for successfully performing a speech act are so minimal as to be trivial. For instance, consider Searle's account of advising (1969). To *advise* another, according to Searle, there is some future act that an advisee could perform (Searle's "propositional content," e.g., buying a ham). The advisor must have some reason to believe that buying the ham will benefit the advisee and that the advisee will not buy the ham in the normal course of events (preparatory condition). The advisor must believe that buying the ham will benefit the advisee (sincerity condition). The advice the advisor gives must count as an undertaking to the effect that buying the ham is in the advisee's best interest (essential condition). When all these conditions obtain, then "I think you should drop down to the store and get a ham to serve the Rosenbergs for dinner tomorrow" counts as a successful act of advising. Of course, the advice might be bad, malicious, not taken, or in some other way be successful, but defective, e.g., if the Rosenbergs are Orthodox Jews, if the advisee had already bought sole, etc. But defective advice is still *advice*, and the speaker performed an act of advising (cf. Searle 1969:67; compare Searle and Vanderveken 1985:202). In all of this, both parties are characterized without identification (Searle labels them S and H, for speaker and hearer) and their relations to each other need be no more than the minimal relations sketched. Save for those circumstances in which the speaker and hearer have special institutional status—e.g., soldiers in an army, umpires, or ministers—or in cases where the speaker intentionally talks both to addressee(s) and "eavesdroppers," this account is sufficient.

But the fact that there is a minimal relation between the speakers and hearers does not mean that relationships "factor out," so that any person can perform any institutionally free communicative speech act. An example from MacIntyre can be adapted to illustrate this point. If one is standing at a bus stop and a person nearby suddenly says, "The name of the common wild duck is *Histronicus*

*histronicus histronicus,"* what is that person doing? Whatever the speaker might be intending to do, the action is unintelligible to the hearer because there is no relationship between speaker and hearer to provide a context for performing that action (MacIntyre 1981:195-96). The speaker may be an actor practicing a part in a play, or a college student engaging in fulfilling the requirements of an odd sort of hazing ritual, or a misinformed, socially awkward naturalist trying to initiate a conversation. But until a hearer responds, "Pardon me?" or "Huh?" and the speaker (or another person who knows what the speaker is doing) performs another speech act of informing the hearer, an act which gives a context for the perplexing act, the latter cannot be understood. Even if the utterance is constituted by a sentence which, if the act were an assertive, would be true, the hearer cannot understand the meaning of the utterance because the hearer cannot know if the speaker is asserting anything at all without some contextual setting which specifies the status the speaker has vis-à-vis the hearer. All communicative acts require some relationship to obtain between the speaker and hearer, even if only some acts require that relationship to be specified by the institutional roles each has.

The problem, then, with the issue of institutionally bound and unbound speech acts is a failure on the part of theoreticians to distinguish institutions (e.g., the army, the church, the political party, the department store) from practices which may be performed in many of these institutions (e.g., ordering, praying, debating, buying) and both from relationships between people which may or may not be produced by their relative places in an institution. While institutions and institutionalized practices may control, constitute, or affect many of the actions we perform, their influence on some of our acts is so minimal as to factor out. While Habermas and Austin alert us importantly to notice the role institutions play in constituting the possibilities for performing many of our actions, they overstate the role institutions play in constituting all of our actions.

In sum, this means that performing a communicative act requires a narrative setting. The speaker and hearer(s) must be in an appropriate relationship to each other, although these relations will vary from act to act. A speaker must have a certain institutional status to be able to perform some, but not all, speech acts. Yet having a certain institutional status is a disabling condition for performing some, but not all, speech acts.

## Perlocutionary Results

Like any other social actions, i.e., actions a person undertakes with the purpose of affecting other person(s), communicative speech acts have results. However, constructing a systematic theory which shows why all social human acts have all the results they do may be impossible. This does not imply that some acts do not have some determinable results. If I punch my wife in the eye hard enough, the result will be a black eye, a predictable biophysical response. The act also makes me at least vulnerable to, and in most circumstances guilty of, a charge of assault and battery, with a predictable resultant change in my social status. I could truthfully say, "I didn't intend to hurt her," but that alone is not sufficient defense against a charge that my act was one of assault and battery: "What else did you expect, dummy, when you hit her so hard?" Were circumstances such that she died as a result of the punch, I would have performed not only an act of assault and battery, but also one of manslaughter. In short, the results of my act may, in part, determine the nature of my act.

In contrast, there may be consequences of my action that could not have been intended. One consequence of the punch might be, in appropriate circumstances, that I "come to my senses," realize that I have not been coping well with the stresses of my job, and begin a course of therapy which saves and enriches our marriage, a result so unexpected that some would call it Gracious (see Adams 1986). Here I might truthfully say, "I didn't intend to save our marriage by hurting my wife, but that's how it worked out." It would be a very strange set of circumstances, including some very suspicious intentions, in which I could *intend* the *result* of saving our marriage by blackening my spouse's eye, even though that might be a *consequence* of my act.

These homely remarks are merely reminders of some very basic facts about human actions often overlooked by speech act theorists: their consequences may be predictable or unpredictable, expected or unexpected, intended or unintended. For performing them, the agent may be responsible or not responsible, and found (by self or others) morally guilty or innocent, legally guilty or innocent. While agents may intend and perform actions and are responsible for those intentions and actions, in normal circumstances[8] agents are generally responsible for the expected and predictable *results* and foreseeable consequences of their acts, even if they do not intend them. They are not responsible for the consequences of their actions to the extent that those consequences are unexpected and unpredictable.

These remarks also apply to speech acts: I am responsible for the intentions I have and the actions I perform, and for the results of those actions to the extent that they are part of the actions or expected and predictable effects of the actions. However, most speech act theorists have paid little attention to the results of speech acts. For instance, Searle notes that issuing a speech act has purposes beyond using language to express a mental state. "For example, the primary extra-linguistic purpose of directives is to get people to do things; a primary extra-linguistic purpose of assertives is to convey information; a primary purpose of commissives is to create stable expectations of people's behavior." But Searle goes on to note that following a conventional procedure cannot guarantee that a person will perform extralinguistic acts or achieve extralinguistic goals. "The perlocutionary effects of our utterances cannot be included in the conventions for the use of the device uttered because an effect which is achieved by convention cannot include the subsequent responses and behavior of our audiences" (1983a:178; cf. Searle and Vanderveken 1985:11-12). Like most speech act theorists, Searle's primary goal is to provide a theoretical explanation of a speaker's intentions and actions. Hence, he has no need to analyze the perlocutionary results of speech acts which are not explicable by a formal theory.

For present purposes, this is insufficient. Communicative speech acts affect other people. To understand what concrete acts are being performed and their significance requires understanding the extra-linguistic context for and results of those actions. Attending to results can reveal that *results* can change the meaning of the act performed, as the difference between "assault and battery" and "manslaughter" shows. Attending to contexts can reveal that differing *contexts* can also change the significance of an act performed (cf. McClendon and Smith 1975:64).

That contexts, as well as results, partially determine what an act is, seems overlooked, not only for communicative speech acts, but also for human acts generally. Philip P. Hallie's comments on Hannah Arendt's portrayal of the banality of Eichmann's evil illustrate the significance of this point:

> Eichmann was a commonplace, trite man if you look at him only in the dock and if you do not see that his boring clichés are directly linked with millions of tortures and murders. If you see the victims of Eichmann and of the office he held, then—and only then—do you see the evil of this man. Evil does not happen only in people's heads. Eichmann's evil happened in his head (and here Arendt is not only right but brilliantly perceptive) *and* (and the "and" makes a tight, essential

linkage) in the freight cars and in the camps of Central Europe. . . .Early in her book she wrote: "On trial are his deeds, not the sufferings of the Jews."

As if "his deeds" could be neatly peeled away from what he did to the Jews! Her *separation* of the mental activity of Eichmann from the pain-racked death of millions that this mental activity brought about made Eichmann's evil banal. Without these actual murders and tortures Eichmann was not evil; his maunderings were those of a pitiable, not a culpable man. His evil lay in his deeds, as Arendt says, but not only in his mental "deeds": it lay in all that he intended and all that he carried out, in his mind and in the world around him (1985:43-44).

If one is responsible only for what one intends to do and not for any consequences beyond what one intends, a myopic moral bureaucrat who sees no links between well-intended deeds and bad results becomes a moral exemplar. As Hallie points out, that won't do. It presumes intentions alone give actions their significance. Yet to ascribe responsibility for "all that he intended and all that he carried out" is so vague that it may be construed as ascribing responsibility to Eichmann for every act performed by others as a consequence of his orders. This presumes that even consequences no one could imagine can give actions their significance. That won't do either.

To avoid the Scylla of pure intentionalism and the Charybdis of unlimited consequentialism, we need to focus on how context provides the connection between the intention to perform an act and the results of performing that act.[9] Consider how context connects just a few crucial speech acts. Had there been no Third Reich to give him his specific institutional status, Eichmann could not have performed the acts he did. If Hitler had not *appointed* (a declarative communicative act) him, he could not have *sworn allegiance* to the Reich (a commissive) and as part of that commitment *ordered* (a directive) others to carry out the final solution to the Jewish problem. Eichmann is responsible for giving his orders and the results of his orders; he is responsible for accepting appointment and swearing allegiance; but others are responsible for appointing him and executing his plans; and, perhaps, still others collectively for creating the institutions which enabled his orders to be effective. Considering even these few speech acts suggests that a speech act theory which connects intents and results through context can provide a way for sorting through the maze of individuals' responsibility, shared responsibility, and corporate responsibility. Such considerations also help untangle the confused notions of individual sin, natural evil, and social evil, notions obscured by the practice of theodicy—or so chapter 9 of this volume argues.

A theory of speech acts cannot neglect to notice that context provides an essential link between the communicative intention and result. It cannot equate the meaning of the act performed to the illocutionary intent of the agent. That would be as flawed as a general theory of human acts which neglected the essential links between act and results or which equated the act performed to the bare intention of the agent. Speech act theory must be open to the possibility that the concrete context in which the agent acts can alter the results of an act enough to change the nature or meaning of the act. If one narrows the focus enough, Eichmann's intentions and actions do not differ in kind from those of any other small-souled bureaucrat—and that is just what makes his banal evil so terrifying. But just such narrowing of vision can be deceptive—or self-deceptive—if it is thought to be the whole story (cf. Anscombe 1957; Hauerwas and Burrell 1977). The institutional and social context of those directives is a necessary condition not only for issuing those commands, but also for those directives to have the power that they did and to be the kinds of directives that they were. A formal speech act theory is not constructed to show, nor should it obscure, how contexts condition acts (cf. Searle and Vanderveken 1985:11).

Hence, part of the meaning of communicative speech acts is their perlocutionary results. Since a formal theory cannot provide a complete account of such results, an analysis of paradigm examples of communicative speech acts suggests where one should look to find perlocutionary results which may have a bearing on the nature of the act performed.

Assertives are differentiated by the strength of the speakers' warrants for and commitments to their assertions. A speaker (S) who asserts $p$ conveys $p$ to a hearer (H). In certain circumstances, if H performs an action for which $p$ is a necessary condition, S bears some responsibility for that action. For instance, suppose that during war an intelligence officer informs a bomber pilot that he knows beyond a doubt that an appropriate military target building, $t$, has unique marks $m,n,o$; a commander orders the pilot to bomb $t$, the pilot finds $m,n,o$ during the mission, successfully destroys only the building they mark, and returns safely. Later, during an investigation it is discovered that $m,n,o$ marked not $t$, but a hospital. The pilot can offer what the intelligence officer said as extenuating circumstances which make his bombing of the hospital excusable. The key focus for the military's investigation then properly shifts from determining the pilot's responsibility for the tragedy to the intelligence officer's responsibility. This suggests that what H can do with $p$, the content of what S asserts, and the authority of S to issue the assertion to another, should be foci in exploring the perlocutionary purpose and results of assertive communicative acts.

Directives are distinguished by the strength of the directive. If General S properly commands Private H to go to battle, S is (mostly) responsible for that action. If friend S properly asks friend H to pass the salt, then H is (mostly) responsible for passing the salt. In both cases, the directive is a necessary condition for H to act, but the main responsibility for the action is different. This suggests that the strength of the directive and the relative status (institutional and personal) of S and H are reasonable foci for investigation.

Commissives are also distinguished by the strength of the commitment. Each has perlocutionary results, including creating expectations and obligations. If S properly promises to H to do the dishes, then S creates both an obligation for S and an expectation in H. If S offers to sell merchandise to H if H will pay part of the price "under the table," S creates an obligation only if H agrees to the deal. The strength of the obligations and expectations will vary with the type of commissive performed.

Successful declarations create new states of affairs. Many of their perlocutionary results are obvious and can be assessed directly. The hybrid declaratives will have results which are determined by both the declarative and the other illocutionary force constituting the hybrid.

Noncommunicative expressives, such as making vulgar sounds at one's computer, are not of any interest for our purposes. Communicative expressives, like commissives, may result in creating expectations in a hearer, especially in institutionally bound situations. If boss S properly congratulates laborer H on doing a job right, *ceteris paribus*, H may come to think that the boss approves of his work in this instance. If psychologist S nods her head and says "Mm-hmm" at frequent intervals to client H, H will reasonably come to think that S is aware of H's problems, and likely will come to think that S is sympathetic to H. Unlike commissives, however, it is not clear that expressives create any obligation for S. Nor do expressives directly convey any *p* to H, for they have no world-word fit.

However, the boss's expression of congratulation presumes, but does not assert, that H did the job right. Can S congratulate H if he believes H failed to do his job correctly? That expressives have presumptions enables H to infer (with a strength determined by the context) that S believes some proposition necessary for issuing congratulations or at least does not believe a proposition inappropriate as a presumption for congratulations. Yet that there is a necessary presumption alone does not give H sufficient warrant to believe that

S believes H did a good job—for the boss may "congratulate" everybody as a motivational technique. Hence, it may be difficult for H to warrant an inference with much reliability because there may be a large range of presumptions sufficient for a boss to "congratulate" a worker. To get the inference right, H needs to know the circumstances—including S's linguistic habits—adequately. Of course, S may be trying to deceive H, not by lying—as an expressive does not assert, so it cannot assert falsely—but by misleading H, getting H to make an inference H cannot warrant.

Similarly, the psychologist may be bored silly by the client's story, but may be dissembling for therapeutic purposes. In fact, it is not clear whether S's utterance is an expressive or a very weak directive-commissive directed to patient H, meaning, "If you keep going, I will continue to listen until your time is up." Thus, the psychologist may be issuing an expressive to create a climate which weakly enables H to perform other actions or may be reinforcing H's trust in the psychologist. In either case, the dissembling of the psychologist is significantly different from the deceptiveness of the boss not because neither tells or fails to tell the truth, but because the psychologist's purposes are to help the patient and the boss's to harm the worker in issuing the expressive.

Subsequent chapters attend to the perlocutionary results of specific speech acts in greater detail. These results make it possible to understand how speech acts are "chained together" into conversations. Analyzing single communicative actions about the 'grammar' of God and evil, such as Augustine's *Enchiridion* (see chapter 5), can clarify the significance of crucial texts for subsequent readers. However, analyzing philosophical conversations about God and evil, such as Hume's *Dialogues Concerning Natural Religion* (see chapter 7) and "pastoral counseling" in the face of evil, such as portrayed in George Eliot's *Adam Bede* (see chapter 8), is even more revealing. Without considering the perlocutionary results of speech acts, such analysis would be impossible.

## Conclusions

Understanding the range of illocutionary points, social contexts, and perlocutionary results for communicative actions provides a framework for understanding and evaluating utterances people make in religious contexts, including those about God and evil. Failing to be clear about differences between the types of speech acts leads at least to confusion about, and at worst to distortion of, what people do when they talk of God and evil. Such failure causes misunderstanding of what the speakers are doing and what their utterances mean, presuppose, or imply when they speak. It obliterates the ways in which extralinguistic conditions, including institutional structures and personal relationships, affect communicative speech acts. It breeds perplexity about what the appropriate results of illocutionary acts are.

Worst of all, being unclear about what we do when we speak may lead us to perform speech acts that are inappropriate enough to be not only ineffective but even destructive or immoral. We may imply things we don't mean and fail to imply what we do. We may criticize actions that are in perfect order or accept actions that are seriously defective. We may deface images which should be seen or silence voices which heal suffering and sin. In the chapters that follow, all these problems are illustrated.

At this point, however, we need to show how speech act theory sheds light on 'religious' speech in general. Other than speech acts bound to religious institutions (e.g., baptism), there are no 'religious' speech acts to be distinguished from 'secular' ones. Rather, speech acts with each illocutionary point can be performed in religious contexts and have been performed in talking of God and evils. Chapter 2 explores speech acts bound to religious institutions and chapter 3 explores 'religious' speech acts which are institutionally free. Then we will be in position to show the significance of the speech acts people perform when they talk or write of God and evils.

## NOTES

1.    The preeminent contemporary speech act theorist is John Searle, who has worked in speech act theory for over two decades. Although the present approach is indebted to his work, it differs from his in significant ways. Searle's approach centers on developing a "formal account of the logic of speech acts" (Searle and Vanderveken 1985:ix). His concerns are essentially linguistic.

The present approach centers on the conditions for and evaluation of actually performing speech acts. My concerns are not essentially linguistic. I will not always mount theoretical arguments to justify my 'deviations' from the Searlean model because my purposes differ from his and because the differences cannot be resolved by the thrusts and parries of philosophical set pieces. Generally, I prefer to let the approach taken here be justified in ambulando by its explanatory power, although I will construct arguments where the an might be illuminating or a position I take especially controversial.

One key difference is that speech act theorists tend to spend little time portraying concrete speech acts. Their interest is generally in providing rules which account for language use. Once the theorist has explicated the rules, there is no need to deal with the messy particularity of speech situations, for these are of no real philosophical or linguistic interest. The *real* interest can then be pursued: forming a philosophy of mind or showing how individual minds acquire the rules that give them the cognitive capacity to use language or perform the mental and speech acts that they perform (see Searle 1983a).

However, such an approach cannot explain speech acts. As Nussbaum suggests, such a move reduces engaging in a practice to following a rule:

> This pattern of argument plainly does conflate the question, 'What is it' with the question, 'What conditions are necessary in order for it to be?', and, similarly the request for the explanation of certain events with a request of an account of the material necessary conditions for those events. . . . This is a way of arguing that is typical of reductionist scientism in all ages. . . . (1986:270)

A speech act theory composed only of rules is reductionistic.

Moreover, attending to specific speech situations reveals that it is impossible to specify *all* the conditions that would have to obtain or rules that would have to be followed for people to perform the speech acts they do. Systematic theorists tend to hide these conditions in seemingly innocuous *ceteris paribus* clauses. But things are not always equal—and to assume they are can lead to unwarranted reductionism.

Generally speaking, the adaptations of speech act theories by philosophers of religion and theologians are not very helpful for present purposes. James Harris's and Ian Ramsey's articles did not mine the distinctive riches of the theory. Donald Evans's book appeared shortly after Austin's lectures had been published posthumously, and so could not take advantage of later nuances. Brümmer and McClendon and Smith wrote important books, but with rather different purposes from mine. Of these, the present discussion is indebted most to McClendon and Smith's work.

Bach and Harnish are preeminent among the linguistic theorists who have attempted to incorporate Austin's basic nonsystematic insights into a linguistic system. They claim their theory provides a "conception of linguistic communication that integrates philosophical, linguistic, and psychological issues" (1979:xii). However, their explanatory system is unsuited for present purposes. It is an abstract and formal system, not very useful for understanding and evaluating concrete speech acts, a point developed in note 3. They omit serious consideration of the nonlinguistic social issues. They also limit the perlocutionary to what the speaker intends (17). As the discussion of Eichmann's acts on pp. 21-23 indicates, this is not satisfactory for moral evaluation of speech acts. Finally, their account is excessively mentalistic. For instance, they construe communicative understanding as the matching of speakers' intentions plus hearers' inferences. Hence, hearers' understanding speakers is "inference compressed by precedent rather than by meaning or convention" (xvii). I see no reason to think that people 'infer' linguistic meaning any more than they 'infer' that blue books are blue. I would take understanding to consist in hearers' appropriate reactions to speakers' communicative actions, learned by mastering communicative practices. I would construe 'mental acts' as possible constituents of some speech acts rather than foundations for all speech acts.

Kearns has proffered a speech act theory which "claims to overthrow many current theories in linguistics—while providing the resources to salvage what is valuable in those theories" (1984:9). He is rightly critical of Searle's exclusive focus on illocutionary acts. However, his theory is cumbersome in that it tries to portray both surface actions and deep structures and to account for some of the perlocutionary results of acts in a formal structure. It is unconvincing in its multiplying of speakers' acts (41-62) and its account of referring (395-98). Kearns promises an illocutionary logic (424), but Searle and Vanderveken have already sketched one. There seems little reason to prefer the approach Kearns takes, at least for present purposes.

2.     Although Austin may have thought otherwise (1962:93, 95, 148), the meaning of an utterance is constituted in part by its illocutionary force. This is because the *illocutionary* force of the utterance determines *how* the speech act is supposed to fit the world. Searle's approach helps clarify this point.

My most obvious difference from a Searlean approach is to reject equating "speech act" with "illocutionary act" (cf. Searle and Vanderveken 1985:12). This not only forces the introduction of a dubious distinction between 'direct' and 'indirect' speech acts (see note 5, below), but also has the potential for obscuring speakers' responsibility for their acts in a number of cases. Searle and Vanderveken's illocutionary logic is not a logic of speech acts, but of the linguistic component of speech acts. It provides a necessary, but not sufficient, account of speech acts.

Second, my most important difference is to construe meaning as a function of action rather than as a function of intention. Blair suggested (1984:38) that Searle shifted his view on the place of intention between (1969) and (1979); be that as it may, it is his present view I differ from. Searle writes that "the problem of meaning in its most general form is the problem of how do we get from the physics to the semantics; that is to say, how do we get (for example) from the sounds that come out of my mouth to the illocutionary act?" His answer is that the mind imposes intentionality on entities that are not intrinsically intentional (1983a:27). Later, arguing against Putnam, he claims that "meanings are precisely in the head—there is nowhere else for them to be" (1983a:200).

Searle's formulation of the problem takes the *physically basic* as *basic action*. He builds a gap between the basic, meaningless, brute noises we make and the meaningful, sophisticated acts of communication we perform, especially those which represent the way the world is. For him, individuals' mental intentions bridge that gap, especially the intention to represent the world. To perform meaningful acts one adds the right intention to brute acts.

The present approach assumes that the most general form of the problem of meaning is understanding human communicative actions. Like Habermas, I see speech acts as a subset of the set of human actions (although I find his separation of communicative from strategic actions unwarranted save as a heuristic device; cf. Geuss:1981). The key is not to bridge a gap between the brute facts of physics and the meaningful acts we perform, or between basic and nonbasic actions, but to understand these human acts by placing them in their social, institutional, and linguistic contexts. Anscombe, MacIntyre, and others have shown how dubious is the project of "building up" the intentional from the unintentional. While one can surely distinguish noises from speech, that does not mean one can understand what an act means by separating out "noise" from "intention" and then analyzing each. Our actions can mean and communicate what we intend, or more or less than we intend, depending on the context in which we perform them; Searle's approach has trouble accounting for the ways in which contexts constitute (in part) the nature of our acts. To learn how to perform meaningful acts, to learn what meaning others' acts have, one learns not how to understand their mental intentions, but how to do things.

3.     In this section, I discuss three of what Searle and Vanderveken identify as the seven components of illocutionary force: illocutionary point, the degree of strength of illocutionary point, and propositional content conditions. I also discuss some aspects of their "sincerity conditions." Like most speech act theorists, I will generally ignore derivative and parasitic uses. Although pretending, dissembling, playacting, etc., are also interesting, one must first get clear on paradigm straightfor-

ward acts before one tackles the more obscure acts.

Bach and Harnish provide a different taxonomy, but one I find less successful for three reasons. First, they presume a complex theory of cognitive competence (1979:92) which has as its goal the explanation of the linguistic competence of speakers and hearers in terms of abilities to perform complex mental acts which are explicable by their following rules or performing cognitive functions. This type of explanation tends to assimilate abilities to activities conforming to an algorithm. I have no special need to explain *why* language must function as it does, but only to note *how* we *use* language. Here, I agree with Searle (1983b:45; 1984:passim) that reducing mental states to formal states of a computational system is unwarranted.

Second, Searle used three main standards (the point of saying something, the ways in which the words fit the world or vice-versa, and the sincerity conditions for performing an illocutionary act) and nine less important ones to construct a taxonomy (1979:12). Searle and Vanderveken reorganized this to see seven components determining the various illocutionary forces. Bach and Harnish use only illocutionary intent (1979:40). Considering intent alone is not sufficient for present purposes: the points made in note 2 about Searle's intentionalism apply *mutatis mutandis* to Bach and Harnish.

Third, Bach and Harnish cannot account for the power of the actions of specific individuals in specific situations. Searle's basic approach is open to such analysis, so adapting it is preferable to using their account, which is not open to important relational and contextual claims, such as the "essential presupposition for the success of a speech act is that the speaker enter into a specific *engagement*, so that the hearer can rely on him" (Habermas 1979:61).

Hence, I generally follow Searle's taxonomy, but not his rationale for it. I see no reason to follow Searle in his further claim that these five genera "must derive from some fundamental features of the mind" (1983a:166). It is as possible that the mind basically generates the indefinite number of illocutionary forces and that 'reducing' them to a manageable number by arranging them in general according to their illocutionary point (only one constituent of illocutionary force) is a simplification we impose to manage the incredible complexity of speech acts.

4.    Generally, speech act theories recognize that an utterance can have more than one force in certain circumstances and that specific verbs in natural languages can be ambiguous or multivalent (cf. Searle and Vanderveken 1985:179-82). Where speech act theories differ is in how to describe the circumstances and account for the multiple forces. Searle recognized the assertive declaration, but not commissive or directive declarations (but compare Searle and Vanderveken 1985:175). (Although declarations may convey a speaker's attitudes, because expressives have no world-words fit and declarations must have such, there could be no pure expressive declarations.) Searle calls many commissive or directive declarations "indirect" speech acts issued *en passant* when some "direct" speech acts are performed. Bach and Harnish also note various implied and embedded speech acts in explicit speech acts. However, Fish (1980:284-92) has shown that Searle's account won't hold water because the conditions Searle invokes for distinguishing direct from indirect speech acts apply to all speech acts. Moreover, the distinction factors out in Searle and Vanderveken's formal work.

Fish's objection applies *mutatis mutandis* to Bach and Harnish. I would further add that the distinction between direct and indirect speech acts requires the validity of the "brute act + intention" view of meaningful action, an assumption criticized in note 2 above. Fish's objection does not undercut the present account because I do not equate illocutionary act with speech act as the others do. Any act a person performs can have numerous forces and varied consequences. These depend on the circumstances in which the person performs the act.

5.   Expressives are a class more complex than this summary suggests. The psychological states expressed can be very rich and multifaceted and have perlocutionary results often neglected in purely formal analyses. Searle and Vanderveken claim that every speech act entails an expressive (1985:178). This seems formally true, but materially empty. They seem to think that the feeling or attitude must relate directly to the content of the speech act. But the "propositional content" and the "sincerity conditions" are not always clearly related. For instance, institutionally bound declarations may entail that the speaker have psychological states, but those states may have nothing to do with the content of the expression. As an example, it seems clear that a judge may not desire that a defendant serve the sentence she must pronounce, and still successfully and nondefectively sentence the defendant. While psychological states are crucial for some speech acts, they are not crucial or determinable for all.

6.   In this section, I deal with what Searle and Vanderveken call the preparatory conditions and the mode of achievement of illocutionary acts, and some aspects of their psychological conditions, where relevant.

7.   Now someone might claim that even if the skill of representing is derivative from the practice of communicating, it does not follow that each intention to perform a noncommunicative speech act is dependent on the practice of communicating. This issue cannot be resolved without getting snared in the philosophical maze of attempting to provide a general account of the relations of individuals' intentions and actions to social conventions and practices. However, one cannot *intend* to do B unless one has some understanding of the practice of which action B is a specific exercise. Moreover, this book is not concerned with providing a general theory of the relations of intentionality and meaning or with discovering the conditions for performing any and every speech act. Hence, it does not need to account for derivative actions outside its purview. It needs only to account for specific communicative speech acts in light of the conventions, practices, and institutions in which they are embedded.

8.   It is probably impossible to give a rigorous or noncircular definition of "normal circumstances." For present purposes only, an act can be said to be performed in normal circumstances just in case an agent's account of that act is not revisionist. That is, it does not include either (1) a distinction between actual results, intended results, ordinarily expected results, and predictable (or probable) results of the act; or (2) an attribution of responsibility to another agent for the act, either or both of which is included in the account of the act to show a difference in the agent's moral or legal responsibility for the act from that which an impartial, but skilled, hearer would ordinarily ascribe to the agent. The burden of proof is always on the person giving such an account to show that the circumstances were abnormal, although the burden of proof may not be heavy. For present purposes, normal circumstances may include unusual circumstances ("Ordinarily I oppose abortion, but because I am . . .") or pathological conditions ("I was drunk when I . . ."). Such may or may not be extenuating circumstances which provide valid excuses for (not justifications of; cf. Tilley 1988) actions in the context of making moral or legal judgments, but extenuating circumstances are not, for present purposes, ipso facto abnormal. Following Hauerwas, I have accepted (Tilley 1985:191-95) a presumption in favor of the agent's account, but that can be overridden if the agent claims abnormal circumstances.

Normal circumstances may include relevant institutional or social conditions. In normal circumstances, shooting and killing another person is murder unless the agent has special institutional status (a soldier in war, an executioner, a prison guard trying to stop an escape) or relations (being the victim of a mugging) to the other person.

9.    Recent work by Michel Foucault and others on the notions of discourses or discourse practices provides concrete analyses of these contextual connections. One fruitful application of their strategies has been Boone's analysis of the "discourse of protestant fundamentalism." The very discourse system which constitutes fundamentalism means that the "authority of fundamentalism arises in the 'reciprocal relations' of text, preachers, commentators, and ordinary readers. And in studying these relations, one confronts the compelling power of a closed system, a power which cannot be localized but is of one cloth, a power woven in and through every thread" (Boone 1989:2-3).

In any discourse system, there are powerful connections between the constituents of the system. A person who enters a discourse practice (for instance, "is converted" to a fundamentalist Christian group or "becomes an intern" in an American hospital) accepts some beliefs as unquestionable. The participant learns how to take some texts (in the former case, the Bible, usually the Authorized Version; in the latter, medical textbooks) and persons (the pastor; the attending physician) as authoritative. The participant recognizes that some practices (boozing, dancing, gambling; fee kickbacks, ambulance chasing, euthanasia) are forbidden or impossible without leaving the discourse practice and other practices (referring all things to God; professional courtesy, diagnosing) as expected. The participant can usually take an institutionally determined place (worshipper in the church, parent and supporter of the Christian school; physician in the hospital, diagnostician in the clinic), which gives him or her a status in the discourse community. Such status and power relationships make it impossible for an ordinary member to give an "authoritative" interpretation of a text or for a nonphysician to render a diagnosis or write a prescription. It is practically impossible for a preacher not to give an authoritative reading of a text: within certain parameters (spelled out by Boone for fundamentalism) the members of the community take the text to mean what the preacher says it means. While not all speech acts performed within a discourse practice are institutionally bound (as discussed in chapter 2), the practice limits the possible speech acts that can be performed by those engaged in it. In these terms, it is Eichmann's position within the discourses that constituted the Nazi discourse system that determines the nature and meaning of (at least some of) his speech acts, whatever his alleged intentions might have been.

Some poststructuralists go beyond this analysis of specific discourse practices and seem to construe modernity itself as a discourse system which needs to be undermined or deconstructed. Among theologians who have taken this approach, Chopp has claimed that "words themselves are fixed neither by their essences nor by their self-referentiality, but by their context, the cultural practices in which they are used, by the interest of the persons using them, and by one sign's relation to other signs" (1989:31). The only disagreement with such a claim that the present approach would make is that its focus on *words* as signs may obscure the actions people perform in giving meaning to those words. Later, Chopp asserts that one "way to cast an analysis of modernity is to consider the deceitful figuration of its major metaphors and tropes: mastery, success, presence, autonomy, and progress. Ways of speaking have been structured into the ways of acting, and vice versa; ways of being in the world have developed out of and in constant close relation to ways of speaking" (93). To complete her circle, one must note that ways of speaking have also developed out of ways of being.

Yet if modernity is a discourse system, how would one know that these figures are deceitful? From within the system, these figurations would be taken for granted; from outside the system, they would be meaningless or irrelevant. Once one left the system, one could not call the figures "deceitful" because one no longer accepted them. One might call the system "deceitful," if one could show that its figures were self-defeating, but it is hard to see how one could both accept poststructuralist semiotics and have a place to stand to render such a judgment on a discourse system in which one did not take part.

Chopp avoids this dilemma by proposing to "rename the world with new words or words used in new ways" (23). These speech acts of renaming are acts in the praxis she calls "emancipatory transformation." These are, in speech act terms, declarations performed by those who are marginalized by the system or who are in solidarity with the marginalized. In most of the discourses of Christianity, women are marginalized; hence, feminists (among others) can perform such acts. They are effective not if a revolution takes place in which the marginalized become the new rulers and the old rulers become marginal, but insofar as the relations of power are undermined and "transformative relations of multiplicity, difference, solidarity, anticipation, embodiment and transformation" are enabled (68).

Chopp is among those poststructuralists who not only show how discourse systems work, but also seek to realize discourse practices which are not necessarily harmful to some who (are forced to) participate in those practices. Their strength is their recognition of the power relations within discourse practices and social-symbolic systems. But they also need to notice that declaring such systems destructive and inaugurating new signifying practices are speech acts which must be performed by people in specific social locations and which, to be effective, must be supported by and supportive of new forms of relationships and community which marginalize no one.

Moreover, it is not clear that any discourse *system* could avoid marginalization. Fundamentalism as a discourse system requires that its participants' relationships with nonfundamentalists be negative and thus marginalizes those others (cf. Tilley 1990). Nonfundamentalists' discourses tend to marginalize fundamentalists. Feminist dicourses marginalize supporters of Enlightenment liberalism and of authoritarianism. Roman Catholic authorities and "establishment" theologians often continue practices of marginalizing women and those men who do not meet the rules for having a place in the ecclesial establishment. The solution to the problem of marginalization seems to be creating a nonsytematic, nontotalizing, discourse practice. A pragmatic speech act theory such as the one presented here is compatible with the possibility of such discourse practices. It may even be more useful than poststructuralist semiotics, as it provides an approach to language which avoids a claim that semiotic systems determine the meanings of words which, if accurate, would seem to render a nonsystematic, but significant, discourse impossible. But to unpack these issues fully is beyond the scope of this book.

*Chapter 2*

# INSTITUTIONALLY BOUND SPEECH ACTS IN RELIGION

"Religion" and "religious" are terms so protean that they defeat attempts to define them. Theorists tend either to define religion so broadly as to include patently irreligious attitudes and institutions, e.g., secular humanism, Marxist political parties, or they define religion so narrowly as to exclude traditions and attitudes obviously religious, e.g., Theravada Buddhism. Some theologians have followed Karl Barth in claiming that Christianity is not a religion, but that presupposes definitions of both Christianity and religion that few find warranted (compare Proudfoot 1985:155, 179-89, and the literature he cites).

Instructed by these failures, the present work does not try to define "religion" or detail an exhaustive account of every possible "religious" speech act. Rather, it lays out the conditions for successfully performing, in clearly religious contexts, speech acts which have each of the five illocutionary points. This chapter considers *institutionally bound* speech acts, acts which only a person having a requisite status or role in a religious institution can perform successfully. The next chapter examines *institutionally free* speech acts, those which can be performed without regard to the person's institutional status or role. This distinction is necessary, for even if one must participate in a religious tradition to have religious experiences and beliefs (as Katz and Proudfoot in different ways have argued for mystical experiences and beliefs), one does not have to occupy a specific place or role in an institutional structure to perform some religious speech acts. For example, in Roman Catholicism, only the pope has the institutional position and authority to *declare* a dogma divinely revealed, e.g., "that the Immaculate Mother of God, the ever Virgin Mary, having completed the course of her earthly life, was assumed body and soul into heavenly glory" (DS:3903). Yet any Christian believing the doctrine might *profess* (an assertive) this dogma in appropriate circumstances.[1] In each section below, I chart and discuss the conditions for performing an institutionally bound speech act with each illocutionary point.

The purpose of both this chapter and the next is to lay the groundwork for subsequent analysis and evaluation of discourses centering on God and evil. The analysis also suggests ways to resolve the incessant debates over the question of whether religious language is "cognitive." In fact, language used in religious contexts is no more and no less "cognitive" than language used in other contexts, for the ways in which speech acts in religion relate to the world are as various as the ways speech acts in general relate to the world. The real questions concern the warrants for the presuppositions, assumptions, and claims people make when speaking in religious contexts (compare Tilley 1985:195 and Proudfoot 1985:196-99). I will discuss these points about cognitivity near the end of chapter 3.

## Speech Acts Bound to Religious Institutions

Many institutionally bound speech acts in religion are hybrids, i.e., assertives, directives, or commissives which are also declaratives. This is due to the institutional position of those making the assertions and to the institutional context in which the speech acts are performed. When institutional authorities make assertions, their audience may take their utterances as directives or declaratives as well. This is because the authorities occupy positions from which others in the institution reasonably and normally expect to hear declarations of doctrine and directives concerning practical matters. Occasionally, authorities in some religious institutions take care to make the illocutionary forces of their speech acts clear when they issue assertives without specific directive force. This alerts their audience that the common expectations the audience brings to its hearing of their utterances may not be in effect.

An excellent example of taking such care is found in the official summary of the 1983 pastoral letter of the American Catholic Bishops, *The Challenge of Peace*:

> We write this letter from the perspective of Catholic faith. Faith does not insulate us from the daily challenges of life, but intensifies our desire to address them precisely in light of the gospel which has come to us in

the person of the Risen Christ. Through the resources of faith and reason we desire in this letter to provide hope for people in our day and direction toward a world freed of the nuclear threat.

As Catholic bishops we write this letter as an exercise of our teaching ministry. . . . In doing this we realize and we want readers of this letter to recognize that not all statements in this letter have the same moral authority. At times we state universally binding moral principles found in the teaching of the church; at other times the pastoral letter makes specific applications, observations and recommendations which allow for diversity of opinion on the part of those who assess the factual data of situations differently. However, we expect Catholics to give our moral judgments serious consideration when they are forming their own views on specific problems. . . .

While this letter is addressed principally to the Catholic community, we want it to make a contribution to the wider public debate in our country on the dangers and dilemmas of the nuclear age. Our contribution will not be primarily technical or political, but we are convinced that there is no satisfactory answer to the human problems of the nuclear age which fails to consider the moral and religious dimensions of the questions we face.

The bishops are careful to differentiate the points and strengths of the utterances embedded in their letter for good reasons. Many within and without their 'flock' may presume that everything they say has the same authoritative strength because it is all said from the same authoritative position. However, both their care to distinguish the multiple forces and strengths within this one letter and the clearly defined realms of institutional authority within the Roman Catholic Church make *The Challenge of Peace* a very useful test case for analyzing institutionally bound religious speech acts. While other religious associations and institutions will have materially different ways of establishing authoritative positions, the formal principles for issuing institutionally bound speech acts remain constant.

## Institutionally Bound Directives

The quotations above from *The Challenge of Peace* include the bishops' beginning by stating their perspective ("Catholic faith") and purposes ("provide hope and direction"). The letter generally has the directive illocutionary point (even though specific utterances within it may have different strengths and points). Its perlocutionary purpose is to inculcate hope. In effect, the bishops are saying that if you will work to change the world in ways we indicate, then you can hope to live in a world free of the threat of a nuclear holocaust. In seeing this as an "exercise of [their] teaching ministry," they explicitly claim an institutional authority for their utterances, underlining the letter as a whole as an institutionally bound speech act.

An analysis of the general conditions for performing an institutionally bound *directive* and their application to the present specific list of case, is displayed in chart on p. 37.[2]

When the bishops "state" *universally* binding moral principles, they imply that every Catholic (and, they would add, every person) should never deviate from them. They also properly "expect" that Catholics will use the letter to form their consciences on matters concerning war and peace, although they recognize that there are legitimate positions other than their own with regard to the application of these principles. This shows the difference in illocutionary strength between "command" and "recommend." Although they have the same illocutionary point, their different strengths mean they have different institutionally bound illocutionary forces.

The same letter also has an institutionally free directive force. When the bishops address non-Catholics in their attempt to "make a contribution to the wider public debate in our country on the dangers and dilemmas of the nuclear age," the *point* of the letter is no different: it is a directive. But because the bishops do not have a specific institutional relationship with all the members of the public, the bishops cannot issue a command or order (of any strength), but can make a request or plea for consideration. Because the letter is promulgated to be read in a variety of contexts by people with different relationships to the bishops, it has a variety of directive illocutionary forces (cf. Searle and Vanderveken 1985:40-41).[3]

However, individuals can avoid having the utterance have the strength of a command or recommendation for them by leaving the institution. Because in the American polity a church is a voluntary association, anyone not willing to follow a command can leave the institutional structure. This does not imply that it is easy for anyone to leave the institution or that there are some people who could no more leave a church than shed their skins. It means that no legal governmental authority can force or forbid one to join or to renounce membership in a church. They may ignore the letter or they may become part of the "public debate," in which context the letter has the force of a *proposal* or a *plea*, not a command.

People can also disobey the command within the institution (and take whatever consequences can be meted out). In this case, the institutional bonds between speaker and audience are not broken

## INSTITUTIONALLY BOUND DIRECTIVES

| GENERAL | SPECIFIC |
|---|---|

*Contextual conditions*

1. Author and audience have roles in an institution constituted such that the author is able to issue a directive of the appropriate strength (order, suggest, request, instruct, etc.) to the audience to perform future act(s) which the audience can perform.

1a. Bishops have a role in the Roman Catholic Church such that they are empowered to instruct other members of that church to perform future acts.

1b. Members of the Roman Catholic Church have a right to be instructed by their bishops.

1c. The instructions have a binding force proportional to the authority exercised under the institutional rules.

*Illocutionary conditions*

2a. The author correctly presumes that the world is not as the author would have it.

2b. Author and audience can and do recognize the speech act as having the illocutionary point of a directive.

2a. The bishops correctly presume that the world is not as peaceable as they would have it be.

2b. Bishops and people can and do recognize the pastoral letter as having the force of an instruction to act.

*Perlocutionary conditions*

3a. Author presumes that audience is able to follow the directive.

3b. Author expects, proportional to the strength of the directive, that the audience will follow the directive.

3c. On the basis of what the author says, the audience takes the author to be issuing the directive with the strength the author intends.

3d. It is obvious to both author and audience that audience would not do what the author directs unless the directive were issued.

3a. The bishops presume that church members can follow the instructions of the pastoral.

3b. The bishops expect Catholics to adhere to *universally* binding moral principles, but only "expect Catholics to give our moral judgments serious consideration when they are forming their own views on specific problems."

3c. On the basis of the pastoral letter, Catholics take the bishops to be instructing them in a matter of morality, and can claim the authoritative guidance of the bishops as a reason for their actions. (Those who are not church members cannot do so).

3d. It is apparent to both bishops and other church members that at least some of the latter would not properly form their views or plan their actions on the issues discussed unless the bishops gave moral instruction or guidance.

nor even necessarily weakened. Yet if enough people refuse to obey a command, that massive refusal changes ipso facto the institutional relationship between the authorities and the rest of the members of the institution. This is exemplified by the overwhelming rejection by Roman Catholics of the teaching on 'artificial' contraception in the 1968 encyclical letter of Pope Paul VI, *Humanae Vitae*. In either voluntary or involuntary institutional relationships, massive disobedience of commands may change the illocutionary force of those directives (cf. Searle and Vanderveken 1985:69).

It might be objected that because some Catholic peace activists would do what the bishops instruct anyway, the letter would not be an instruction for them because they would do what the letter directed even if the letter were not issued. However, if the letter were not issued, specific condition (3d) above could not be followed. More to the point, many Catholics took the letter precisely as an instruction. Greeley (1985:93-100) has reported (to his surprise) a statistically significant shift of position among Catholics on issues of war and peace, according to samples taken before and after the pastoral letter was discussed and promulgated. Given the specific conditions for the pastoral letter, it apparently was not merely nondefective, but a true paradigm of an effective institutionally bound directive.

## Institutionally Bound Assertives

In issuing *The Challenge of Peace*, the bishops also performed other speech acts. These speech acts are embedded in the letter, but are not therefore "indirect." Each has a specific purpose contributing to the force of the letter as a whole. For instance, they perform institutionally bound *assertives* frequently throughout the text. These assertives are institutionally bound in that the bishops occupy a privileged position which gives them an authoritative status for issuing them.[4] The following is an example:

> In light of the framework of Catholic teaching on the nature of peace, the avoidance of war, and the state's right of legitimate defense, we can now spell out certain moral principles within the Catholic tradition which provide guidance for public policy and individual choice. (I-C-2)

Here the bishops are not performing a declarative speech act in which church teaching is made. Rather, they spell out, or assert explicitly, what the church teaches. But because they do so from an authoritative position, they *cannot* merely surmise or opine or report what the church teaches. They must *state* their position. Their authoritative status also implies that their speech act necessarily has some important perlocutionary results which are different from analyses of or reports on that teaching. College professors, newspaper reporters, religious educators, etc., do not have the same privileged institutional status as bishops and so their assertions cannot have the same force or strength as the bishops', even if the content of their speech acts were identical.

The chart on p. 40 illustrates the conditions for performing an institutionally bound assertive and their importance in the present context.

In contrast to institutionally bound directives, where *both* illocutionary and perlocutionary forces of the utterance partially depend upon the institutional status of the audience (see specific conditions (1a-1c), (3c) on p. 37, *only* the perlocutionary force of the institutionally bound assertive partially depends upon the institutional status of the audience (see specific condition (3c), on p. 40). Also in contrast to some directives, institutionally bound assertives have no obvious institutionally free force.

An implication of this analysis is that one can understand Roman Catholic theologians who "dissent" from teaching which bishops have promulgated as challenging specific condition (2a) (for both the present example and the previous one). But a challenge does not undercut bishops' authority to speak nor Roman Catholics' right to hear those bishops (conditions (1a), (3b) and (3c)). Such a challenge only implies that on specific issues, a specific utterance or set of utterances is not fully successful. Such a challenge is not a challenge to authority, but a challenge to what authorities presume in performing specific institutionally bound assertive or directive speech acts. How authorities and audience ought to respond in light of those challenges is hotly debated, and beyond the scope of the present work.

## Institutionally Bound Commissives

Throughout *The Challenge of Peace*, the bishops also make commitments. In discussing institutionally bound commissives, we must distinguish between commissives made *in*, *of*, or *for* the institution. Consider the following three quotations from different sections of *The Challenge of Peace*:

> As a tangible sign of our need and desire to do penance we, for the cause of peace, commit ourselves to fast and abstinence on each Friday of the year. . . . (IV-B-4)

## INSTITUIONALLY BOUND ASSERTIVES

### GENERAL

### SPECIFIC

*Contextual conditions*

1a. Author has a position in an institution such that the author is empowered to state the policy of the institution.

1b. Audience recognizes the author's position as such.

1a. A bishop, by appointment to that office, can state Catholic teaching on matters of faith and morals.

1b. Audience recognizes the speaker as a bishop.

*Illocutionary conditions*

2a. Author represents the way things are, with sufficient accuracy given the topic and occasion, in issuing the assertion.

2b. Author and audience can and do recognize the speech act as having the assertive illocutionary point.

2a. Bishops represent Catholic teaching, with sufficient accuracy given the topic and occasion, in issuing the statement or instruction.

2b. Bishops and audience can and do recognize the speech act as having the specific illocutionary force of a statement.

*Perlocutionary conditions*

3a. Author presumes that the audience is able to understand the content of the assertion.

3b. The audience presumes the statement is adequate and accurate and can report the content of the statement on the authority of the author.

3c. The audience can, in proper circumstances, act on the content of the statement on the authority of the authors.

3d. It is not obvious to either author or audience that the audience is currently aware of the content of the statement.

3a. The bishops presume that the audience can understand the content of their statement.

3b. The audience presumes that the bishops' statement adequately and accurately represents Catholic teaching and can report the statement to others as Catholic teaching on the authority of the bishops.

3c. Catholics can claim the authority of the bishops as a reason for their accepting the statement as the teaching of their church concerning a matter of faith and morals and act on the basis of that statement. Those who are not church members cannot claim the bishops' authority for their own beliefs or acts.

3d. It is not obvious to either the bishops or their audience that the audience is currently aware of the content of the statement.

Any claim by any government that it is pursuing a morally acceptable policy of deterrence must be scrutinized with the greatest care. We are prepared and eager to participate in our country in the ongoing public debate on moral grounds. . . . (II-D-2)

### To Men and Women in Defense Industries

You also face specific questions because the defense industry is directly involved in the development and production of weapons of mass destruction which have concerned us in this letter. We do not presume or pretend that clear answers exist to many of the personal, professional and financial choices facing you in your varying responsibilities. In this letter we have ruled out certain uses of nuclear weapons, while also expressing conditional moral acceptance for deterrence. All Catholics, at every level of defense industries, can and should use the moral principles of this letter to form their consciences. We realize that different judgments of conscience will face different people, and we recognize the possibility of diverse concrete judgments being made in this complex area. We seek as moral teachers and pastors to be available to all who confront these questions of personal and vocational choice. *Those who in conscience decide that they should no longer be associated with defense activities should find support in the Catholic community.* Those who remain in these industries or earn a profit from the weapons industry should find in the church guidance and support for the ongoing evaluation of their work. (IV-C; emphasis added)

While the first of these expressed commitments is both public and exemplary, it is not an institutionally bound commitment: given the Catholic tradition, anyone could promise to abstain from meat without regard to his or her institutional status. Nor is it, as marriage vows are, a commissive declarative which changes their institutional status. It is a commitment merely made *in* the institution and does not warrant special attention here as it is not institutionally bound.

The second is a commitment *of* the institution. The bishops corporately pledge to participate in the ongoing discussion of the morality of deterrence, a pledge which they have kept. For present purposes, the differences between various commissive forces are not important (see Searle 1969:58-59; Searle and Vanderveken 1985:192-98). The chart on p. 43 presents the conditions for issuing this speech act in this context. This commitment of the bishops to intervene in the ongoing debate presumes that the debate will continue (as in (2a) on p. 43). It also presumes that they do not enter the debate merely as individuals, but as authorities in the church with the power to make a commitment for themselves and for their successors as ecclesial authorities to participate in the discussion of deterrence.

The third excerpt makes a specific commitment *for* the institution, i.e, that the Catholic community should support those who leave their positions in the defense industry for moral reasons. I excerpted a whole section of the letter in order to show the context for the making of the commitment. The specific conditions charted on p. 43 can be adapted *mutatis mutandis* to cover this commitment. Yet two points should be noted.

First, the type of support to be given to those who leave the defense industry is not specified. However, the sorts of losses that they would have are financial, personal and professional, as the bishops imply earlier. Given the position of the bishops in the community, given that they can make commitments *for* the community, and given the context, the implication is that they have committed the Catholic community to aid those who leave defense jobs for conscience' sake.

Second, if the bishops in the course of subsequent participation in the public discussion should abandon their "conditional moral acceptance" of using nuclear weapons for deterrence (a position which has come under attack by ethicists who dissent from their teaching by advocating either a condemnation of deterrence or a more wholehearted endorsement of deterrent strategy), and if those who accept using nuclear weapons in a war situation could not show how those weapons could be used morally (cf. *The Challenge of Peace*, II-C, II-D), then the bishops would have to find that there could be no morally justifiable use for nuclear weapons, even to deter an attack. In that case, the bishops would be obliged to instruct Catholics that there were no longer any grounds for "different judgments of conscience." Should these possible future events occur, then the ability of the bishops both to direct Catholics and to make commitments for the Catholic community would be put to the test.

## Institutionally Bound Expressives

It might be argued that the section in *The Challenge of Peace* addressed to defense workers is not a commissive, but is an expressive, such as a wish. For expressives, there is no implied words-to-world fit. Thus, the section would neither commit the bishops (nor direct the audience) to perform any future action. As an expressive, it would not imply that the church had any obligation to those who

## INSTITUTIONALLY BOUND COMMISSIVES

| GENERAL | SPECIFIC |
|---|---|

*Contextual conditions*

1a. Author has a role or status in an institution such that the author is able to commit the institution or a member of it to a future course of action in an extra-institutional context.

1b. Audience recognizes the author's position as such.

1a. Bishops have a role in the Roman Catholic Church such that they can speak for the church (see previous chart) and can commit the church to participate in future public discussions of deterrence.

1b. Audience within and without the church recognizes the bishops' position in the church which enables them to make such a commitment.

*Illocutionary conditions*

2a. Author represents a possible future undertaking of the author and/or author's institution with sufficient accuracy (including appropriate strengths in and conditions for the commitment) in making the commitment.

2b. Author and audience can and do recognize the speech act as having the illocutionary point of a commissive.

2a. The bishops' intervening in "the ongoing discussion of the morality of deterrence" is a possible future act which they represent with sufficient accuracy to be taken as a promise; the audience takes the commissive as a promise (rather than a threat, vow, etc.).

2b. Bishops and their audience can and do recognize the speech act as having the illocutionary force of a promise.

*Perlocutionary conditions*

3a. Author presumes that the audience is able to take the speech act with the intended specific illocutionary point and strength.

3b. The audience can and does expect the author to fulfill the commitment to perform the future act in the appropriate circumstances.

3c. The audience can act in a manner which presumes that the author will keep the commitment as made.

3d. It is not obvious to the audience that the author is committed to the proposed course of action unless the speech act is performed.

3a. The bishops presume that their audiences can take their commitment as a promise.

3b. The audience within and without the church can and does expect the bishops to keep their promise to participate in the public discussion of the morality of deterrence.

3c. The audience within and without the church can act in a manner which presumes that the bishops will keep their promise.

3d. It is not obvious to the audience that the bishops are committed to further public discussion of deterrence unless they make this promise.

left their jobs for conscience' sake. To test this interpretation, we will discuss the material addressed to defense workers (quoted on p. 41) in light of the analysis laid out in the chart on p. 45.

In an institutionally bound expressive, the contextual and illocutionary conditions parallel the other types of speech acts. As noted in chapter 1, those who perform expressive speech acts must presume a state of affairs to obtain even though they do not assert that the state of affairs does obtain, if their acts are not to "misfire" (e.g., "The church thanks you for your generous donation." "What donation? I wouldn't give you a plug nickel for *anything*!"). The time at which the state of affairs is presumed to obtain depends on the concrete expressive point: one cannot express regret for a future act or wish for a past one.

However, the perlocutionary conditions differ from those of other types of speech acts. Since institutionally bound speech acts normally tend to be taken as directives, commissives, or declaratives, and since expressives have no words-to-world fit, it is crucial that institutionally bound *expressives* neither imply nor assert a words-to-world fit. Obviously, commissives and directives can and often do express a speaker's attitude toward a state of affairs or provide evidence for inferring that attitude. However, expressives cannot commit, declare, direct, or provide support for actions. If the perlocutionary conditions are not met as stated, given the normal expectations that authorities speak with authority, then the speech act fails to meet the "sincerity" preconditions (see note 2) and fails to be a pure expressive.

One might attempt to show that my claim that institutionally bound speech acts normally tend to be taken as directives, commissives, or declarations, and its obvious implications, that other expectations are 'abnormal,' is unwarranted. But to undermine these claims, one would have to explain why people (for example, the bishops) sometimes take such care in getting clear on the force of what they say. Either they are letting people know they are deviating from the normal or they are presuming we live in an illocutionary anarchy in which the force of every speech act needs to be spelled out. But if the latter is true, then one needs to explain why people spell out illocutionary forces only *sometimes*. Hence, the bishops are at least being precise so that they won't be misunderstood (implying that what is "normal" may not be clear to their audience) or at most issuing what may be 'abnormal' instructions.

Of course, institutional officials often trade on the confusion between speech acts which imply specific words-to-world fit and

---

## INSTITUTIONALLY BOUND EXPRESSIVES

---

| GENERAL | SPECIFIC |
|---------|----------|

### Contextual conditions

1a. Speaker has a role in an institution such that speaker can express an institutional attitude ("thank," "congratulate," "apologize," "deplore," "welcome" are typical expressive verbs [Searle 1979:15]) to a state of affairs.

1b. Audience recognizes the speaker's role.

1a. The bishops can express the institutional attitude of the church toward a state of affairs.

1b. The audience recognizes the bishops' roles.

### Illocutionary conditions

2a. Author expresses an attitude to a state of affairs with sufficient exactness such that the audience can recognize the author's attitude.

2b. The state of affairs presumed by the expressive obtains, has obtained, or might obtain, and the expressive correctly presumes the status of the state of affairs.

2a. The bishops express a wish that those who leave their jobs in defense industries as a matter of conscience might find support in the Catholic community.

2b. That those who leave their jobs in defense industries as a matter of conscience find support in the Catholic community is a possible future state of affairs.

### Perlocutionary conditions

3a. Author presumes that the audience can take the speech act in the context in which it is issued as *only* expressing the attitude intended.

3b. The audience, on the basis of this speech act, takes the author *only* to be expressing an attitude and not to be issuing a commissive, directive, or declarative.

3a. The bishops presume that the audience can take the speech act as *only* expressing a wish that the future state of affairs will come to pass, and neither committing nor directing the Catholic community to support workers who leave defense jobs for conscience' sake, nor declaring the Catholic community to be a support community for people who leave their jobs for conscience' sake.

3b. The audience, on the basis of this speech act, takes the bishops *only* to be expressing a wish and neither committing nor directing the Catholic community to undertake future acts, nor declaring the Catholic community to be a support community for people who leave their jobs for conscience' sake.

---

which reveal an author's attitude, and expressives which do not imply any specific words-to-world fit. Governments' diplomatic notes expressing "regret" over international incidents are usually such pure expressives, which sound good in the world press but have no forces which carry any commitments (compare Nussbaum 1986:43). Those with special roles or status in an institution can easily trick hearers into taking expressions of disgust or delight as commissives or directives concerning the states of affairs over which those officials express disgust or delight. They can also (intentionally or unintentionally) mislead hearers into drawing inaccurate inferences about the presumptions of expressions of delight or disgust. Then, if a hearer asks why the officials have taken no action to which the officials committed themselves or their institution, the officials can reply that they really made no commitments but merely expressed an attitude. If hearers cite official sanction for their own actions, officials can reply that they issued no directives, but merely expressed disgust, and the hearer ("unfortunately," "inappropriately," etc.) drew unwarranted inferences from them. This common political weaseling probably contributes to the breakdown of institutional authority, but it does not necessarily undercut the possibility of issuing institutional expressives. It rather shows that pure institutionally bound expressives may be rare, and that there is much room for duplicity on the part of authors and also for misunderstanding on the part of audiences. Sadly, in our era, when hearers attend to institutionally bound speech acts, it seems that the motto must be: *Caveat auditor*.

We now return to the bishops' address to defense workers. If the bishops at this point were performing an expressive speech act rather than a complex of commissives and directives, then (3a) and (3b) as on p. 45 would have to obtain. But since the bishops use "should," ordinarily associated with commissives or directives, rather than the wish-expressing "might" in their writing (see specific condition (2a) on p. 45), this exhortation is not properly taken as an institutionally bound expressive, but could be taken as a commissive (a promise to defense workers), a directive (an instruction to the local churches), or possibly as a hybrid declarative with both directive and commissive components. From the context the address might fit any of the three latter, but its substance clearly does not fit well as an expressive.

## Institutionally Bound Declaratives

*The Challenge of Peace* does not clearly issue any institutionally bound declaratives. As suggested in the introduction to this chapter, it is the prerogative of the pope to *declare* what doctrine is. Bishops can declare (perform the speech act of declaring) a person to be excommunicated, a church to be dedicated, etc., but can only promulgate (perform an assertive or directive speech act) doctrine. Each of these is possible because the agent has specific institutional status.

Moreover, Catholic theologians have recently been debating the status and authority of national bishops' conferences. In present terms, there is some debate over what acts (including speech acts) a national body of bishops is empowered to perform, an uncertainty which explains the ambiguity over the exact status of the address to defense workers discussed in the previous section: it is not at all clear that the bishops as a national conference have the power to make a declaration, although each bishop could certainly make such a commitment or issue such a directive within his own diocese. Thus, to find a clear institutionally bound declarative, we shall leave *The Challenge of Peace*, and consider the sacrament of baptism as a paradigm for analysis.[5] The conditions for performing a declarative are summarized in the chart on p. 48.

The perlocutionary results of declaratives are more obvious than those of other speech acts. This is because if persons are the subjects of declaratives, they are often thereby placed in positions in which they can perform acts they could not otherwise have performed and have status which gives them rights and responsibilities they would not have otherwise had.

In addition to pure declaratives, there are also hybrid declaratives. As noted in chapter 1, these must meet conditions for both declaratives and (1) assertives, (2) directives, or (3) commissives. The first two can be illustrated without difficulty: in the Roman Catholic Church the pope and only the pope has just the institutional status required to be able to perform definitive assertive declarations with regard to matters of faith and definitive directive declarations with regard to moral matters, each to be held by the universal church whether or not the faithful consent to what is declared. That is the 'cash value' in speech act terms of the declaration of papal infallibility promulgated by the First Vatican Council in 1870.[8]

Commissive declaratives are not so simple. Religious marriage vows are an excellent example. Since two declarers must jointly perform the ritual acts, analyzing them is more complex, but nonetheless revealing. The chart on p. 49 spells out the general conditions within the Catholic Church for receiving the sacrament of matrimony by making marriage vows. Of course, the secular law and other religious communities may have different conditions for a valid marriage, but that just shows how different institutional structures affect the possibility of performing institutionally bound actions.

---

## INSTITUTIONALLY BOUND DECLARATIVES

---

| GENERAL | SPECIFIC |
|---|---|

*Contextual conditions*

| | |
|---|---|
| 1a. Declarer has a position in an institution such that declarer is empowered to perform the declarative. | 1a. The minister has a position in the church such that the minister is empowered to baptize.[6] |
| 1b. The objects (recipients) of the declaration have a position vis-à-vis the institution such that they can be declared what the declarer declares them. | 1b. The person to be baptized has not previously been baptized. |
| 1c. The audience, if any, accepts the declarers' and recipients' positions. | 1c. The audience, if any, accepts the minister's and candidate's position as such. |

*Illocutionary conditions*

| | |
|---|---|
| 2a. Declarer performs the action with sufficient precision (including performing nonlinguistic actions). | 2a. Minister performs ritual gestures (immersion or pouring water over candidate's head) while saying appropriate words. |
| 2b. Declarer and audience can and do recognize the speech act as having the illocutionary point of a declarative. | 2b. Minister and candidate (and rest of audience) can and do recognize the act performed as a baptism. |

*Perlocutionary conditions*

| | |
|---|---|
| 3a. Declarer presumes that the subject is appropriate for the declaration and that the audience is able to understand the declaration. | 3a. Minister presumes that the subject is unbaptized and desires baptism,[7] and that the audience is able to understand the action performed as a baptism. |
| 3b. The audience can presume that the declaration was performed properly and can report the declaration performed in the appropriate circumstances. | 3b. The audience can presume that the baptism was performed properly and can testify to the status of the baptized person in appropriate circumstances. |
| 3c. The subject or recipient becomes and is entitled to be treated in the future as he, she, or it is declared to be. | 3c. The baptized person is a Christian and treated as such (e.g., can receive other sacraments, cannot be rebaptized). |
| 3d. It is not obvious to declarer, subject, or audience that the recipient would have whatever attributes the declaration gives unless the declaration were made. | 3d. Without baptism, the person would not be or properly be treated as a Christian. |

---

## INSITUTIONALLY BOUND COMMISSIVE DECLARATIVES

| GENERAL | SPECIFIC |
|---|---|

*Contextual conditions*

1a. Declarers have a position in an institution such that the they are empowered to perform the commissive declarative.

1b. The declarers are in a position vis-à-vis the institution to take the status to which they declaratively commit themselves.

1c. The audience, if any, accepts the declarers' positions.

1a. At least one of the two declarers is a Roman Catholic; both are properly prepared; they are not too closely related.

1b. Both declarers are unmarried, of different sexes, are of an age and mind to give free consent, can consummate the marriage, are not bound by religious vows.

1c. An ordained minister and at least two others witness the making of the marriage vows.

*Illocutionary conditions*

2a. Declarers make the commissive declaration with sufficient precision (including performing nonlinguistic actions).

2b. Declarers and audience can and do recognize the speech act as having the illocutionary point of a commissive declarative.

2a. Declarers both participate in and complete a recognizable marriage ceremony.

2b. Declarers and witnesses can and do recognize the ritual as having the illocutionary force of marrying which changes the marital status and the rights and obligations of the couple.

*Perlocutionary conditions*

3a. Declarers presume that the status to which they declare themselves committed is appropriate and that the audience is able to understand the commissive declaration.

3b. The audience can and does presume that the commissive declaration was correctly performed and can and does expect the declarers to assume the declared status and to keep the commitments appropriate to that status.

3c. The declarers become what they declare themselves to be and become entitled to be treated as such.

3d. It is obvious to both declarers and audience that declarers would not have the status or commitments they do unless they make the commissive declaration.

3a. Declarers presume that they are both free to marry, that they can and will keep their vows, and that the witnesses can officially witness the marriage.

3b. The audience can and does presume that the couple married each other and thereby acquire the rights and obligations proper to that status.

3c. The couple are married and become entitled to be treated as such.

3d. It is obvious to the marrying couple and audience that the couple would not be sacramentally married had they not participated in the marriage ritual.

Although marriage might seem a case of an act merely performed *in* an institution, in fact the declaration as spelled out changes the status of the couple vis-à-vis the institution. As a sacramental marriage could not be performed outside this institution (or another with very similar rules), and as the rules of the institution in which it is performed regulate when the attempted act is defective enough not to be the act attempted (see note 7 for a parallel discussion regarding baptism), it is an institutionally bound speech act. Because the declaration gives the declarers a status which carries rights and obligations, it is best understood as a commissive declarative, for those who make it are ipso facto committed to having those rights and keeping those obligations.

## On Being Responsible for
## Institutionally Bound Speech Acts

In general, the fact that we act when we speak puts what we say "on our moral account." The specific force of our actions determines just how we are responsible for what we say. But we need to note four points relevant to understanding the force (and thus the morality) of institutionally bound speech acts.

First, extra-institutional contexts can partly determine the illocutionary forces of an institutionally bound speech act. Institutionally bound directives may, in some circumstances, also properly have a strength relevant to addressees outside the institution as well as those within the institution. The example of the multiplicity of directive forces of *The Challenge of Peace* can be extended. For instance, if religious leaders publicly command their followers to vote a certain way in a secular election, in a liberal democracy the act they perform may be a hybrid: it may also have the force of a threat or warning. However, in a totalitarian polity such a command might also be a challenge to secular authority or even sedition.

Second, institutional status partly determines both the force and the strength of the acts people can and do perform. The ability to instruct authoritatively in Roman Catholic doctrine belongs to those with the status of bishop and others designated by them. The ability to analyze doctrine requires a different status: bishops *qua* bishops cannot analyze or report doctrine, but proclaim it.

The significance of this distinction is to locate precisely the true issue between teaching authorities and "dissenting" theologians within a religious tradition. The theologians point out problems in and "dissent" from the presumptions in or content of the teaching, not from the authority to teach. Their scholarly investigations may lead some to disregard authoritatively imposed teaching by showing its content unwarranted. However, this is not properly a result of the theologians' investigations, but a consequence due to the social or intellectual contexts of the teaching and the investigation. Revealing the flaws in what authorities teach may be like pointing out the truth about the emperor's new clothes. How people respond will be various. Theologians, like the boy who points out the emperor's nakedness, are responsible for the act of revealing and for the direct results of that action, but not for the conditions revealed or for the indirect consequences of revealing those conditions. Obviously, an unscrupulous theologian might intend to embarrass ecclesiastical authorities or a revolutionary one might intend to overthrow them and begin a new church. But those acts would be different from investigating (and challenging) what the authorities teach. Those would be direct attacks on the authorities. Although there are gray areas, revolutionary or unscrupulous attacks upon the institution or its authorities must be distinguished from appropriate dissent within an institution to what the authorities assert or direct.

Moreover, if people with specific status speak in contexts in which the addressees expect certain types of speech acts (e.g., directives, commissives) and actually perform other types of acts (e.g., expressives), flawed communication can result. Unscrupulous people can exploit this by trading on the audience's expectations. Careful speakers make the force of what they say clear. The difference between what people intend to say and what they are taken to say results because status and context  sometimes only partly determine what act one can perform.

Contexts also can make it practically impossible for people with certain roles or status to perform specific acts. Bishops cannot give opinions about doctrines. More importantly, the evil of Eichmann's acts, subjectively considered, may have been as banal as anyone's, and the acts he intended as meek as any other bureaucrat's. But the acts he performed, objectively considered, were neither banal nor trivial, because with the institutional status he had and in the institutional context in which he spoke, trivial acts of negligible strength and such minimal results could not be performed. One cannot neglect the role of institutional status and context in understanding and evaluating institutionally bound speech acts.

Third, institutionally bound speech acts can be undercut if one can leave the institution or if the institutional structures change sufficiently to make it impossible to perform a specific act. If institutional structures cannot be changed, individuals can leave voluntary associations; and mass exodus can destroy them. Either outcome renders institutionally bound speech acts ineffective. Voiding institutionally bound speech acts for voluntary associations such as most contemporary churches rarely presents insuperable difficulties. However, undercutting authoritative acts performed in institutions such as governments requires the intrinsically risky or difficult practice of revolution, reformation, or emigration.[9]

Fourth, speech acts are open to moral evaluation not only on the basis of the institutionally determined illocutionary force and strength of the act performed, but also on the basis of the perlocutionary results of the act. For example, the bishops who issued *The Challenge of Peace*, are and can be held responsible for providing "hope for people in our day and direction toward a world freed of the nuclear threat." If they provide illusory hope and bad direction, so much the worse for them and those who follow them. If they provide real hope and good direction, so much the better. But however one evaluates their acts, it makes no sense to claim that they are morally neutral.

# NOTES

1.   Lindbeck makes a rather different set of claims for religious utterances. He rightly implies that context and purpose both determine the illocutionary force of an utterance and that the illocutionary force determines how it is to be related to the world. But by wrongly suggesting that nonreligious "performatory" (here declaratives) have no words-to-world fit (1984:65) reduces them to mere expressives, hardly the status he intends for them. He also sharply distinguishes between first-order religious utterances (generally, assertives), which make ontological truth claims, and second-order religious doctrines (directives), which make none, but regulate the sorts of first-order utterances which can be made within a religious tradition. This presumes that directives have no assertive force. Lindbeck's denial of ontological truth-status to doctrines, a focus of dissatisfaction over his cultural-linguistic approach to theology, could have been avoided had he noted either that there are hybrid declarative-assertives which have both ordering and asserting aspects or that declarative-regulatives must be correct in their presuppositions to be fully felicitous.

2.   In this and subsequent discussions, it will be assumed that normal "preconditions" (McClendon and Smith 1975:59-60) or "input and output conditions" (Searle 1969:57) obtain: speakers and hearers (authors, audience, and recipients of declaratives) have sufficient language in common to understand each other, no physical impediments (e.g., aphasia, deafness) and no psychological impediments (e.g., illiteracy) obtain. It will also be assumed that people are not communicating in a code with contrived rather than public meanings, that speakers are not acting in a play, or trying to deceive or dissemble, or taking roles to which they are not entitled, etc., and that hearers are not eavesdroppers, spies, etc. Hence, the "can and do" of these conditions is meant to cover both the conventions or constitutive rules which make it possible to perform such acts felicitously and the (subjective) intentions to perform

"sincerely" the acts those rules make possible (see p. 215, note 7 on sincerity). This does not exclude the possibility that a person might perform relatively successful acts which do not meet all the conditions and thereby create a new kind of act or a new way of performing an established act).

The present lists of conditions differ from other theories in two important ways. First, an effort has been made to include social and institutional conditions clearly and explicitly. Bach and Harnish generally find them relevant only to "conventional illocutionary acts" (1979:109-19), roughly the class here defined as "institutionally bound." McClendon and Smith did not elaborate them, and Habermas, although seeing speech acts as essentially institutionally bound, did not analyze ideal or real social or institutional conditions for specific speech acts. Martinich included "status" conditions, but his analysis is limited to sacramental acts. Most of the social and institutional conditions are subsumed in Searle and Vanderveken's "modes of achievement" and "degree of strength" with which the illocutionary point is achieved (1985:40-43). These earlier theories have obscured most social and institutional conditions for satisfactorily performing concrete speech acts.

Second, the conditions which make perlocutionary effects possible have been included. Searle (1969:71) takes care to avoid reducing the illocutionary act to its perlocutionary effects. Yet in subsequent work, the concept of the perlocutionary all but disappears, until (in 1983) the speech act is practically equated with illocutionary intention. This loss of the perlocution and its constituted and contextual determinants distorts his account seriously. As the discussion of Eichmann's acts in chapter 1 illustrates, reducing a person's acts to her or his explicit intentions makes the acts performed unrecognizable. Speech acts reduced to explicit intentions are also unrecognizable, because they also may be sufficient, given social and institutional circumstances, to enable subsequent actions to be undertaken. Martinich makes this clear in his discussion of the sacrament of penance, and I will exploit this point especially in chapter 8. Searle and Vanderveken ignore perlocutions because they are "not essentially linguistic" and thus not conventionalizable (1985:12). An account concerned with the morality of speaking, rather than the conditions for speaking, cannot ignore perlocutionary purposes, acts, and results.

3.    Not all institutionally bound directives can have a variety of forces. The pastoral letter can also be contrasted with a different sort of directive, the general commanding the private, "Soldier, tuck your shirt in." If the general addresses a civilian thus (say, on the street in time of peace), the directive is so defective as to be no *command* at all. The institutional relationships between the general and the civilian are not such that the general can *issue* a command in these circumstances. Unlike the bishops' letter, which envisions variously constituted audiences, this order is addressed to a specific institutionally bound hearer; if the hearer does not have the proper institutional status, the act is a failure. This command cannot have another directive force. It takes multiplicity of addressees or of purposes to create multiplicity in the illocutionary forces of an utterance. Using Searle and Vanderveken's work, this could be accounted for by recognizing that one act had multiple modes of achievement and varying strengths of illocutionary points. Or, following Anscombe, one could see multiple intentions with which the letter was issued and that none is swallowed up by a greater (1957:46-47). Hence, a single act with a single point effectively intended for different audiences can be said to have many illocutionary and perlocutionary purposes and forces.

4.    Not all privileged positions are institutionally bound. See the discussion of this with regard to preaching in chapter 3, pp. 63-67.

5.    Austin saw baptism as a model performative, an analysis followed by McClendon 1966. Martinich did important work using speech act theory in analyzing

the general and specific conditions for sacraments. The present work differs from Martinich especially in that it takes Searle's taxonomy of speech acts as a model, rather than Austin's. Here sacraments are taken as either pure or hybrid declaratives, while Martinich took them as either declaratives or another type of act (see Searle and Vanderveken 1985:175). What is especially important in Martinich's analysis is his recognition that all sacramental acts require specific institutional status conditions (see Martinich 1975:408), although just what those conditions are is debatable. While persons who do not have the requisite status may surely perform or participate in acts similar to sacraments, what makes those acts sacraments is their being acts fulfilling the conditions for sacramentality in the religious community in which they are performed.

For present purposes, whether God must directly be an actor in a sacrament (as McClendon hints) or must authorize others to act effectively in the name of God (as Martinich sees it) will be left aside, as it does not directly affect the present work.

6.     In the Roman Catholic tradition the minister of baptism in ordinary circumstances must be ordained, but in times of emergency when an ordained person is not available, any person is empowered to administer this sacrament. This reminds one of the fact that noninstitutional circumstances can affect what institutionally bound acts a person can perform.

7.     Martinich (1975:301) recognizes the problems at just this point with baptism of infants and proposes to ignore infant baptism and concentrate only on adult baptism. Given that (historically) infant baptism is derivative from believers' baptism, it is reasonable to construe it either (1) as deviant enough from the norm to be so defective as to be no baptism at all or an empty performance (as many 'radicals' of the Reformation and their theological descendants have done; cf. McClendon 1966:406-7, 415-16); or (2) as a practice undertaken in special circumstances (such as a conversion of an entire household to Christianity in a society in which the head of the household was expected to give the whole household's intention) which became (for various reasons) normal and generated a separate sacramental action (confirmation) to preserve the crucial individual intention to be incorporated into Christ's church.

8.     For present purposes, accepted standard Catholic teaching on papal infallibility is presumed. The problems with the historical foundations, the logical and ecclesiological status of the doctrine, and the validity of the council which promulgated it, though of intrinsic interest, are beyond the scope of the present investigation.

9.     Speech act theory per se does not address the questions of whether given institutional structures ought to be changed or whether the conventions of given discourse practices can or ought be overthrown or undermined. In noting that conventions and institutions enable or disable specific speech acts, speech act theory is not "conventional" in the sense of "conservative" or "cheritical." Indeed, by describing correctly the conditions for performing specific speech acts and their results, speech act analysis can show just where reform is needed or just what abandoning a practice might imply and thus show just where the moral issues lie.

*Chapter 3*

# INSTITUTIONALLY FREE SPEECH ACTS IN RELIGION

This chapter concludes the formal speech act analysis by laying out the conditions for performing institutionally free religious speech acts with each of the five illocutionary points. A speech act is institutionally free just in case the conditions for performing it do not require that the speaker have a specific role or status in an institution. A religious speech act is institutionally free just in case the conditions for performing it do not require that the speaker have a specific role or status in a religious institution. This is not to say that institutionally free speech acts cannot be performed in an institutional setting, nor to deny that specific speech acts may presuppose the existence of some institutions to be performed. The existence of institutionally free practices,[1] those practices not essentially linked to any specific institution, provide sufficient background to give the social context necessary for many institutionally free speech acts. An example will help clarify this.

Anyone who understands the practice of betting can make a bet. To place a bet is, among other things, to perform a speech act. "Five dollars on Native Dancer to show," said in the proper circumstances, *is* the making of a bet. The circumstances may be standing before a betting window at a race track waving a five-dollar bill, playing a child's game with dice or spinners and phony money, making a phone call to a bookie, etc. The practice of betting is institutionally free: it may be performed in so many (and, perhaps, outside of any) institutions that there are no specifiable institutional conditions essential for engaging in the practice. Speech acts of placing bets are also institutionally free: to perform them requires no special status or institutional role, but only that one know how to engage in the practice of betting and exercise that knowledge.

Similarly, anyone who understands the practice of praying can perform a speech act of prayer. "Oh God, let Native Dancer win!" said in the proper circumstances, *is* praying. Admittedly, some prayers, especially petitionary prayers, may be very shallow, but that does not make them some other sort of act. Those circumstances may be standing before a betting window at a race track waving a five-dollar bill, playing a child's game with dice or spinners and phony money, making a phone call to a bookie, etc., as much as visiting a church. The practice of praying is institutionally free: it may be performed in so many (and outside of any religious) institutions that there are no specifiable institutional conditions essential for engaging in the practice, although the practice of prayer is properly nurtured and deepened in the setting of a religious community. Speech acts of praying are also institutionally free: to perform them requires no special status or institutional role, or even membership in any religious institution (and I will argue below that even belief in their intentional object is not necessary to offer petitionary prayers), but only that one know how to pray and exercise that knowledge.

As in the previous chapter, I have charted the general conditions for performing an institutionally free speech act with each of the five illocutionary points and the conditions for performing a specific speech act with those points in a religious context. The use of speech act theory provides a new angle of vision on some religious practices and suggests solutions to problems that vex accounts of those practices. A concluding section redeems the promise made near the beginning of the previous chapter to discuss the cognitivity of religious language and to suggest some of the moral dimensions of speech revealed by speech act theory.

## An Institutionally Free Directive: Petitionary Prayer

As suggested above, prayer can be undertaken in many circumstances. It is a prime example of an institutionally free directive performed in a religious context. The chart on p. 57 lists the conditions for a simple petitionary prayer such as "Oh God, let Native Dancer win!"[2] The subsequent discussion analyzes some central issues clustered around the propriety of prayer because resolving those issues for prayer provides a pattern for resolving them more generally for uses of language in religious contexts. (Although it may seem

## INSTITUTIONALLY FREE DIRECTIVES

| GENERAL | SPECIFIC |
|---|---|

*Contextual conditions*

| GENERAL | SPECIFIC |
|---|---|
| 1. Author and addressee have a relationship such that the author is able to issue a directive (order, suggest, request, instruct, etc.) to the addressee to perform future act(s) which the addressee can perform. | 1. Petitioner and addressee have a relationship such that the petitioner is able to pray to the addressee to perform (or refrain from performing) future acts which the addressee can perform or to allow certain states of affairs to obtain without intervention. |

*Illocutionary conditions*

| GENERAL | SPECIFIC |
|---|---|
| 2a. The author correctly presumes how the world is and implies that the world is not as the author would have it.<br><br>2b. Author and addressee can and do recognize the speech act as having the illocutionary point of a directive. | 2a. The petitioner correctly presumes that the world is not (yet) as the petitioner would have it be (i.e., the race is not decided).<br><br>2b. Petitioner and addressee can and do recognize the words uttered as having the illocutionary force of prayer. |

*Perlocutionary conditions*

| GENERAL | SPECIFIC |
|---|---|
| 3a. Author presumes that audience can follow the directive.<br><br>3b. Author expects, proportional to the strength of the directive, that the addressee will follow the directive.<br><br>3c. On the basis of what the author says, the addressee takes the author to be issuing the directive the author intends.<br><br>3d. It is not obvious to both author and addressee that addressee would do what the author directs unless the directive were issued. | 3a. The petitioner believes, hopes, or wishes that the addressee can do what the prayer asks.<br><br>3b. Petitioner believes, hopes, or wishes that the addressee will answer the petitioner's prayer.<br><br>3c. On the basis of the prayer uttered, the addressee takes the author to be praying.<br><br>3d. It is not apparent to both petitioner and addressee that addressee would do what the petitioner prays for if the petitioner had not prayed to the addressee. |

stilted to use "addressee" rather than "God," I do so because all prayers are not addressed to God or a god. Prayers may be addressed to saints, ancestors, angels, etc.) On the present analysis, some philosophical and theological issues about petitionary prayer can be clarified.

As a practice, petitionary prayer must presuppose that the intentional object to whom the prayer is directed is real, that is, that there is an addressee who can "answer" the prayer (conditions (1), (3a-d)). The practice is pointless without that presupposition, so each time one prays, one must presuppose the reality of the addressee. It might be claimed that prayer is pointless because one cannot show the existence of the addressee, or that petitionary prayer is improper because its presuppositions may be false. However, presuppositions may be of two types. They may be procedural *presumptions* or they may be substantive *assumptions*. All too often challenges to practices conflate these two types of presuppositions: An inability to demonstrate the truth or probability of a substantive claim (e.g., the existence of God) is taken as a reason to believe that a practice (e.g., praying to God) is confused or decadent. What follows shows why arguments against the rationality of assuming the existence of God do not undermine the practice of prayer which procedurally presumes the reality of its addressee, even if the presuppositions of prayer cannot be fully justified.

First, consider the alternative that presupposing the reality of an addressee is a procedural presumption of petitionary prayer. How can one justify such presumptions? Getting into position to check on a presumption independently of participating in a practice which presumes it may be impossible. This may seem odd, but consider a nonreligious example. When one is involved in a criminal court trial, the defendant is presumed innocent until proven guilty. When one is not engaging in the practice of a criminal trial, one need not make that presumption (although one may believe the accused innocent). "Checking" such a presumption is impossible. It is a procedural rule (formally given in the law—in speech act terms, an institutionally bound declarative directive) which is not "true or false" but "observed or ignored." One cannot engage in the practice of a criminal trial, although one might engage in "vigilante justice" or other practices, without observing it. To engage in a criminal trial, one presumes the defendant innocent; a prosecutor bears the burden of proof against the presumption while engaging in a practice which presumes it (compare Flew 1976).

Analogously, if presuming that the intentional object of prayer is real is a procedural presumption of prayer, then checking on it independently of participating in a religious practice which makes that presumption may be impossible. One cannot engage in the practice of prayer without observing that presumption, and unless one is engaging in prayer or some other practice with that presumption, one need not make the presumption (although one may believe) that the addressee exists. The truth or falsity of the "propositional content" of that presumption is not at issue. To engage in prayer, one presumes the reality of the addressee; to drop that presumption requires one to abandon the practice. The presumption is not "true or false" but "observed or ignored."

Now one might want to argue that practices such as criminal trials or prayers are vicious, warped, destructive, etc. But here the challenger clearly bears the burden of proof against an established practice. Moreover, the goal of the challenger's argument must be either "wholesale," i.e., to show the practice *as a practice* to be vicious, warped, destructive, etc., or "retail," i.e., to show that specific acts or types of prayer or specific trials are vicious, warped, destructive, etc. But note that the focus of the argument must be on the wisdom of engaging in the practice or on the results achieved by engaging in the practice, not on the presumptions of the practice. In neither legal nor religious examples does one argue over the truth of the presumptions necessary to engage in those practices. One may argue to accept the practices and, necessarily, their presumptions. Or one may argue to reject the practices and, necessarily, their presumptions. Or one may argue to reform the practices and possibly to change those presumptions. But to separate the presumptions from the practices and to argue about the "content" of those presumptions is a purely academic exercise with no obvious practical implications.

Second, consider the alternative that presupposing the reality of the addressee is a substantive assumption of petitionary prayer. How would one go about checking on such an assumption? One might argue that belief in the existence of an addressee with certain qualities made prayer appropriate or possible. If the addressee did not exist, then prayer would be (objectively) pointless. If the petitioner did not believe in the addressee, then the practice would be (subjectively) pointless. What a person who prayed would need to do, if he or she would pray justifiably, would be to show that the addressee exists and has the qualities needed. Then we could tell whether prayer is appropriate. Yet the arguments to support this alternative are conceptually flawed.

(a) The argument cannot be that one must be able to give a justification of belief in an addressee before one can justifiably pray to that addressee. In general terms, given what we know of nonliterate cultures and the development of children in our own culture, it seems ludicrous to argue that one must be able to give warrants for presuppositions of one's practices before one participates in those practices. To argue that any person must first justify the assumptions of practices before participating in them is far-fetched. This is the point of Wittgenstein's dictum that belief comes before doubt. The challenger must either show that the class of religious practices should be an exception to this general "tolerance" or that the general approach of "tolerance" is wrong. The latter is beyond our scope, and I know of no arguments for the former.

(b) The argument cannot be that belief in an intentional object, such as the addressee of a prayer, is conceptually prior to engaging in a practice. Prayer as a practice does not presuppose the existence of any specific addressee of prayer any more than nuclear physics as a practice presupposes the existence of any specific subatomic entities. Specific acts of prayer, like specific scientific investigations, do presuppose the existence of specific entities as their intentional objects. What validates or invalidates those presuppositions is the very engagement in the practice, an engagement which gives reason to believe or disbelieve in specific intentional objects. Performing an act of prayer or a specific scientific experiment is how one uncovers reasons to believe in a god or in specific subatomic events/particles. But assuming the reality of, having belief in, a specific intentional object is not conceptually prior to engaging in a practice. In fact, it is sufficient to wish, hope, hypothesize, etc., the reality of intentional objects if one engages in prayer or experiment. Most religious believers believe that someone hears their petitionary prayers, but that belief is neither formally nor materially necessary for praying. In sum, that an addressee hears one's prayers is a necessary procedural presumption of prayer, and may be a common, but not necessary, substantive assumption made by those who pray. Hence, to be effective, the challengers' arguments must be directed not against belief in God as an assumption, but against presuming the reality of God when one prays.

To show that a presumption necessary for a practice is inappropriate, one might argue that the practice is conceptually incoherent. To succeed, one would have to show that the class of intentional objects of the practice cannot exist or very probably does not exist. With regard to religious practices, such a burden of proof has not been borne even by rigorous materialists like Feuerbach, Marx, and Sartre. Another approach would be to show that the practitioners cannot intend those objects by engaging in the practice, that is, that exercises of the practice must be unsuccessful. This would require showing that those who engage in petitionary prayer cannot pray to the addressees any more than army privates can issue orders to army generals. I know of no such argument.

One might try to undermine the practice of prayer by wielding an Ockhamite razor: Since one can explain prayer naturalistically, and since one ought not multiply entities beyond necessity, one has no need to postulate supernatural entities to account for prayer. Scientific investigations require a procedural presumption of parsimony, analogous to a procedural presumption of innocence in a criminal court; a subatomic entity cannot be declared to exist unless the declarer bears the burden of proof. But at this point the analogy between the practices of prayer and science breaks down. The practice of prayer does not have a procedural presumption of parsimony. Two considerations show why this is so.

First, the goal of scientific investigation, like the goal of a criminal trial, is to have the investigating team, like the jury, be in position to perform speech acts which are assertive declarations: "The entity exists," "The accused is guilty." The proper motto, in speech act terms, to account for the importance of Ockham's razor is something like, "One ought not declare to be what one cannot prove to be." However, the goal of petitionary prayer is not to have the petitioner get into position to perform any speech act, but to get the addressee to act. Since the razor is a tool suitable for use in reaching appropriate declarative goals in the context of theory construction, and the goal of prayer is not to declare something to exist, it is not clear that the razor is a useful tool in this context. Its utility for one purpose does not imply that there is good reason to believe it is a useful tool for reaching a different goal.

Second, one can engage in the practice of prayer to many addressees—say, in the context of polytheism or Catholic prayer to saints as well as to God, in the hope that at least one of them will act. While there may be theological arguments about such practices, I do not know any philosophical arguments that would show them to be incoherent. The practice of prayer is not necessarily parsimonious.

If one's prayers are not answered, a person might give up on praying to the specific addressee, just as in other circumstances a person might abandon an investigation or declare a mistrial. But as not finding a particle to fit one's scientific hypothesis or not reaching a verdict in a criminal trial are not reasons for giving up on the practices of nuclear physics or criminal trials, so not having one's petitionary prayer answered is not a reason for giving up on the practice of prayer. Hence, arguments which attempt to show that prayer inevitably is unsuccessful fail. The practice of prayer and its necessary presumption of an addressee have not been shown to be conceptually incoherent or otherwise essentially flawed.

Thus one does not have to "prove" the existence of the addressee before (historically or conceptually before) one prays. Moreover, one does not have to believe that the addressee exists to pray to that addressee, any more than one has to believe that muons exist to find out that they do exist and have certain properties. The contextual conditions for prayer do not require belief in the addressee and perlocutionary conditions (3a) and (3b) are such that the petitioner does not have to believe in God. Pojman (1986) has argued that hope, not belief, is an attitude sufficient for a religious person. I would go further and note that merely wishing that there be an addressee is sufficient for petitionary prayer. Admittedly, "O God (if there be a god), save my soul (should I have a soul)" is not much of a prayer. But it can be a minimal prayer, perhaps a first exercise in a strange practice, a practice in which a person can develop an ability to pray more deeply. Minimal prayers, like wartime prayers of "atheists in foxholes," cannot be disparaged by declaring them no prayers at all nor be used to show that there are "no atheists in foxholes," since those praying do not have to assume the existence of their intentional object.

Of course, someone eavesdropping on the prayer (a hearer who is not an addressee) might then infer that the person praying "believed in" the addressee of the prayer. This seems an "expected" or "normal" epistemic attitude for a praying person to have. However, such an inference is no more warranted than the inference that the boss who utters the motivational expressive, "Good work," is approving the worker's job. The circumstances may make both inferences unwarranted. The circumstances of prayer may be unusual enough—e.g., atheists in foxholes, doubters in church—that a hearer might be unwarranted in inferring that the person praying had the "usual" epistemic attitude. But the reliability of that inference varies with the circumstances in which the prayer is offered and someone making such an inference would be wise to check it ("I didn't think a guy like *you* would believe in God." "Oh, I don't, *really*, but when ya' hear the shell coming, ya' wish there were Someone who might deflect it").

What gives many "philosophical" objections to prayer their interest is that we cannot ascertain whether all the conditions for engaging in nondefective petitionary prayer actually obtain. We cannot demonstrate that the requisite relationship (contextual condition (1)) does or does not exist, that the addressee can and does, cannot or does not, hear the prayer (illocutionary condition (2b)), and that the addressee can and will, cannot or will not, answer the prayer (contextual condition (1), all perlocutionary conditions). A praying person may believe any or all of these and have good reasons for believing them, but cannot get into position to check them. Such inability to "prove" that prayer is appropriate seems to open the door to challenges and may leave some people who pray uncomfortable at their inability to justify their prayer to their nonparticipating friends.

However, the fact that it is possible that the conditions for praying do not obtain does not mean that there is good reason to believe that they do not obtain and to stop praying, any more than the fact that it is possible that science does not portray reality means that there is good reason to believe that science is useless and to stop investigating. Scientific practices, like prayer, may not be rooted in reality, but neither has been shown to be purely instrumental or illusory. Thus, analyzing the conditions for performing the speech act of petitionary prayer has shown that prayer is a practice as "foundationless" as science. The question of whether and how one should participate in either cannot be settled by academic argument about the rationality of the realistic "propositions" abstracted from the presumptions of these practices.

## An Institutionally Free Assertive: Religious Preaching

In most religious traditions, members are in position to say what they believe. While this can be proclaiming, professing, testifying, etc., depending on the circumstances, such communicative actions can often be performed without regard to a person's institutional status. In some traditions preaching is institutionally bound (just in case those not ordained or otherwise authorized are not permitted to preach). However, preaching as a practice is institutionally free (in the sense relevant to this investigation), for it can be found in many traditions and can be undertaken in many traditions without regard to institutional status. It remains, perhaps, the most widely recognized example of religious assertion. As a sample of preaching, consider the formulation of the Four Noble Truths from the First Sermon of Buddha at Benares, where he is portrayed as addressing a group of five monks:

> The Noble Truth of suffering is this: Birth is suffering; ageing is suffering; sickness is suffering; death is suffering; sorrow and lamentation, pain, grief and despair are suffering; association with the unpleasant is suffering; dissociation from the pleasant is suffering; not to get what one wants is suffering—in brief the five aggregates of attachment are suffering.
> The Noble Truth of the origin of suffering is this: It is this thirst (craving) which produces re-existence and re-becoming, bound up with passionate greed. It finds fresh delight now here and now there, namely,

thirst for sense-pleasures; thirst for existence and becoming; and thirst for non-existence (self-annihilation).

The Noble Truth of the Cessation of suffering is this: It is the complete cessation of that very thirst, giving it up, renouncing it, emancipating oneself from it, detaching oneself from it.

The Noble Truth of the Path leading to the Cessation of suffering is this: It is simply the Noble Eightfold Path, namely right view; right thought; right speech; right action; right livelihood; right effort; right mindfulness; right concentration (*Samyutta-nikaya* lvi, 11 [Rahula's translation], as in Bowker 1970:238-40).

The chart on p. 65 lists the specific conditions for preaching a sermon, yoked with the general conditions for issuing an assertive.

In contrast to the case of petitionary prayer, the audience and the preacher's relationship with it present little problem. Preaching is one obvious verbal way of persuading the audience to accept what one says.

As with all assertions, to be fully successful, the assertion must be true (compare Tilley 1985:182-212) and its asserters must be able to show how they came to hold the assertion with the strength they do. A person may properly give very weak backing for a surmise, hunch, or untested hypothesis. A person may give only controversial backing for controversial claims. In recent years, religious experiences have again been recognized to provide warrant for religious believers, as they may be properly basic for those who have those experiences (see Tilley 1990 and the literature cited therein). Buddha could certainly have cited the events of the fourth watch of his night devoted to contemplation at Bodh Gaya as giving rise to his properly basic beliefs. According to the Scriptures, when he reached the depth of his insight, the earth swayed, gentle zephyrs caressed him, flower petals showered from the heavens, and all living beings were glad. These are surely evidences of true insight. Given the Buddha's standing in the religious traditions of India, he may be justified in taking the Four Noble Truths as properly basic. Hearers of sermons or testimonies (not Buddha's monkish hearers, of course) may reject Buddha's insights or find the miraculous accompaniments incredible, or doubt whether his belief is *properly* basic, but no preacher would be surprised by such rejection.

Perlocutionary conditions (3a) and (3d) are presumptions necessary if someone is to preach, and (3b) is necessary if the audience is to be in position to accept what the preacher said as possibly true. Condition (3c) generally accounts for the fact that you can take what I say and act on it on my authority, appropriate to the strength of the illocutionary force of what I say. If I claim that $p$ is absolutely

## INSTITUTIONALLY FREE ASSERTIVES

### GENERAL

### SPECIFIC

*Contextual conditions*

1. Author has a relationship with audience such that audience can recognize the specific assertive act performed.

1. Preacher has a relationship with audience such that the audience can recognize that the author is preaching.

*Illocutionary conditions*

2a. Author represents the way things are in issuing the assertion, with sufficient accuracy given the force, topic, and occasion.

2b. Author is in position to warrant what is said sufficient to the force of the utterance.

2c. Author and audience can and do recognize the speech act as having the illocutionary point the author intends.

2a. Preacher represents the way things are, with sufficient accuracy for preaching the sermon at that time and place.

2b. Preacher is in position to say why he believes what he preaches.

2c. Preacher and audience can and do recognize the speech act as having the illocutionary force of a sermon.

*Perlocutionary conditions*

3a. Author presumes that the audience is able to understand the content and force of the assertion.

3b. The audience presumes the assertion adequately and accurately represents the way the world is, given the topic, the occasion, and the specific illocutionary force and strength of the utterance, and can report the content of the assertion as accepted by the author with the strength shown.

3c. The audience can presume the truth of the assertion proportional to the illocutionary force and strength of the assertion and, in proper circumstances, act on that presumption.

3d. It is not obvious to either author or audience that the audience is currently aware of the content of the assertion.

3a. The preacher presumes that the audience can understand the content of the sermon.

3b. The audience presumes that the sermon adequately and accurately represents what the author believes about the world and can take the sermon as evidence for the preacher's views.

3c. The audience can (but does not have to) accept the truth of the sermon and, in proper circumstances, can act on that presumption.

3d. It is not obvious to either preacher or audience that the audience currently accepts what is preached with the strength the preacher believes appropriate.

certain, and you have no good reasons to doubt what I say, you are empowered by me to act on $p$.[3] Of course, if I surmise that $p$ or guess that $p$, or if you have good reason to doubt the reliability of my warrants or my sincerity or veracity, then you may not be in position to act on my claim. If you "should have had" good reason to doubt my warrants, then you may not be able to justify acting on my authority. Condition (3c) specifically shows that if the monks accept what Buddha says, they are then empowered to act upon it: to walk the Noble Eight-Fold Path to Enlightenment.

Such epistemic transmissibility is often presumed to require institutionally bound authority. However, not all assertives which transmit content require that the speaker have a specific institutional status, as McClendon and Smith have pointed out:

> Although I can surmise, I cannot state what the British prime minister wore to bed last night, since I was not there—but someone who was there can perhaps state that he wore pink pajamas, and I may then be able to state that on the other's authority. The president's physician cannot state, is not in line to state, current U.S. policy in some Lebanese crisis, while the president and secretary of state are and can (1975:58).

In the former example, the privileged position is not an institutionally bound one, while in the latter it is. While people in various positions (detectives, butlers, friends, spouses, guards, etc.) might be situated to describe the P.M.'s nightwear, only a person authorized to state policy can do so. Only when that policy is authoritatively stated, can it properly be reported as policy. Of course, a policy statement can be "leaked" to the press, but wise reporters will proportion their use of the leaks and the strength of their published claims both to the status and veracity of the "leaker" and the circumstances in which the "leak" springs. In general, then, assertions carry transmissive perlocutionary force proportional to the illocutionary force of the act performed.

Buddha's authority is, in Weber's sense, charismatic (as opposed to institutional). He occupied no special institutional position to warrant his view. He was not even a Brahmin. Nonetheless, he does not surmise the Four Noble Truths, or hypothesize them, but preaches them as *truth*, giving them as strong an assertive force as possible on the basis of his personal authority. If a hearer accepts what Buddha says on his authority, the hearer has a right to act on it. Buddha, like any speaker, to the extent to which he explicitly or implicitly claims authority, and to which that claim is accepted, is at least in part responsible for the results: the hearer's acceptance and actions based directly on what Buddha said.

## An Institutionally Free Commissive: Pledging

Although vows are often made within institutional settings and can both give persons making the vows obligations in the institution they did not previously have and change their status in the institution (as marriage vows do), much simpler commitments can also be called vows. Supernatural entities make various commitments to humans, from dire threats to absolute promises. People make promises, pledges and other commissives to and in the explicit presence of gods, saints, angels, etc. Some of these commissives are absolute, others conditional. Pledges, vows, contracts, covenants, agreements, treaties, and other institutionally bound and free commitments can be made both within and without religious institutions. Hence, the conditions for religious vowing will not be much different from those for nonreligious vows.

Consider the following text:

> After these things the word of the Lord came to Abram in a vision, "Fear not, Abram, I am your shield; your reward shall be very great. . . . Look toward heaven, and number the stars, if you are able to number them." Then he said to him, "So shall your descendants be." And he believed the Lord; and he reckoned it to him as righteousness (Gen. 15:1, 5-6).

The chart on p. 68 lays out the conditions for commissives and the specific conditions for this pledge of the Lord addressed to Abram.

In the present example, considerations similar to those made about institutionally free directives generally and prayer specifically apply. The contextual conditions and perlocutionary condition (3c) have presumptions as "independently uncheckable" as those for petitionary prayer. Checking on whether a relationship in which pledging and accepting a pledge between God and a person obtains may require participating in the practice of pledging, or in the communities which accept the pledge. Illocutionary condition (2a) presumes that God has the power to ensure that the pledged state of affairs will come about. Indeed, the Jewish and Christian communities have often understood their very existence as a fulfillment of that pledge.

To show that these presumptions are unwarranted requires making the same sorts of arguments as those discussed above. The presumption can be defeated if a person participates in the practice and bears the burden of proof against the presumption, or shows that one cannot accept a pledge from a divine being, or shows that there

---

### INSTITUTIONALLY FREE COMMISSIVES

---

| GENERAL | SPECIFIC |
|---|---|

#### *Contextual conditions*

| | |
|---|---|
| 1. Author and recipient have a relationship such that the recipient can recognize and accept the specific commitment the author makes. | 1. The Lord and Abram have a relationship such that Abram can recognize that the Lord is making a pledge to him and accept such a pledge. |

#### *Illocutionary conditions*

| | |
|---|---|
| 2a. Author represents a possible future undertaking of the author with sufficient accuracy (including appropriate strengths in and conditions for the commitment) in making the commitment.<br><br>2b. Author and recipient can and do recognize the speech act as having the illocutionary point of a commissive. | 2a. God pledges without conditions that Abram shall not only have an heir of his loins, but many descendants.<br><br>2b. God and Abram recognize God's word to Abram as a pledge without conditions. |

#### *Perlocutionary conditions*

| | |
|---|---|
| 3a. Author presumes that the recipient is able to take the speech act with the intended specific illocutionary force.<br><br>3b. Recipient can and does expect the author to fulfill the commitment to perform the future act in the appropriate circumstances.<br><br>3c. Recipient can act in manners which presume that the author will keep the commitment as made, including reporting the commitment to others in appropriate circumstances.<br><br>3d. It is not obvious to the recipient that the author is committed to the proposed course of action unless the commitment is made. | 3a. God presumes that Abram takes God's word as a pledge to Abram.<br><br>3b. Abram can and does expect God to keep the pledge God made without reservation if Abram accepts it.<br><br>3c. Abram can rely on God's pledge without reservation (cf. Gen. 22), and can testify to the pledge to others in appropriate circumstances.<br><br>3d. It is not obvious to Abram that what God pledges will come about unless God pledges it. (cf. Gen. 16-18:15, 21) |

---

are no coherent concepts of God's power on which God can fulfill his pledge. Obviously, perlocutionary condition (3a) admits of no direct checking, but if God can fulfill the pledge, one presumes that God could make it. Perlocutionary conditions (3b), (3c), and (3d) are necessary for the pledge to work as a pledge. In the absence of sound counterarguments, a person may be epistemically justified in believing that God made a pledge to Abram.[4]

## An Institutionally Free Expressive: Swearing

Taking the name of the Lord in vain is, among Christians and Jews, a violation of a commandment in the Decalogue. While some take the commandment to preclude any nonreligious use of "God," most find swearing upsetting. Consider the following theological discussion of why people swear and what it means:

> Now it is in situations of high frustration when nothing seems to yield; when a man realizes his powerlessness or finitude; when he is caught up in an entanglement of relationships that he may be heard to swear. In such words are his cosmic protest, his label for this situation where in some way his existence is shown in its 'authentic' character; when he sees the 'existential' claim in his life; when he knows what 'being-in-a-situation' is. Swearing expresses 'heroic defiance'; it is an assertion of a man's 'being *pour soi*' and so on. So swearing is rightly condemned by religious people because the logic of swearing is so very close to the logic of God. Both appeal to a characteristic situation of discernment and depth, but when a man swears, 'God' is replaced by a word which, even if it is the same token word—made up of the same letters or sounding identical—has no logical connection with a theistic scheme. Swearing is rightly condemned when, in a situation of discernment, an oath takes the place of 'God' (Ramsey 1957:22).

What is right about Ramsey's discussion is his recognition of the types of situations which may provoke (or are the contextual conditions in which a person can do) some serious swearing. What Ramsey remains confused about is the use of "God." It is not that the word somehow magically changes from one context (say prayer of adoration or thanksgiving) to another (such as swearing). What is different is the speech act in which the linguistic token, "God," is ingredient. Because the token does not change, even though it does have a different context, meaning, and (possibly) reference, anyone who performs such an act may not be saying anything to which religious belief is relevant. But the swearing person may give offense to religious people because they take the very sound of the word "God" as sacred.

Speech act analysis can show just where the problem is between them. Charting the conditions (as on p. 71) for "God damn her" or other expressives will help to begin unraveling the problem.

Like all expressions of attitudes, swearing presumes states of affairs and is defective if those presumptions are wrong. One cannot felicitously swear at a person who has given one no cause for irritation. That would be an act of swearing, but a defective one. If there is no God nor any damnation, the expressive is neither unsuccessful nor defective: it still expresses the speaker's attitude, however vulgarly. The existence of God is irrelevant to the expression. Atheists can swear because their use of "God" in swearing no more presumes the existence of God than does teachers' use of "Ceres" in classroom discussions presume the existence of Ceres.

What makes religious people so opposed to swearing is a defect with regard to conditions (2a), (3a) and (3b). A religious person may simply be unable to hear any utterance with "God" in it as not referring to the God that a religious person worships. The religious person hears the swearer as taking the name of God in vain. However, the person who swears is using the token "God" to ventilate her or his feelings. In speech act terms, the person swearing rarely, if ever, means to be issuing a directive to God ("God: Take that person and torture her eternally, please"). To do so is to utter a curse. But a religious person may be unable to hear "God damn her" as anything but a curse, a directive speech act. At this point there is a stalemate: it cannot be shown that either person has the only possible reasonable position on this matter. However, the problem is not with the illocutionary intention, but with a profound disagreement either about the possibility of performing an expressive illocutionary act using the word "God" in it or about the morality of doing so. One might say the swearer and the believer participate in different, irreconcilable discourses, and that this creates the failure to communicate.

## An Institutionally Free Declarative: Confession

Even though one often finds preaching, pledging, and praying in religious institutions, I have argued that each of these speech acts can be institutionally free. However, finding institutionally free declaratives is much more difficult. Searle put the matter thus:

> Notice that all of the examples we have considered so far involve an extra-linguistic institution, a system of constitutive rules in addition to the constitutive rules of language, in order that the declaration may be successfully performed. The mastery of those rules which constitute linguistic competence by the speaker and hearer is not in general sufficient for the performance of a declaration. In addition, there must exist an extra-linguistic institution and the speaker and hearer must occupy special places within this institution. It is only given such institutions as the church, the law, private property, the state and a special position of the speaker and hearer within these institutions that

---

### INSTITUTIONALLY FREE EXPRESSIVES

| GENERAL | SPECIFIC |
|---------|----------|

*Contextual conditions*

1. Speaker is in a situation which provokes her or his expression of an attitude, e.g., "thank," "congratulate," "apologize," "condole," "deplore," "welcome" (Searle 1979:15) toward a state of affairs.

1. The person is in a situation such as described above in the quotation from Ramsey.

*Illocutionary conditions*

2a. Author expresses an attitude to a state of affairs with sufficient exactness such that the audience can recognize the author's attitude.

2b. The state of affairs presumed by the expressive obtains, has obtained, or might obtain and the expressive correctly presumes the status of the state of affairs.

2a. The person expresses disgust, frustration, etc., over an act another person has performed, a characteristic she has, a state of affairs, etc.

2b. The state of affairs evoking the expressive reaction obtains, has obtained, or might obtain and the expressive correctly presumes the status of the state of affairs.

*Perlocutionary conditions*

3a. Author presumes that the audience can take the speech act in the context in which it is issued as the *only* attitude intended.

3b. Any audience, on the basis of this speech act, takes the author *only* to be expressing an attitude and not to be issuing a commissive, directive, or declarative.

3a. The speaker presumes that any audience can take the swearing as *only* expressing the reaction/attitude intended.

3b. Any audience, on the basis of this speech act, takes the speaker *only* to be expressing the reaction/attitude intended.

---

one can excommunicate, appoint, give and bequeath one's possessions or declare war. There are two classes of exceptions to the principle that every declaration requires an extra-linguistic institution. First there are supernatural declarations. When, e.g., God says "Let there be light" that is a declaration. Secondly there are declarations that concern language itself, as for example, when one says, "I define, abbreviate, name, call or dub. . . ." Declarations are a very special category of speech acts (Searle 1979:18; compare Searle and Vanderveken 1985:57).[5]

The only institutionally free declaratives Searle recognizes, then, are those which create something out of nothing, in either ontological or semantic realms.

Yet there is at least one speech act that is a declaration, but requires no specific extralinguistic institution for its performance nor that its speaker and hearer have specific institutional positions. It is the assertive declaration which is a confession, an act sufficient for resolving one of the problems of evil, as chapter 8 shows. (Indeed, in chapter 8 I identify at least one other institutionally free assertive declaration, that of "forgiving.") The prototype of this declarative is Augustine's *Confessions*.

The claims scholars have made about the psychology of the author of the *Confessions*, its literary force, and its religious significance are as varied as those made of any classic. Consider, for example, some of the bewildering variety of claims that Peter Brown, Augustine's masterful modern biographer, has made about the *Confessions* in a very few pages:

> At first sight, it was easy to place the *Confessions*: they were patently the work of a Neo-Platonic philosopher. They were . . . written in the form of a prayer to God that was common to a long tradition of religious philosophy (1967:165).
>
> The *Confessions* are a masterpiece of strictly intellectual autobiography (167).
>
> The *Confessions* are a manifesto of the inner world . . .(168) . . . the *Confessions* is an autobiography in which the author has imposed a drastic, fully-conscious choice of what is significant. The *Confessions* are, quite succinctly, the story of Augustine's 'heart', or his 'feelings'—his *affectus* (169).
>
> Augustine wrote the *Confessions* in the spirit of a doctor committed only recently, and so all the more zealously, to a new form of treatment (176).
>
> It is this theme of *Confession* that would make Augustine's treatment of himself different from any autobiography available, at the time, to his readers. For the insistence on treatment by 'confession' has followed Augustine into his present life. The amazing Book Ten of the *Confessions* is not the affirmation of a cured man: it is the self-portrait of a convalescent (177).

How can a coherent and classic book be a prayer, a philosophical treatise, a manifesto, a strictly intellectual autobiography that is paradoxically the story of its author's feelings, and a form of therapy written by someone not fully healed?

This is all possible because in the *Confessions*, Augustine is *declaring himself to be who he is*. This assertive declaration is a speech act both necessary and sufficient to make the new Bishop of Hippo

Regius who he is. It is necessary in the same way that the public declaration at an A.A. meeting, "I am an alcoholic," is necessary for a person to be a recovering alcoholic: only those who declare themselves such can be on the road to recovery. Like Augustine's confession that he is a sinner, the alcoholic's declaration is also a drastic, fully conscious assertion of what is significant in one's life. It is sufficient in that once the audience (including Augustine himself later) reads or hears the Confessions, Augustine is to them as he portrays himself. He can be no other. Only another confession (or an analysis which explains who Augustine was better than he did) can change this.[6]

The following chart lays out the conditions for performing an assertive declarative generally and a confession specifically. In it the term "confessor" has the classic sense of the person who performs the act of confession, not the more recent Roman Catholic usage, where the minister of the sacrament of penance is sometimes called the confessor.

The conditions for performing an institutionally free assertive declaration are very similar to those for performing an institutionally bound declaration. The key difference is that the contextual conditions in the present instance do not specify that the declarer's position is institutionally privileged, but simply privileged.

When judges find criminals guilty, they can perform that declaration successfully only because they have institutionally privileged positions in the criminal justice system. If there were no institution which gave them their office as judge, they could not perform the declarations. They might say the same words, but they would not thereby make a person liable for legal punishment. However, when a person confesses her life, the privileged position the confessor holds is not institutional. Having a specific official status in an institution is not a condition for successfully confessing. Nor is the privileged position epistemological (having some private access to information or data as one may allegedly have "private access" to one's pains and tickles). Rather, the privileged position is assumed when one takes up the proper attitude and places oneself in a social context in which she can perform, and be heard to perform, the declarative act of confessing.

For example, in Augustine's case, he must lay all his life bare before God, to be seen by God and by the many who will read his Confessions (X/2, X/1). To do so, he had to see himself not as a healthy person, but as a convalescent (Brown 1967:177) committed to a new form of therapy (Brown 1967:176). A person who did not see himself as diseased, sinful, sick, could not undertake therapy

## INSTITUTIONALLY FREE DECLARATIVES

| GENERAL | SPECIFIC |
|---|---|

*Contextual conditions*

| GENERAL | SPECIFIC |
|---|---|
| 1. Declarer has a privileged position such that the declarer's utterance is necessary and sufficient in the context in which it is uttered to create a fact or state of affairs. | 1a. The person is in a position to declare who she is as she confesses the story of her life.<br>1b. The confessor previously was not and was not taken to be who she declares herself to be. |

*Illocutionary conditions*

| GENERAL | SPECIFIC |
|---|---|
| 2a. Declarer performs the action with sufficient precision (including performing nonlinguistic actions).<br>2b. Declarer and audience can and do recognize the speech act as having the illocutionary point of a declarative. | 2a. Confessor confesses by narrating her life story with sufficient accuracy to show who she is.<br>2b. Confessor and audience can and do recognize the story told as an assertive declarative of confession. |

*Perlocutionary conditions*

| GENERAL | SPECIFIC |
|---|---|
| 3a. Declarer effects a state of affairs by issuing the declaration.<br>3b. The audience can report in the appropriate circumstances the reality of the new state of affairs.<br>3c. It is not obvious to declarer or audience that the declared state of affairs would have obtained if the declaration had not been issued. | 3a. The confessor becomes and can be taken to be who she declares herself to be as she confesses the story of her life.<br>3b. The audience can report in the appropriate circumstances what the confessor has become in making her confession.<br>3c. It is not obvious to the confessor or audience that the person would be who she declared herself to be if the confession had not been made. |

since he could not see the need for it. He must correctly identify the disease as "sin," for a misidentification would incline one to undertake the wrong therapy or, at best, the right therapy by accident. There also must be an audience for the confession, since an unheard confession, like any other unheard or unrecognized declarative, fails to be a successful action. The primary audience would be God, but the readers of the *Confessions* provide a secondary, and perhaps practically necessary, audience.

In the similar case of the A.A. member, he assumes the privileged position by seeing himself as an alcoholic, preparing to lay bare his life in front of his fellow convalescents (A.A. has no "graduates"), correctly identifying the condition which needs therapy, and by having or finding an audience (fellow sufferers who understand) who constitute a therapeutic community. In general, although one can express many things, e.g., remorse, recrimination, guilt, etc., one cannot confess unless one places onself into a position in which the declaration can be effective. In both cases, getting into the proper position to perform the action is not taking up an office in an institution, but being a member (whether institutional official or not) of a community which can recognize the speech act.

One cannot merely get into position to act, one must act once one is in position. Augustine had not only to prepare to act by thinking of himself as he did, but had to perform the act of confessing in writing the *Confessions*. Augustine adapts the assertive form used by some Neoplatonic philosophers (Brown 1967:165), but transforms it into an assertive declaration. By Book X, it becomes obvious that this is no simple assertion. (Whether Augustine created the form of confession, this specific kind of speech act, is irrelevant to the present discussion. Either he invented it or he gave the type its first masterpiece.) To narrate *his* life, the story must be an intellectual autobiography (167) for that is his "inner world" as much as his "heart," "feelings," or *"affectus"* (169). Had he left either part out, the story would be insufficient to say who he was. Nonetheless, Augustine "has imposed a drastic, fully-conscious choice of what is significant" (169). But this is the characteristic of all autobiography, and perhaps even of all memories of one's own past.

Augustine's becoming a problem to himself (*Confessions* X/16) is part of the paradoxes of memory, the problems of remembering and forgetting which are central to Book X. Yet the question is not whether choices are made, but whether the author is comprehensively accurate enough to avoid self-deception.[7] If writing the *Confessions* is understood as issuing an assertive declaration, part of the paradox of memory may be reconceived (and possibly resolved).

The problem is not how things get into the storehouse of memory (*Confessions* X/8, X/10), or how one can bring out from that storehouse what one has forgotten, but whether one's confession faithfully declares what-has-been to be what-is. It is not the mind of another which "stored" memories, but one's own (*Confessions* X/10). What is deep in memory is hard to find.[8]

Augustine also needed an audience for his confession. The successful confession made him who he was and made it appropriate for him to be taken as one sick with sin, and afflicted with temptation, but being cured by the power of God (*Confessions* X/30-39) through Christ (*Confessions* X/43). He might again fail through pride (*Confessions* X/38) or complacency. These are sins of forgetfulness, of failing to remember who had healed him and to remember how comfortable forgetfulness can be (*Confessions* X/39). But acts of remembering his *Confessions*—whether performed by himself or others who could recall his memories for him—provide a prophylactic against his refusing to remember again. Once he had made his confession, his audience would take him to be who he declared himself to be. This attitude toward him (condition (3a)) could enable him to recall his declaration of who he was. It also might haunt his audience with the possibility that Augustine's declaration also might declare who they were.

If the arguments in this section are on target, then there can be institutionally free assertive declaratives (*pace* Searle), and construing Augustine's *Confessions* as performing such an act both illustrates the specific type of speech act and illumines the text. Chapter 8 shows how performing such acts can resolve some of the problems presented by one type of suffering.

## The Morality of Speaking and the Cognitivity of Religious Language

If the analyses in these two chapters have been accurate, two points should emerge. First, the morality of speaking is complex. One might think that discussions of the rights and wrongs of telling what one believes to be false or not telling what one believes to be true would be sufficient loci for moral debate about speaking (see Bok). If one considered speaking merely as explicit or implicit asserting, that expectation would make sense. But speech act theory generally shows that we perform a variety of acts when we speak. Even assertives are rarely "mere assertions." Moralists rarely consider these acts. They debate the conditions in which one may break a vow more than the morality of making vows. They discuss the conditions in which disobedience to directives is appropriate more than the morality of issuing directives. They agonize over dissembling with regard to content, but all too infrequently discuss the duplicity involved in a speaker's getting an audience to take an expressive as a commissive or directive. They leave aside debates in the areas of the ethics of belief (see McCarthy 1986) as if they had little to do with ethics. If speech act theory is on the right track, these omissions constitute defalcations of the intellect. The following chapters of *The Evils of Theodicy* cannot remedy those general defects. However, the investigations in Part 2 provide some hints for exploring that mostly uncharted area, the morality of speech acts.

Second, there is no wholesale way to decide on the 'cognitivity' of religious language. Each type of speech act performed in a religious context has different "cognitive requirements." Arguing over "propositions" abstracted from religious speech acts and divorced from religious practices is merely academic, unless one is trying to show that a person is unjustified in performing an *assertive* speech act with the strength it has. Thus, general discussions of the cognitivity of religious language are undercut by the false assumptions on which they proceed.

For directives and commissives, it must be the case that the presumed relationship between author and addressee obtain if these speech acts are to be successful. If such is not the case, they either are failures or can't achieve the perlocutionary effects the author intends. For instance, if the being to whom one prays does not exist, or does not have the ability to answer one's prayers, the prayer fails to be fully successful a communicative action. But as argued above, wholesale rejection of prayer because there cannot be any such relationships is unwarranted, and rejection of specific prayers on grounds that the specific relationship does not obtain is at least controversial and probably essentially and irresolvably contested. Similarly, warranted wholesale rejection of institutional religion would undercut any institutionally bound directives or commissives, but that is not forthcoming. Rejection of the right of specific institutional authorities to direct other members of their institution or to make commitments is hardly more likely to be warranted. Directives and commissives can demonstrably go wrong when they commit the author or direct another to do what logically, morally, or practically cannot be done—but that possibility is shared with all speech acts, religious or not. Hence, the only area in which the "cognitivity" of those speech acts which do not directly portray "the way the world is" can be *settled* is the possibility of the future action ingredient in the speech act; other issues are "cognitive," but unsettled and perhaps unable to be settled.

For assertives, the presumptions of relationships do not differ materially for present purposes from directives and commissives. What differs is the need to be justified in asserting what one asserts. However, to *be* justified and to *give* a justification are two different things. Institutional authorities must be *able* to give a justification for what they say, even if no one challenges them to do so. Their burden of justification may be limited to showing they are authorized to make the claims they do. If those who make assertions without specific institutional status cannot defend their position (give justifications) in the face of challenges, they may be unable to have their audiences accept what they say, but that does not mean they *are* unjustified.[9] Again, many of these claims may not be amenable to being settled.

Moreover, it is neither necessary nor sufficient for every successful assertive that its content be true or be demonstrable as true. Some true assertions may be unjustifiable and some assertions that a person can justify may be untrue. Some false assertions may be justifiable and some assertions that a challenger can show to be unwarranted may be true. While any assertive which asserts what is false is defective, that does not cause its failure. If a challenger can show an assertive to be seriously defective, that may undercut its effectiveness. If an asserter can justify the assertion, that may enhance its effectiveness. However, neither of these rhetorical moves affects the truth of what is asserted. Religious assertives including references to transcendent being(s) may not be fully justifiable, but it is not clear what a challenger would have to do (other than show the assertive to be incoherent or radically inconsistent with other assertions a speaker made) to demonstrate such a claim to be defective enough to be not worth accepting (see McClendon and Smith 1975:69-74). Thus, the cognitivity of a religious assertive is like that of any other assertive: issuing an assertive implies that the claim asserted is true, but its success does not depend on its being true nor on its being fully justified, but only on its being justifiable and being as justified as the context demands.

Religious expressives make no cognitive claims, and so their explicit cognitivity is not an issue. No cognitive claims are implied, even though expressives may be defective if some of their presumptions are not true. If all language used in religious contexts were purely expressive, then religious language would not be "cognitive" in any interesting way.

For pure declaratives, the issue of cognitivity is simple: they neither reflect, report, nor predict, but create facts. If their presumptions are flawed or their execution inept, they may fail, but it is not clear that this is a "cognitive" or "noncognitive" failure. These terms don't seem to fit. For commissive and directive declaratives, what has been said above about commissives and directives obtains, with the proviso that their cognitive failures may provoke speech act failure. For assertive declaratives, failures of the speakers to "do their homework" and portray the way the world has been or is in their declarations may make them failures. Augustine may have been self-deceived, but his declarative still was effective. A teaching authority in a church may declare a point of doctrine, but be ineffective (as the papal encyclical *Humanae Vitae* [1968] was with regard to "artificial" contraception). Hence, declaratives have cognitive presumptions and assertive declaratives imply truth claims, both within and without religious contexts. If those presumptions are seen to be unjustified, some may fail to be the acts the speaker intends, while others will be successful, but defective. However, as chapter 9 shows, assertive declarations which falsify states of affairs may, by doing so, create new evils.

In sum, there is no wholesale way to decide on the cognitivity of religious language because the speech acts performed in religious contexts are so varied. Each must be judged on its own.

\* \* \*

This completes Part 1, an exploration of the implications of the claim that "words are deeds." It has recognized five basic illocutionary points made in communicative actions. It has argued against Searle that there are not one, but at least three, types of hybrid speech acts. It has analyzed the conditions for performing both institutionally bound and institutionally free speech acts within and without religious contexts. Along the way it has argued that understanding the varying forces of different speech acts not only provides avenues for clarifying and resolving some institutional disputes, but also shows the complexity of the issue of the "cognitivity" of religious language. We are now in position to analyze and evaluate various classic communicative actions in which God and evil are the key topics.

# NOTES

1.   Following MacIntyre (1984:175), a practice can be defined as "any coherent and complex form of socially established human activity through which goods internal to that form of activity are realized . . ." MacIntyre stipulates other conditions for an activity to be a practice (concluding the previous definition): ". . . in the course of trying to achieve those standards of excellence which are appropriate to, and partially definitive of, that form of activity, with the result that human powers to achieve excellence, and human conceptions of the ends and goods involved, are systematically extended." MacIntyre's stipulation of other conditions defines "degenerative" or "vicious" practices out of existence. His purpose is to show that participating in practices can be a school for virtue, a move useful for his project, but not necessary to understand what a practice is. Hence, the basic understanding of a "practice" need not include "good-making" qualities (cf. McClendon 1986:160-77).

   This point especially applies to discourse practices, which do make possible the realization of certain goods and may even constitute those goods. Yet those goods are internal to the practices and unless one adopts a complete moral relativism which accepts as morally good all the goods obtained in any practice, one must find that the goods thus obtained or even note the acts performed may be morally defective.

2.   As in chapter 2, it is assumed that normal "preconditions" (McClendon and Smith 1975:59-60) or "input and output conditions" (Searle 1969:57) obtain. I accept Stump's defense of the consistency of engaging in petitionary prayer with belief in an omnipotent, omniscient, omnibenevolent God (1979, 1985). I do not find Hoffman's objections (1985) sufficient to upset Stump's contentions.

3.   Harré (1987) has explored the issue of truthfulness and the reliability of scientists' claims (in the sense that they can be accepted and acted upon) in similar ways. What gives specific claims in the scientific community their standing is as much (or more) the character and training of their authors as the "procedural" warrants given in the specific experiments. Although there is no obvious single way for extending his insights to religious believers' claims, he effectively shows that the positivistic and impersonalist views which underlie much philosophy of science are not warranted. Hence, applying them to religious cases is not clearly warranted.

4.   Of course, this does not imply that a person must accept the claim that God made a pledge to Abram as true simply because there are no arguments which show it impossible. If that were the case, both Buddhist and Abrahamic claims would have to be accepted as true, as both *can* be true. Nor does one who accepts such a claim have to understand it in a "literalistic" manner, rather than in a more "symbolic" way. Both claims are relatively well justified, but that does not mean they are true.

5.   Such declarations are clearly relevant to the causal theory of reference which Searle rejects. While extended discussion of this issue is out of place here, it seems to be just Searle's dropping of the necessity of perlocutionary (uptake) conditions for successfully performing speech acts that prohibits him from considering the causal theory as a viable alternative to his own preferred descriptive theory of reference (cf. Searle 1983:231-61).

6.   Of course, the alcoholic's specific declaration could not have been performed without the support of the A.A. group. In this sense the declaration requires an institutional setting, although alcoholics could still admit their status to themselves. Yet the declaration requires no specific institutional role or status other than the generic one of membership, i.e., belonging to the institution or association. Confessions, like other declarations, are intrinsically public acts. Hence, they are usually found in institutional settings. However, no specific institutional setting is

necessary for the practice of confession and no specific institutionally defined role is necessary for the speaker or hearer of a confession. As with all speech acts, relationships must obtain between speaker and hearer if the act is to be performed; and for the purposes of the confession the speaker must have the role of confessor and the hearer must assume a role which includes involvement, support, and empathy. Nonetheless, the practice of making and listening to confessions is not essentially institutionally bound.

7.    Hauerwas and Burrell (1977) suggest in their fine treatment of Speer that it is just the ability to see who one is that distinguishes authentic confession from self-deceptive ones. Indeed, performing a confession properly may be telling the sort of story that halts the human slide down the slope of self-deception (also see Tilley 1985:196-201).

8.    This "spatial" metaphor for memory may mislead Augustine. The present "performative" analysis suggests that uttering what one remembers can be a declaration. To remember, then, is to engage in a practice. What is "hard to get out of memory" is what is hard to recognize, hard to own, hard to declare one's own. What makes confession difficult is not that the memories which must constitute its narrative form are "things" buried so deep under other memories, but that confession is a rare and difficult act of declaring correctly what-has-been to be one's own memories. Confession is an act which distinguishes what one owns and owns up to out of all that happened to one. That accounts for the selectivity in the *Confessions*. That Augustine performed it well is the key to its being a classic text.

9.    But because they cannot give justifications does not mean that they are unjustified in (have no justification for) holding or asserting their views. The burden of proof in this case is on the challenger. See Tilley (1984) and chapter 5 below for applications of this point to defenses against the charge of incoherence between belief in God as traditionally conceived and belief that there is genuine evil in the actual world.

# PART TWO:

# REMEMBERING DISMEMBERED TEXTS

# Introduction to Part Two

To remember is a practice which requires selecting what is significant from the mass of data thrown from the past into the present. As Augustine had to search in the storehouse of memory to remember who he was, so theologians choose from a stockpile of past works to construct a theological tradition. Like other intellectual traditions, theological traditions are made more than found, created more than discovered, taken more than given. Moreover, the act of constructing a tradition, like other acts, is performed for a purpose.

Theodicy is a practice within Christian theology. Its purpose was articulated quite clearly by one of its early Enlightenment exponents, Archbishop William King. King has concluded "that the World is as well as it could be made by infinite *Power* and *Goodness*" (1731:53). Hence, King needs to explain how

> [Evils] may be reconcil'd with the Government of an infinitely powerful and beneficent Author of Nature. For, since there is such a Being, 'tis ask'd, as we said before, Whence come Evils? Whence so many *Inconveniencies* in the Work of a most *good*, most *powerful God*? Whence that perpetual War between the very *Elements*, between *Animals*, between *Men*? Whence *Errors*, *Miseries* and *Vices*, the constant Companions of human Life from its Infancy? Whence Good to Evil Men, Evil to the Good? If we behold any thing irregular in the Works of Men, if any Machine answers not the End it was made for; if we find something in it repugnant to itself or others, we attribute that to the Ignorance, Impotence, or Malice of the Workman: but since these Qualities have no place in God, how come they to have place in any thing? Or, Why does God suffer his works to be deform'd by them? (73-74)

In other words, King aims "to have at last discover'd the true Origin of Evils, and answer'd all the Difficulties and Objections that are brought on this Head, against the Goodness, Wisdom, Power, and Unity of God" (80). King's purpose is to solve an intellectual problem for those thinking about evil in God's world, not to explain the meaning of evils afflicting suffering individuals (*pace* Berger's claims about theodicy; see p. 2 above).

In light of this purpose, King, like other theodicists, picks materials to construct his theodicy from the stockpiles of history and theology. In doing so, theodicists both shape a tradition and participate in a tradition. Theodicists participate in a tradition of construing all discourse about God and evil, from the author of Job to David Hume, as commensurable. They "read" the earlier texts in the Christian tradition as assertives, all addressing the "same" perennial problem King addresses. But the problem is not perennial: it is the problem of Enlightenment theism. The discourses are not commensurable: these texts are addressed to different problems, in different contexts, for different purposes. The texts are not all, in speech act terms, assertives whose content can be facilely abstracted and used. It is these differences that the tradition, the discourse practice, of theodicy obscures.

It is my purpose in this section of the book to use speech act theory as a tool for remembering some of those texts in a way that retrieves and valorizes their differences, not only in "content" but also in their illocutionary forces. These chapters show how philosophers and theologians who use these texts often abuse them by ignoring or obscuring their rhetoric and logic. However, construing them as communicative actions reveals their power.

Chapter 4 analyzes the stories of Job. The argument shows that no matter how one construes the text and the speech acts portrayed therein, Job remains a stumbling block for any theodicy. Job may even undermine the possibility of consolation for its readers, for either God in the text or the reader of the text must silence Job's voice. If Job is to be 'rescued' as a text supportive of religious belief, it cannot be taken as an assertive which conveys doctrines. At best, it is a biblical directive which warns those who included it in their canon of religious texts not to seek ultimate answers.

Chapter 5 looks at Augustine's *Enchiridion* as an institutionally bound communicative act. It rejects the usual practice of building an 'Augustinian' theodicy from a pastiche of Augustine's texts dealing with God and evil. Close analysis of the logic of his arguments shows that, in contemporary terms, *Enchiridion* is a defense, not a theodicy. As an instruction containing Bishop Augustine's response to a layperson's problem, *Enchiridion* is a speech act which deserves a central place in the traditions which look to Augustine as an authority on how to speak of God.

Chapter 6 examines the speech acts in the 'pharmaceutical' dialogue Boethius inscribed in and as *The Consolation of Philosophy*. As a text, this medicine for melancholy is both prescription for and proscription of ways of speaking. Within the text, Lady Philosophy both gives the prisoner the ability to perform proper speech acts and leads the prisoner to proper silence. The *Consolation* is a script which gives and receives power only if readers speak both voices as their own and learn to speak properly of fortune.

Chapter 7 hears Hume's voices in the *Dialogues Concerning Natural Religion* as performing unexpected communicative acts. Close analysis of the rhetoric and logic in the conversation portrayed in Parts X and XI reveals that not all who believe in God are challenged by Epicurus's Old Questions, and explains the shifting alliances between the three participants. Demea's position emerges relatively unscathed and Philo's alleged agreement with Cleanthes in Part XII is shown to be no real shift at all. Finally, it shows that the key to understanding the *Dialogues* is not finding *who* speaks for Hume, but what *action* Hume performed in inscribing the *Dialogues*.

Chapter 8 begins by investigating the confrontation in a jail cell between "Methody preacher lady" Dinah Morris and Hetty Sorrel, her shallow, guilty, silent cousin who is condemned to be hanged. Through her powerful speaking, Dinah gives Hetty a voice to confess and to forgive. George Eliot's brilliantly crafted characters show how one oppressed character was released from her bondage by being given a voice. The analysis shows the abilities Dinah must have to be able to give Hetty a voice which overcomes Hetty's fear of death without denying death's power. It also brings out how Eliot's novel also portrays the social power of confession and forgiveness, and protests against the arbitrary and destructive silencing of those whose speaking enables others to overcome evil.

In sum, these chapters show how the practice of theodicy drowns out other voices. In Part 3, we will see why this is one of the evils of theodicy.

*Chapter 4*

## CONSIDERING JOB: DOES JOB
## FEAR GOD FOR NAUGHT?

*Hast thou considered my servant Job*
*that there is none like him in the earth,*
*a perfect and an upright man,*
*one that feareth God and eschewed evil?*
Then Satan answered the LORD, and said,
*Doth Job fear God for naught?*
—Job 1:8-9, KJV

The Book of Job is both the masterpiece of Wisdom literature and the most problem-plagued text in the Bible. Its rising poetry climaxes when the overwhelming voice of God speaks from the whirlwind. Its compelling story of one man struggling with God and God's world ensures its place as "arguably the greatest achievement of all biblical poetry" (Alter 1985:76). The power of the "Job story" makes Job a religious and cultural classic which demands "interpretation, never mere repetition nor simplistic rejection" (Tracy 1981:154).

Yet theodicists typically neither interpret nor repeat nor reject Job. They ignore the text and silence Job's voice. Even those who refer to the text minimally (e.g., cf. Farrer 1962:16-17, 158, 186) prefer to write off Job. As I will argue in chapter 9, a key part of the evil of theodicy as a discourse practice is its effacement of the Book of Job, its erasing of the divine sadism the Book of Job portrays (not Job's masochism, *pace* Berger 1969:75).

Rather than glossing over either its difficulties as a text or the problems of its content for "theodicy," this chapter construes those problems as key not only for interpreting the text itself, but also for discerning and evaluating the verbal and other acts portrayed in the text. After briefly discussing the structure of the text, the chapter analyzes the speech acts performed therein from Job's perspective and from the framework perspective. This chapter shows how the story of Job's confronting the problems of understanding and enduring suffering in a world created by God does not provide doctrines to be asserted, but forces those who take it as a religious or cultural classic to confront their own understandings of God and God's world. Theodicists fail to confront Job: that is part of the problem theodicy creates.[1]

## Job: A Text Made, not Found

Job's story was not woven by one writer, but stitched together by one or more writers who took strands from many sources. A general consensus about the components in the book can be summarized in the following:

(1a)   Chapters 1 and 2 form a five-scene prose prologue, alternating between earth, where the upright and blameless Job's property is destroyed, his children killed, and his body afflicted; and heaven, where God twice taunts the Satan about the fidelity of Job and twice gives the Satan leave to test Job.

(2a)   Chapter 3 begins the brilliant poetry of the three cycles of Job's "laments" and the "comforts" of his wordy friends, the three comforters, Eliphaz, Bildad and Zophar. The poetry continues more or less intact until chapters 24-27, where the speeches in the cycle of Zophar, Bildad, and Job seem scrambled. Various unscramblings have been proposed.

(3)   Chapter 28 is a hymn to Wisdom.

(2b)   In chapters 29-31 Job declaims a peroration.

(4)   Chapters 32-37 contain speeches of Elihu.

(2c)   YHWH responds to Job in chapters 38 and 39, YHWH challenges, and Job responds at the beginning of chapter 40; YHWH talks a second time and Job responds again, ending at 42:6.

(1b)   42:7-end is an epilogue in prose. The prologue and epilogue together seem to rehearse an ancient folktale of divine testing and restoration.

Acknowledging the difficulties of ascribing authorship for the Book of Job,[2] we will use a holistic or canonical approach which takes the text as a whole inscribed by one author.[3]

Canon critic Brevard Childs suggests that "Job poses two sets of questions, one for the reader who views the ensuing dialogue from the perspective of the framework, the other for the reader who chooses to share Job's stance of ignorance of the divine will in order to pursue his probing questions" (1979:534). He further suggests that the two perspectives may provide different solutions for different problems rather than incompatible solutions to the same problem. The next two sections follow up on this suggestion by using speech act theory to analyze the text. But both perspectives raise insoluble problems.

## *The Book of Job from Job's Perspective*

One option is to "view the dialogue" from Job's perspective. One would not necessarily do so because one chose to share Job's ignorance. Purely academic questions do not drive one to Scripture for answers. One might find oneself in Job's position, an innocent person victimized by terrible loss and suffering. One might then enter into Job's story, for "there's always someone playing Job" (MacLeish 1958:12). Yet to understand the text from Job's perspective is not to take a spectator's position, but to take Job's role in the story. To "view the dialogue from the inside" is not to say Job's lines, but to perform Job's speech acts, from his lamentable curse to his heaven-shaking oath.[4]

In the prologue (*1a*), Job, the prosperous moral and religious exemplar, appears in three scenes. In the first, he offers sacrifice for his children, in case they had sinned. In the second, after the destruction, he worships God: "The Lord gave, and the Lord has taken away; blessed be the name of the Lord." The narrator declares that Job did not sin or charge God with wrong. In the third scene, Job's wife urges him to curse God and die (be relieved by death), but Job rejects her advice and rhetorically asks whether we should receive good from God, but not evil.

In the "dialogues" (*2a*), Job begins by cursing the day he was born and lamenting the portion he shares with other unfortunates (3). Eliphaz then reproves Job gently, reports a revelation, "Can mortal man be righteous before God" (4:17), testifies to its validity, appeals to Job to commit his case to God, praises God, and assures Job that God heals and binds in order to correct (4-5). Job responds by describing how God has attacked him. He expresses his wish or hope for God to help him, indicts his friends and denies their wisdom: "Job castigates his friends as fickle. Their consolation is insipid pious pap" (Habel 1985:141). He then turns to complaining about the human condition and the terrible pain he experienced, expresses his rejection of life, and questions God's motives (6-7).

Bildad impugns Job's words and asserts that his children must have sinned, since God could not pervert justice. He urges Job to throw himself on the mercy of the just God (8). Job then picks up Eliphaz's mention of righteousness and Bildad's of justice. He describes God in terms which anticipate God's speech from the whirlwind and predicts that if he did summon God to court, "I do not believe he would hear my voice. He would crush me with a whirlwind and increase my wounds without cause" (9:16b-17, trans. Habel 1985:179). He laments the futility of trying to bring God who "destroys both the blameless and the wicked" (9:22) to court. He outlines his case against God who brought him to life to smear him with filth and torment him (9-10).

Zophar proclaims that God is beyond human understanding, and advises Job that if he reaches out to God, God will heal him (11). In 12-14, Job then expresses disdain for the comforters while asserting that he knows as much as they. In biting satire, he describes God's perverse power and wisdom (12:13-25), and insults the three as whitewashing liars and "worthless physicians" (13:5). Job interrogates the comforters, previewing what it would be like for them to testify, and screws up his courage to "arraign" God (13:19; cf. Habel 1985:231, Pope 1973:100). He commits himself not to hide from God's face while requesting God to remove his pressure and not to let God's dread dismay him (13:20-21). Although God hides, Job commits himself to argue his case to God (even though it be hopeless) and to respond (13:22-23). He concludes with a litany of legal lament incorporating a dream of vindication (14:13-17).

Eliphaz accuses Job of infidelity to the tradition and challenges Job's wisdom. He then recounts a vision of the wicked man with "verbal irony and barbed innuendo designed to expose how Job testifies to characteristics in himself that are typical of the wicked man"(Habel 1985:251-52). Job responds in kind by demeaning the efforts of his "miserable comforters." He accuses God of destroying his world and ripping him open, breaching him, chewing on him like a wild beast, while testifying to his innocence: "although there is no violence in my hands, and my prayer is pure" (16:17). Job implores the earth not to cover his blood and wishes for a witness in heaven to be his advocate. He then accuses his friends of being "mockers" and concludes with a cry of despair (16-17).

Bildad defends the comforters' wisdom and threateningly portrays the fate of the wicked. Job again attacks his comforters and returns to accusing God of waging a military battle against him and his friends of deserting him. Job begs for pity from his friends, expresses a wish for God to hear him, for an avenger, and to see God, and warns the others that the judgment is coming (18-19).

Zophar returns to rehearse the fate of the wicked tormented by God, picking up many of Job's battle metaphors. Job requests his comforters to listen to him. He responds to their portrayals of the fate of the wicked by showing how the wicked prosper (20-21). He entreats the "friends, who have shown no capacity to understand his plight from anything but a traditional doctrinal perspective" (Habel 1985:324).

Eliphaz then takes off the gloves and accuses Job of numerous sins, and urges him bluntly to return to God for his own sake and perhaps even that of others. Job laments God's hidden "unarraignability," avers his innocence, laments that God is nonetheless against him, and expresses his fear (22-23). He goes on to rehearse the ways the guilty oppress their victims while God thinks nothing is amiss (24).

Bildad praises the might of God and rhetorically asks how a human can be clean and just before God (25-26). Job challenges his friends about their help to the weak and declares his innocence again (26-27).

Zophar contradicts Job on the prosperity of the wicked by claiming that God raises them up and lays them low, and challenges Job to prove him wrong (27,24). The truncated third cycle of speeches is concluded by a poem on the inaccessibility of wisdom (3), which appears as an (not the) author's commentary on the "dialogues," rather than a part of them (cf. Habel 1985:392-94).

Job's final monologue (2b) has been labeled a "Confession of Innocence" (Alter 1985:93), but is more accurately a tripartite "formal testimony . . . addressed to a public assembly. . . . but intended for his divine adversary to hear" (Habel 1985:404,405). Job testifies to his honored position and his righteousness, especially to the outcast (29), contrasting that with the way people now insult and assault him, and concluding with the agent of destruction: "God casts me into the mire and I become dust and ashes" (cf. Pope 1973:218, 223). He then charges God with not listening to his cries in his oppressed state (30). The third part includes a far-ranging and awful oath which declares his innocence, and his challenge to God to respond to his signed, sealed, and delivered testimony (31).

Habel suggests that, to this point in the poetry, Job has moved from curse, lament, and complaint to considering legal "action, even if that action is an impossible dream" (188). However, this is over-simplified. Job has moved from the "weakest" type of speech act, his expressive lament, to the strongest, his terrible declaration of his final oath and the audacious directive of his challenge to God. How his actions shifted from lament to oath can be illumined by considering the speech acts he performed along the way.

Job's assertions focus on three content areas. First, they center on his miserable situation. Job constantly asserts that God is the cause of his misery (e.g., 9-10), using violent metaphors of wounding (6:4, 16:12-14), assault (19:7), dethroning (19:9), and battle (19:12) to accuse God, although Job maintains his innocence (e.g., 9:21, 27:7). Second, Job frequently recalls the miserable human plight of the God-given human condition he shares (7:1-10, 12:5-25, 14:1-6, 21, 24). Third, Job generally agrees with much of the comforters' theology, but compares their torments with those God inflicts on him (19:22) and directly contradicts Eliphaz's key assertion of retributive justice (24). Save for the third group, there is little development in Job's assertions.

Nor is there much development in Job's directives. He frequently challenges God or his friends to inform him, he sometimes begs pity of both, and his final oath concludes with a defiant challenge to God.

Yet Job's expressives change remarkably. He begins with curse (3:1) and lament (3, 6:2-3), but no further curse is expressed and subsequent laments over his suffering are brief (e.g., 10:1) or conclude descriptions of the human condition (7:11-16). His expressive lament seems supplanted by assertive accusations. He later begins his speeches expressively insulting and deriding his comforters (12:2-5, 13:1-5, 16:1-5, 26:2-4). He expresses some hope for a witness (16:18-17:1) but soon utters a cry of despair (17:11-16). But when he returns to lament (23), he no longer centers on his suffering, but now laments God's immunity from arraignment. It is as if the legal metaphors which structure Job's speeches in his dialogues with the comforters (e.g., 14:13-17) shift the focus of the feelings to which Job gives vent.

Job makes three declarations in his speeches. They are linked with the only commissives he issues. They are also linked with directives. His first is his "arraignment" of God in 13:19 to contend against him. He asks God to withdraw his pressure and dread and demands that God tell him his offense and sin (13:23). He also commits himself to follow the procedural order God prefers (13:22).

Obviously, Job finds himself in no position to perform the act of arraigning God successfully, as he frequently laments God's eluding him. Job's action fails as a speech act because he cannot perform an institutionally bound declaration (he is not a judge) on God (who, as discussed below, is not 'bound' by human justice).

His second declaration is both an illocutionary denegation (an explicit declaration that one is *not* performing a speech act; cf. Searle and Vanderveken 1985:176) and a positive declaration: he refuses to find his comforters right and maintains his innocence (27:5-6). He commits himself not to speak falsehood. This speech seems truncated and there is no associated directive, unless one reads 27:7 as a directive curse rather than as an expressive "swearing." Yet this declaration merely anticipates the final one.

His third declaration is his oath/confession of his innocence. After his rehearsal of his situation, he declares his innocence, not only with a "signature" (31:35) which formalizes his declaration, but also with imprecations (7-12,38-40). He challenges/summons God, his adversary at law, to appear, and commits himself to flaunt whatever God writes—an inscription which the text leaves ambiguous, for God may write an indictment of Job or a verdict of acquittal (cf. Habel 1985:438-39, Pope 1973:238).

Then, after an anticlimactic intrusion by Elihu (4), a redundant young "fool who claims to be wise" (Habel 1985:444), whose primary literary purpose seems to be to defend a traditional theological answer and whose primary dramatic purpose seems to be to delay God's responding to Job, God startlingly speaks to Job from the whirlwind. God's two majestic poems begin with a challenge to and a summons of Job the litigant (38:2-3, 40:7-14). God responds first to Job's clouding of God's design (38:4-39:30) by sarcasm, challenging Job to see the world from God's perspective with "each existing thing having its own intrinsic and often strange beauty. . . . [moving] through aeons from creation to the inanimate forces of nature to the teeming life on earth" (Alter 1985:97). God responds second to Job's perverting of divine justice (40:6-41:26) by asking Job if *Job* could thunder like God, crush the wicked, and subdue Behemoth and Leviathan.

God's speeches clearly respond to Job. Habel has shown the parallels between the content of Job's accusations and laments and of God's first speech (1985:530-32). But God shockingly also responds to Job's act of summoning God (and perhaps the purpose of the interpolated Elihu speeches was to obscure this startling event). There is a parallel between 38:2 and 13:19; and in 31:35 Job summons his adversary at law, while in 40:2 God uses the same noun to stand for Job. God may also accept Job's procedural commitment, as 38:3 parallels 13:22. But God does not "draft a document" (the verb also is used for the act for making a covenant) and so God does not respond to Job's challenge and conditional commissive in 31:35-37. Nor does God respond to Job's request of 13:21-22, for Job is at least cowed by God's first response and after God's second speech alludes to the dust and ashes Job mentioned in 30:19. God's response to Job, then, is selective. God seems to accept some of Job's acts, but does not concede that God is bound to human practices of justice.

At the end of the first poem, Job's response to God "has a double edge. 'I am small' implies: I am reduced to smallness, I am humbled by the speeches of God, just as I was humbled by his afflictions (cf. 7:1-6) and sought to escape by employing a curse (3:1)" (Habel 1985:549). In the parallel response at the end of the second poem, Job admits he uttered what he did not understand and then performs his final speech act in 42:5-6, "I had heard of thee by the hearing of the ear, but now my eye sees thee, therefore, I

(a)     despise myself and repent in dust and ashes" (RSV)

(b)     abase myself and repent in dust and ashes" (Gordis 1965:305)

(c)     am poured out and dissolved/smitten and am become dust and ashes" (Qumram Targum; Pope 1973:349)

(d)     will be quiet, comforted that I am dust" (Mitchell 1987:88)

(e)     repudiate and abandon dust and ashes" (Gutierrez 1987:86-87)

(f)     retract and repent of dust and ashes" (Habel 1985:575)

(g)     retract all I have said and in dust and ashes I repent" (JB)

(h)     recant and repent in dust and ashes" (Pope 1973:347).

The state of the text is such that any of the above are possible renderings of 42:6.

To understand the meaning of the text from Job's perspective, it is necessary to understand this climactic verse, Job's final utterance in the text. But to understand this utterance, one needs to understand what Job does in uttering 42:6. What speech act does he perform? Does Job declare his worthlessness (as option (a) renders it)? Does he reject his view and accept reconciliation with God (as in (b); also cf. Alter 1985:110)? Does Job declare that he has been silenced by God and that God has reduced him to dirt (c,d)? Does he repudiate lamentation (e)? Does he repudiate both accusation and lamentation (f)? Does he repudiate his accusation and declare his penitence (g,h)? Each of these positions has been argued, but, as a review of the arguments shows, Job is reduced to silence, if not by God, then by the interpreters of the text.

To understand Job's final speech act, his position must be considered. He is a victim, tormented by God and made a scapegoat by his 'comforters.' Job "suffers to see God: Sees God because he suffers. Beautiful!" (MacLeish 1958:50) But what sort of victim is he?

Does he, like torture victims, adopt the language and perception of his torturers? He clearly picks up the legal language of his 'friends,' who "resemble more and more a circle of police around a suspect" (Girard 1985:170; my translation). Does he undergo that most terrible experience for a victim: "to believe himself exposed to the personal hostility of the divinity" (Girard 1985:190)? His laments indicate this, especially with their metaphors of breaching, violence, and loss. His wishes for the relief of death parallel Amnesty International's finding that "Suicide is a not uncommon result of torture" (1984:25). His physical suffering and the interrogations of him by God and his 'friends' seem bonded together in a manner that fits the profound comments of Elaine Scarry:

> There is a . . . cruel bond between physical pain and interrogation that further explains their inevitable appearance together. Just as the interrogation, like the pain, is a way of wounding, so the pain, like the interrogation, is a vehicle of self-betrayal. Torture systematically prevents the prisoner from being the agent of anything and simultaneously pretends that he is the agent of some things. Despite the fact that in reality he has been deprived of all control over, and therefore all responsibility for, his world, his words, and his body, he is to understand his confession as it will be understood by others, as an act of self-betrayal. In forcing him to confess . . . the torturers are producing a mime in which the one annihilated shifts to being the agent of his own annihilation (1985:46-47).

Options (a) and (b) render Job's last act a self-betraying, self-destroying confession extracted from him by his friends and his God through torture. God seems to have responded to Job's summons, but then flaunted the divine power in Job's face and showed him that God was in control. Job is tortured into becoming an 'agent' of his own annihilation where his voice is not his own, but his torturers' production.

The epilogue (1b) reinforces reading 42:6 as a tortured confession.

Not only is Job absolutely silent therein, but also God's comment on Job's words is directed not to Job, but to Eliphaz, one of the three 'comforters': God finds that they may have spoken wrong of him, but tortured Job spoke right. But *what* speech act God performs here in the text remains to be seen. All we know is that God never lets Job know that he spoke rightly. And no one who is in the position of the characters in the text knows that the horror God inflicted on Job was only a test.

Options (c) and (d) also render Job a victim. Rendering (c) alludes to the terrible pain and its result; (d) testifies to the loss of voice characteristic of the torture victim. Both depict the conclusion of Job's speech as Job asserting he has been made dust. Habel's comments on 30:19, where Job also asserted that he had become dust and ashes, in the context of assaults by God and others, apply also to these renderings of 42:6:

> By asserting that he had become as "dust and ashes" (v.19b), Job announces that he has been reduced to nothing. He looks like the lifeless clay from which he was formed and the very ashes which marked his humiliation (2:8). Thus, like the previous unit (vs. 12-15), this unit ends with a forceful statement of Job's return to nothingness and loss of identity (cf. vs. 15 and 19) (420).

If Job has "become" or "is" dust and ashes, then he has reached a death-like state, where he has no voice, world, or agency—but, perhaps, is only a body in pain. Here Job also appears as the victim of torture. But here he has been destroyed not by his confession, but by God.

This reading is also reinforced by the restoration in the epilogue. Perhaps the "amoral deity" as portrayed in Job might simply be restarting the whole cycle of prosperity and annihilation again (cf. Priest 1985; MacLeish 1958:141-48). Job is unheard in, absent from, the epilogue. He neither acts nor speaks, but is only spoken of. He has become an object of others' discourse, not an agent. He is a silent victim. He *is* become dust and ashes.

Charles Muenchow has offered a reading that sees Job in the dust, not as destroyed and tortured, but as shamed. The key to understanding this verse is that it is written in a society structured by competition, an "agonistic society, where honor is the reward for a publicly sustained claim to some sort of precedence, shame is correspondingly the penalty that must be paid for a claim to precedence that has been rebuffed" (1989:601). Job has challenged Jahweh's honor and precedence in (2b). Yahweh responds by shaming Job in (2c). Job, then, acknowledges his shaming. Muenchow claims that "Shame structures relationships between individuals of unequal status. It maintains the basic inequality, to be sure, but it nonetheless serves to keep the bond intact" (611). Muenchow concludes: "On his knees in the dust and dirt, Job nonetheless has been acknowledged and affirmed by his lord. In Yahweh's very acknowledgement of Job's lowliness, Job finds his derivative worthiness" (611).

Muenchow's argument that conventions of shame and honor structured the original reading/hearing of Job 42:6 is plausible. But despite Muenchow's finding an affirmation of Job by God in this scene, this reading renders God in Job as a bully, the top dog in an agonistic society, who affirms a man by shaming him. This God is petty enough to engage in the sport of one-upmanship over one who cannot top him. If this version is more faithful to the original meaning of the text, then Job is a victim of divine pride pricked when a mere man resorts to law. Job may be quiet and comforted that he is dust; but his comfort comes from his accepting his silenced status as shamed by a sadistic petty potentate.

Options (e) and (f) are similar in that they both have Job, in his final speech act, renounce "his lamentation and dejected outlook" (Gutierrez 1987:87). The main purpose of the suffering and the speeches, then, was to correct Job's views:

> If the process of deliverance had not reached this point, Job would have retained a bit of the theology of retribution and, with it, a myopic view of God. The irony in God's speeches is, as it were, the scalpel that cuts into Job's wounded flesh and makes it impossible for the evil to remain and put forth new shoots. This critical juncture has been difficult and painful, but the result is worth the suffering. . . . Job still has many questions, but the unknown is no longer a monster that threatens to devour everything, including his few and fragile certainties. The beast that is his ignorance has not vanished, but like Behemoth and Leviathan, it is under control because of what he now knows about God and God's love.

Job can renounce that "myopic view of God" which is "imprisoning God in a narrow conception of justice" (Gutierrez 1987:91).

However, to make his point, Gutierrez has to resort to imaging God as an enemy and a friend. He does not take the "subjective" escape route by saying that God appears as or is experienced as both enemy and friend. He explicitly states that these "are two sides of the one God" (65). He also confuses theological and logical issues when he suggests that God accuses Job of trying to imprison God in his theological concepts (75). But if one asserts contradictory claims about God, as Gutierrez does, one's speech act of assertion self-destructs (cf. Searle and Vanderveken 1985:151). Similarly, if one evacuates concepts applied to the divine of any positive connection with analogous human concepts, one simply can't assert anything about God, but merely express one's own feelings. These are just the tensions in Job's claims which spawn the dialogues with the comforters. If one asserts or declares that God is beyond all theological concepts, then what can one say about God next? The answer is "nothing"—which is just what Gutierrez is able to assert given a claim that God is beyond any human concepts.

So just what *does* Job "know about God's love"? Gutierrez simply reads divine love into a text where God's love is never mentioned. The divine love is the purifying phallic scalpel that tears into Job allegedly to root out evil. To make knifing the central symbol of divine love portrays God in this text as a sadist (compare Soelle 1975:28-32 on other texts). The evil is not hidden in Job; the evil is God's violating him. Evil does not need to be rooted out; it needs to stop. Perhaps readers might think they learn something about God's love from reading this text, but Job could learn only that love is abuse. But a reader taking Job's position would learn only of divine sadism.

For Gutierrez, the suffering of this innocent one was educative. But Job learned nothing. He only unlearned his belief that vice and punishment, virtue and reward, were connected in God's world. God gives no direct answers from the whirlwind, but, at best, shows that if there be any control in the world, Job doesn't exercise it. No more can be asserted on the basis of the text. One might make claims about God's freedom (cf. Gutierrez 1987:89, 90; Habel 1985:65), but hardly about God's love—unless one takes sadomasochism as the model of love (see Soelle:17-22).

Like Gutierrez, Habel rejects the image of a submissive and repentant Job. His theological claims are more nuanced than Gutierrez's, possibly because he sees bringing the legal bout to closure as central:

> In addition Job "repents of the dust and ashes" with which he has been identified as a litigant and humiliated sufferer. . . . Job has decided to "change his mind" about proceeding with litigation or lament, and is ready to return to normal life again. Yahweh's advent and answer have vindicated Job's innocence and revealed the futility of pursuing litigation based on a moral law of reward and retribution. Job makes no confession of sin, guilt, or pride. His integrity is intact (1985:582-83).

Job's final speech act is one which declares his lawsuit against God dropped. Therefore, there can be "normal relations restored" between them (Habel 1985:579). But what does this leave us with?

What both Habel and Gutierrez do, finally, is to silence the voice of the innocent. For Gutierrez, the suffering of the innocent becomes merely educative. While his work is more a reflection on the text than an exegesis of it, it is hard to see how one can consistently accept Gutierrez's view of 42:6 and his claim that "Job shows us a way [to preach the love of God amid profound contempt for human life] with his vigorous protest, his discovery of concrete commitment to the poor and all who suffer unjustly, his facing up to God and his acknowledgement of the gratuitousness that characterizes God's plan for human history" (1987:102). Gutierrez's interpretation of 42:6 blames the victim of suffering for complaining about his suffering and railing against its human and divine agents. If Job is indeed a torture victim, Gutierrez has joined the torturers in silencing their victim. If Job is taken as simply an ordinary confused human being, baffled by a tragic turn of events, Gutierrez is asserting that suffering sets the stage for God to educate a person. But that simply reiterates the problem. What does God in Job teach the man Job? Moreover, neither view fits with any endorsement of Job's speech actions.

For Habel, the whole thing "cancels out" when Job withdraws his suit. For both, the distinctive voice of the suffering innocent person is evacuated of significance in favor of a devotion to the mystery of God, who neither comforts the unjustly afflicted nor afflicts the unjustly comfortable. For Habel, we are simply returned to the perspective of the prologue. Job accepts God's ways and his own innocence and so the show is over. The lament and accusation are effectively canceled. MacLeish's God-figure in *J.B.*, Zuss, provocatively depicts this sort of reading as J.B. forgiving God and accepting God's will (1958:139-40). But not only is there no such affirmation in Habel's rendering of Job, but also J.B.'s powerful acceptance and affirmation is not of *God*, but of whatever love we can create in this world, having learned that a caring and just God is absent from this world. Habel also silences the voice of Job: Job says nothing worthwhile.

Options (g) and (h) have all the problems with (e) and (f), but also explicitly leave Job where he was. Here, as in (e) and (f), Job performs the act of declaring his suit or his words retracted. Yet Job is neither reconciled with God as Habel has claimed nor hopeful of God's love as Gutierrez has argued. He does not malign himself as in (a) and (b), or identify himself with dust and ashes as in (c) and (d), but he does not leave the dust and ashes where he has sat since

2:8 in the prologue. It seems as if the whole of Job's speaking in the dialogues has been an exercise in futility. Renderings (g) and (h) silence Job, more by making his remarks pointless than by torturing him into submission. But again Job is silenced.

In sum, if one takes Job's position when one comes to read the text of Job, or if one takes Job's perspective as the key to reading Job, and if one enacts Job, then one is silenced. Moreover, it is God as portrayed in Job who does the silencing. But this seems to contravene the finding in 42:7 that endorses Job's speaking. However, that endorsement is worthless.

## God's "Verdict" on Job's Speaking

Almost all commentators on Job take the point of 42:7 and 42:8 to be that God has vindicated Job when God says to Eliphaz, "My wrath is kindled against you and against your two friends; for you have not spoken of me what is right, as my servant Job has" (42:7). But if God does vindicate Job, does God vindicate Job for naught? Writers take this as an implicit or explicit verdict given by God (cf. Childs 1979:538; Habel 1985:34,575,583; Gutierrez 1987:86; Pope 1973:350). Then they can debate over just what God found right in what Job said and/or how he said it (Gordis 1965:14-15; Pope 1973:350).

The endorsement may be part of the folktale behind (1ab). In that text, God seems to endorse the piety of Job in the prologue. But what happens to the poetry in (2abc)? Is it ignored? Or perhaps the verdict is based on Job's last speech in 42:1-6, so that God endorses the wisdom of Job's "submission." Or perhaps the verdict is based on all that has gone before (everything but (1b)), so God endorses all Job says, including his defiance in the dialogue. Arguments usually center on what God found right, and presume that God's act of finding seems rather clear. In short, this act of vindication is taken to be an intratextual divine legitimation of something Job said.

The speech act God performs seems to be—or to be like—an institutionally bound assertive declaration, a judicial verdict. It is institutionally bound because only a judge (or someone acting like a judge, an action parasitic on the institutions and practices of justice) is in the proper authoritative position to render a verdict. It is an assertive because to be fully successful it requires that the facts be correctly represented. It is a declaration because in uttering it, a judge gives the person or the person's suit a new status: the judge's decision determines whether the person is guilty or innocent, the suit won or lost.

Indeed, throughout the poetry, Job constantly cries out for justice. Judicial metaphors structure his speeches. His declamation in chapters 29-31 concludes with a call for his legal adversary to meet him and with an oath denying that he is guilty of any of the sins and crimes his "comforters" could accuse him of committing. His apparent retraction of what he had uttered, implicit in 42:3 and explicit in one possible rendering of 42:6 (Habel 1985:576), keeps legal language to the fore. The legal language of the poetry seems to set the reader up to expect a verdict here.

But can this be a verdict? In fact, if Job has presented a suit, he has apparently withdrawn his suit, so "ironically" nothing remains to be the subject of a verdict (Habel 1985:585). Moreover, in the text God addresses Eliphaz, rebukes the comforters, and compares what they said unfavorably to what Job said. Pope comments on v. 8 that the "friends are no longer present. Perhaps in the folk tale they had gone home after a time and left Job in his misery" (1973:350). But for the text we have, Pope has it exactly backwards. At least one friend is present as the audience to which God's rebuke is directed. Throughout the epilogue (1b), it is *Job* who is absent. Neither the patient Job of the prose prologue nor the feisty Job of the poetic dialogues is present. With both the suit and the litigant withdrawn from the scene, how could a judge be in position to render a verdict?

And *who* performs this speech act? MacLeish's Satan figure in *J.B.*, Nickles, has it right: "But this is God in *Job* you're playing" (1958:7). The God who speaks here *is* God as depicted in *Job*. What sort of God speaks? The God who speaks here is the God portrayed in the epilogue of the text. Presumably, this is the same God who, taunted by Satan, allows Satan to test Job, as portrayed in the prologue (1a). If so, God never lets Job know that the horror he went through, including the murder of Job's children and servants "without any earthly reason" (Crenshaw 1984:57), was only a test to show up the hollowness of the Accuser's taunt, or to win a bet with that son of God.[5] Crenshaw has plausibly suggested that (1ab) shows a movement from tranquility through utter dismay and finally to calm restored. But what sort of character disturbs the tranquility of a person who "is at peace with self, seeks others' well-being, worships God with sincerity, and does no harm to fellow beings" (Crenshaw 1984:59) just to test that person's faith and later to restore that person's possessions double? An "amoral deity. . . . this guilty Lord ties all loose ends together neatly, totally oblivious to the misery he has caused" (Crenshaw 1981:104). Or so God is portrayed in (1ab).

Perhaps the picture of God is to be tempered by that of God in (2abc). But this is no better. This God confronts Job with a litany of naked power which has won supremacy not only over the universe, but even over mythical (evil?) beasts, Behemoth and Leviathan. Is a God who nakedly displays his power worthy of worship? Bertrand Russell put it succinctly and precisely: "Such is the attitude inculcated in God's answer to Job out of the whirlwind: the divine power and knowledge are paraded, but of the divine goodness there is no hint" (1957:108). It is not merely that God does not bow to a human principle of justice, but that "God's anger and favor show no positive correspondence with human acts of villainy or virtue" (Crenshaw 1981:125). Many call this divine freedom; but a closer analogy than "freedom" to human characteristics would call this divine capriciousness at best, divine sadism at worst.

The Book of Job shows a God to whom human practices and concepts of justice are irrelevant. Indeed, this seems to be the most charitable interpretation available of God's responses to Job from the whirlwind. But "rendering a verdict" is part of the constellation of practices that constitute human concepts of justice. And human justice doesn't apply to God. So on what grounds could one affirm that God in Job renders a verdict? The subject is ambiguous. The litigant is absent. The suit may have been withdrawn. The prima facie act is not verdictive. The context says human concepts of justice don't apply to God. In fact, there is no warrant to support a claim that God justly finds that Job spoke rightly. Moreover, if God be as God is depicted in Job, what would such a judicial finding be worth? In short, God's action cannot be a successful declaration of the rightness of Job and his speech. Whatever action God performs, it is not a verdict. God's "verdict" on Job's speech, although accepted as such by many commentators, is no verdict at all. It is merely part of a rebuke to the comforters and a commissive to listen to Job's prayers.

Hence, if God's "verdict" determines the meaning of the text, and if it is not only impossible to agree on what its subject is but also impossible for it to be a verdict, then perhaps it would be more fruitful to consider the Book of Job, not from Job's perspective but from the perspective of a reader who does not seek to take Job's position, but to understand the text as a whole. This strategy is suggested by Childs in his consideration of the "canonical function" of Job, which, in speech act terms, takes the Book of Job as a communicative action performed for and on its readers. This is the second option Childs suggests.

## The Book of Job from the Framework Perspective

If one views the dialogue from the perspective of the framework, a significant problem of coherence emerges. "Does Job fear for naught," the Satan's taunt, "is the crux of the issue, the question which provoked the cruel experiment" (Pope 1973:12). As a speech act, Satan's taunt is a hybrid. Although it presumes God's description of Job, it both asserts the Satan's doubts and (weakly) directs God to overcome them. God then twice declares his protection of Job removed and thus enables the Satan to test Job. The Satan tests Job, Job does not "sin with his lips" (2:10). And then, in the end, God restores everything double, save Job's children, who are simply replaced (42:10).

Why does God restore Job? The text is open to various readings. Habel says it is purely gratuitous (1985:66-69, 584). Gordis takes it to be compensation for loss (1965:305). Peake suggests it was a reward (1905:108). Pope thinks it was "in a temporal and perhaps causal nexus with his intercessory prayer for his friends" (1973:lxxxi). But Mitchell catches the paradox in the text most precisely: God "rewards Job for having said that the righteous aren't rewarded . . ."(1987:xxix). But no matter which it is, this does not solve any problems.

On the one hand, if God restoring Job is not a result of Job's speaking or other actions, then God's restoring Job is as capricious as God's tormenting Job (or permitting the Satan to do so). Both torment and restoration are unrelated to anything Job does. God's acts are irrelevant to human delights and sufferings, to human virtue and viciousness. The Book of Job, then, as a speech act, cannot answer a reader's questions about the meaning of suffering or direct a reader to act in a specific way, for suffering and delight seem randomly distributed by God to the virtuous and the vicious. In sum, "gratuitous restoration," in disconnecting crime from punishment, reward from merit, provides no positive solutions to problems readers bring to it.

On the other hand, if God restoring Job is a result of Job's speaking rightly or praying properly, the reader is caught in a trap. Given the example of Job, who went through torment sufficient to make him loathe his life (10:1) and to give up the notion of retributive justice, the reader now knows that God rewarded Job because of his righteousness. How can the narrative act on a reader? Taking restoration as "deserved reward" undercuts the point of the rest of the book. It reinstitutes Job's problem. It says the virtuous are rewarded. It implies Job was tested, passed, and would be rewarded. If the text asserts that, and enables the reader to accept it as true on the text's authority (cf. pp. 40 and 65 above), how could a reader "gain the ability to cherish God's presence for naught" (Crenshaw 1981:125), to see suffering as other than a *test* of one's fidelity, which, if one passes, earns one a reward? In this reading, the text would urge (if a directive) or portray (if an assertive) the propriety of cherishing God for naught and promise (a commissive) a reward for cherishing God. Having heard the promise of reward, how can a person honestly love/fear God "for naught" rather than "as if for naught"? In sum, "deserved restoration" reinstitutes the problem by creating a threat to the readers' integrity, whatever the readers' goal: they must love God for naught to earn a reward, and know they will get a reward even and only if they seek to love God for naught!

On either hand, if we take the book as a whole as a speech act which we hear from the perspective of the framework story, the action that constitutes the Book of Job is self-defeating.[6] It either portrays God as practically capricious, or it makes what it seems to advocate impossible to perform and what it seems to promise self-contradictory. Construing Job as either an assertive or a directive-commissive communicative action gives the unexpected result of intensifying, rather than resolving, the problem of inconsistency in the Book of Job, presuming the perspective of the framework. It is not surprising that interpreters like Girard and Gutierrez simply cannot face the book as a whole and erase or ignore parts of the text in considering Job.

## Considering Job

Attempting to view the Book of Job from the framework perspective, then, is as problematical as viewing the story from Job's perspective. Taking the latter approach, the Book of Job could not function as an assertive speech act addressed to the community because it was internally inconsistent. Internally inconsistent assertive speech acts are self-defeating. They misfire by both affirming and denying the same proposition simultaneously. Taking the former approach, all the conclusions that can be drawn from the text are fraught with logical problems of consistency and many of the "conclusions" are more read into the text than drawn from it. Assertions made on the basis of the Book of Job, then, carry little warrant from the text.

In considering Job, commentators traditionally try to understand the "meaning" or the "teaching" or the "message" of the book as a cultural or religious classic. Yet Job eludes all their claims. Perhaps this is because they presume that Job is, in speech act terms, an assertive. If the foregoing analyses are correct, that view won't hold. But unless one simply erases much of the book, the inconsistencies and incongruities embedded in Job make it appear to be a self-defeating assertion.

Theodicists, even when they consider the Book of Job, neglect the fact that the actual text of the book is the "most vexed in the Old Testament" (Pope 1973:xliii). In fact, at crucial points, the text of the book is so indeterminate that the "text" of Job is, to a significant extent, made, not found. Not only is 42:6 problematical, but consider Job 13:15. The classic King James translation is "though he slay me, yet will I trust in him." This rendering is also problematical, for the difference in Hebrew between a text well rendered by the King James Version, and a translation such as the Revised Standard Version, "behold, he will slay me, I have no hope" is "a very minor matter of orthography" (Pope 1973:xliv). The difference is one vowel point in Hebrew. The scribes who transmitted the Masoretic texts evidently "corrected" a text they thought corrupt by moving the vowel point. "The Masoretes were able to twist the sense of the passage radically. . . . The elimination of the negative particle enabled the Masoretes to turn Job's defiant and bitter protest against divine injustice into an affirmation of complete trust and submission" (Pope 1973:xliv-xlv; 97-100 offers another translation; compare Habel 1985:223-25). Those who take the twisted sense of this passage as rendered by the KJV to be the key to Job's faith (e.g., L. Roth 1969; Kaufman 1987:56) defuse the power of the text. Job 13:15 becomes a proof text for religious sadomasochism, for submission to a God who kills and tortures merely to prove a point (cf. Soelle 1975:22-28).

This sadistic God's killing of children is also rarely noted by scholarly commentators on 1:18 and 42:13. They comment on the number of children and the fact that they are a special gift, but the horrible fact that they are murdered merely to teach Job a lesson is rarely noticed (for example, cf. Pope 1973:14-15,352-53; Habel 1985:78,92,577,585). Only MacLeish (1958:53-82) gets truly clear on the significance of their death, and how that reflects on the character of God as portrayed in (*1ab*). He does so in a play, not a textual commentary. Crenshaw makes the murder his point of entry for an essay on Job (1984:57), but on the following page explains their suffering away, as they "were no more than extras in a biography of God's favorite."

Some philosophers of religion write as if the biblical text is *not* vexed, as if they can accept without question whatever version they read (cf. J. Roth 1981:17-18). But in fact one has to choose between versions—and that choice makes a significant difference. Even beyond the issue of amending the text, as at Job 13:15, questions about what the text *is* arise at exceedingly crucial points, as at Job 19:25-27 (cf. Pope 1973:lxxvi) and Job 42:6-8 (as above). Some literary critics often write as if some historic form of the text, especially the King James Version because of its past cultural influence, is to be treated as a definitive text. Such criticism may be of historical interest. But even at its best, it cannot raise the questions of whether the Bible *should* be taken seriously enough today to make the work of finding the best form of the text worthwhile, or if those who do take the Bible as a classic *ought* to be influenced by a specific rendering of the text. And at its worst, such nostalgic criticism makes the Bible a book of merely historical interest because it shaped Western culture in the past. In sum, if one is interested in understanding contemporary philosophical and religious issues, one must consider normative textual questions and attempt to understand the illocutionary force of the text.[7]

However, even after one establishes a text, it is not always easy for commentators to square inconsistencies in the text of Job. To take a fairly simple problem, in (*1a*), Job's opponent is not God, but God and the Satan, the accuser in God's court. In (*2abc*), God is Job's accuser and afflicter. In (*1b*), Satan goes unmentioned. In (*2abc*), retributive justice is what Job asks for and God never gives, yet God retributively restores Job's possessions in (*1b*). Interpreters who seek to reconcile these evident inconsistencies tend either to erase part of the text or to deny the validity of strands in the text. In fact, many commentators explicitly or implicitly erase part of the text (cf. Childs 1979:532). For instance, among recent interpreters, Gutierrez (1987) simply ignores (*1b*) and (*4*); and Girard explicitly rejects all but (*2ab*) because the rest must be 'additions' which obscure the power of the text as they only "make Job acceptable for various orthodoxies" (1985:212; my translation). Such interpretations may be acceptable as partial interpretations of Job, but must fail as full interpretations of Job as a "classic."

In light of the textual problems, in recognition of its internal inconsistency, and in an effort to avoid distorting the text, we must construe Job as having the illocutionary point of a directive. The illocutionary conditions for successful directives do not require accuracy in representing the way things are, but only a 'negative' presumption that things are not as the author would have them be (cf. conditions 2a on pp. 37 and 57). Job does not defeat itself if taken as a directive. Moreover, such a placement accounts for the many specific functions attributed to Job (as taking it as a mere expressive would not).

Job warns against the possibility of providing a theodicy. It warns against expecting to achieve the "systematic totalization" (Ricoeur 1985:640) a theodicy requires. Job warns against silencing the sufferer's voice, even the curses and accusations.

More importantly, Job warns against our joining the company of comforters, theologians sure that they have the whole truth which they can "deliver" as answers to those who are plagued with questions. The comforters come to Job, but then leave him alone. They stand outside the circle of suffering. At best, they stand with the impetuous young fool, Elihu, who is full of hot air. At worst, they are "not quite torturers, but all the forms of intimidation, all the psychological conditionings, are good for them to obtain the famous 'spontaneous confessions' so dear to dictatorial societies" (Girard 1985:170; my translation). In either case, the comforters are 'academics' in the worst sense of that term, ineffective observers of the terrors of human suffering, or tormenters who intensify that suffering by the ways they respond to it. It is no wonder that theodicists try to erase Job, for Job reveals the real value of academic responses to real evil: they resolve no problems, but create new ones.[8]

Most importantly, Job is a warning (too little heeded by those who take the text as an assertive) against religious sadomasochism. As a directive, the Book of Job offers no "transmissible" claims. It provides no warrant for speaking of God or the meaning of human suffering. It gives no "revelational data" for theologians to build on or transmit. It offers no solutions to problems of suffering. As I have shown above, those strategies for reading Job fail. Job is not a book of answers, but a text of warning, perhaps even a text of terror. It does not prescribe nor describe, but proscribes, ways of relating to God by portraying the sadism of a divinity who at minimum destroys a man's family and property to shame him, or at most tortures a man who is innocent.

As a part of the Jewish and Christian religious canons, it revealingly warns that ways of speaking of God and suffering won't do. As a part of the cultural canon of the West, it warns against neglecting suffering when trying to understand the way things really are or standing outside of the realm of suffering and telling the suffering how they could solve their problems. As a part of the canons of scholars, its scramblings, ambiguities, and uncertainties suggest that closure of the meanings of texts or canonization of a "final" text may not be possible for as long as scholars devote themselves to considering Job.

To take the alternative path of construing the Book of Job as an assertive is to play God and to silence the voices of Job in the ongoing conversation about God and evils, the path taken by much of the Western theological and philosophical tradition. But to silence a suffering voice may be to participate in one of the most despicable practices theodicists (or anyone else) can perform. Silencing sufferers assists those who would continue the torture by silencing innocent victims' calls for help, prayers for deliverance, and recriminations against God. Silencing sufferers also makes impossible both the dialectical therapy for the unfortunate which educates the voice (as in chapter 6 below), and the confession of the guilty which creates a healing voice (chapter 8). Silencing sufferers consoles those who are deaf to the endless cry from the dust and ashes of the world. Silencing sufferers is part of the "foolishness of theodicy [which] has led us to search for the meaning of suffering. We have supposed, as a result of this long search, that suffering may be justified for retributive, therapeutic, pedagogical or redemptive reasons" (Noddings 1989:26). Failure to listen to the voices in Job has led theodicy to this long search in the wrong direction. Although people may be redeemed, suffering is irredeemable.

Theodicists find warrant for theodicy in the Christian tradition, especially by emulating Augustine. But he cannot be used to warrant the practice of theodicy, for he did not author a theodicy. Or so chapter 5 argues.

# NOTES

1. The secondary literature on Job is enormous. The present reading is especially indebted to Alter 1985, Crenshaw 1984, Habel 1985, and Pope 1973, although these differ substantially in their readings of Job. Among others consulted are Childs 1979, Crenshaw 1983, Duquoc and Floristan 1983, Eissfeldt 1965, Girard 1985, Gordis 1965, Gutierrez 1987, Mitchell 1987, Priest 1985 and Sanders 1968.

2. The Book of Job especially exemplifies the problems of what is to be construed as the text and who its authors are/is. Generally speaking, scholars take (2abc) as written by one writer; separating (2c) as a later addition has been proposed, but is not satisfactory (Gordis 1965:14). That writer or a later redactor adapted a folktale, (1ab), to frame the poetry. That writer and/or redactor or even later editors interpolated (3) (very probably not composed by the writer of (2abc)) into an extant text composed of (2abc) or (1a,2abc,1b) or (1a,2ab,4,2c,1b) and 4 (possibly composed much later than (2abc) by the writer of (2abc)) into an extant text composed of (2abc) or (1a,2abc,1b) or (1a,2a,3, 2bc,1b).

Who is/are the true authors? Are 'improvers' of the text the true authors? Or is the writer of (2ab(c)) the true author? Or the redactor of (1a,2abc,1b)? Or the contemporary critics who rearrange the scrambled passages, choose among numerous crucial variant readings, and construct a 'canonical' text? For instance, as Childs points out about the text of the Old Testament, "the Masoretic text is not identical with the canonical text, but is only a vehicle for its recovery. There is no extant canonical text" (1979:100). Are those who construct a "canonical" text the authors? Hence, deciding who its authors are is a vexed logical and practical question.

3. Sometimes holistic readings approach fundamentalism by presuming that the only "text" is the whole Bible (a Protestant version) and that it is authored by God. I would merely note that the question of divine authorship is not at issue here: if God be the "author" of the text, "author" is used in an analogous sense. What biblical scholars would be investigating on such a presumption is *how* God has worked through the human authors.

4. The subsequent analysis is indebted especially to Habel, save that I have found Pope's unscrambling of chapters 24-27 generally more convincing. Pope better preserves the essential thematic parallels Habel cites and also provides a better balance for the truncated third round of speeches. I regret I cannot convey the beauty and power of the poetry. For this see Habel 1985, Alter 1985:76-110, and especially Mitchell 1987 (although he omits some material from his translation for dubious reasons).

5. "The accuser," that is the Satan, is a member of God's celestial court, even a son of God (possibly a lesser deity). This is a title, not the later proper name of the devil. As with God, so with the Satan: they must first be understood as the text presents them, not as they are seen in later developments or other contexts (cf. Pope 1973:9-10).

6. Job will not work as a directive that solves any material problems. Presumably, those coming to Job for solutions need no directive to tell them to try to solve their problems, so Job can't function as a 'formal' directive (see pp. 37 and 57, conditions 3d). Job doesn't make things the way they are, so it is not a declarative. If it is merely an expressive, it can have no representative force.

7. Ancient scribes and contemporary scholars emend, rearrange, and "'improve'" (Pope 1973:xliii) Job to an extent rarely appreciated by nonscholars. So which is the true text of Scripture, the text Christians and Jews ought to accept as authoritative: a Masoretic 'correction' to an earlier text or a scholarly 'retrieval' of another text? If we are to understand and evaluate the speech acts performed in the text, we need to decide what the text is. Textual questions are vexed, but ought not be ignored by those who use the texts in their work.

Some believe that a text closer to the original ought to be accepted because it is more original. But this begs the question of what "original" means. Is initial oral material, a first writer's text, a final redactor's text, or a text and canon of a specific time and place not our own properly the *norma normans* for our constructing an "original" text? While it may be worthwhile to find what an "original text" is, criteria for determining success are rarely argued and, if argued, rarely resolved.

One way to solve the problem is to construe a "received text" as the "true text." What is handed on, because it is handed on, is authoritative. This resolution casts scriptural texts in stone. They become "sacrosanct," fixed, and thus unalterable by rabbinic or theological recasting. There can be no fiddling with vowel points or inserting explanations of perplexing stories as Jesus' parables were explained (cf. Tilley 1985:73-96). Once texts are fixed, in order to understand their meanings and to explain their problems or obscurities, rabbis and theologians must write commentaries explaining the texts. Such practices can be traced at least to rabbis in the first century B.C.E.

In our era, however, we recognize that texts are not fixed and originals not determinative of meaning. We need to argue for renderings or to judge which scholarly arguments best support a rendering. Philosophers and literary critics who take texts as "given" are simply failing to recognize the crucial textual issues.

8.    James Crenshaw reminded me that not only do academic theologians erase Job; so do those who fix the readings for liturgy, which comprises the *real* canon for most Christians. Job is obliterated, presumably because "texts which contain serious literary, critical, or exegetical problems or which the faithful may find difficult to understand have been omitted from the readings for Sundays and solemnities" (*Lectionary for Mass* [New York: Catholic Book Publishing Co., 1970], 10). With such a principle of exclusion, it is surprising that any biblical text is read in church.

In the Sunday cycles of the new Roman Missal, only two selections are taken from Job: 38:1,8-11 (God's declaration of power from the whirlwind, paired with Jesus stilling the storm [Mk. 4:35-41]) and 7:1-4,6-7 (a lament skillfully edited to erase both the agent who brought about Job's condition (God), and the infestation of his flesh by worms and dirt, paired with some of Jesus' healing [Mk. 1:29-39]). The weekday cycle so severely truncates Job (the first test, two laments, "hope for a redeemer," divine power, confession, and 'verdict') that the story becomes a very simple one of testing, perseverance, and reward. Job 19:23-27 is an optional reading in the Mass for the Dead, and verses from chapter 31 (in which Job affirms his generosity) form an optional reading for a votive Mass for those suffering from famine or hunger. Also see Rouillard 1983:8-12.

The *Common Lectionary* (New York: Church Hymnal Corporation, n.d.[1983]) is no better. It uses texts from Job thrice: 7:1-7 (including worms and dirt, but excluding the divine agent), 28:20-28 (part of the wisdom hymn), and 42:1-6.

*Chapter 5*

# AUGUSTINE'S AUTHORITATIVE DEFENSE

*Thus, by one man sin entered the world,*
*and by sin, death:*
*and so it passed over into all men,*
*in that all sinned.*
—Romans 5:12; as quoted in
Augustine, *Enchiridion* 26

## Augustine and Augustinian Theodicy

The broad outline of the theodicy attributed to Augustine is well known. The all-powerful, all-good, all-knowing God created the world, including some rational creatures (angels, humans) whose nature was wholly good, but not perfect (since only God was perfect). These creatures were given free will, an ability to choose either to remain in or to leave their proper place in God's creation. They could keep their place by keeping their hearts set on their creator or they could change their place by giving their creator's place in their hearts to lesser goods, i.e., themselves or other creatures.

Some angels freely chose to make themselves the centers of their universes. As each was not the center of the universe, this was an evil choice, destructive of the order God made. By this choice they placed themselves before God in their own esteem, and thus those choices were sinful, prideful choices. They fell from their proper places. Their natures, originally good, became permanently twisted and distorted: evil became "second nature" to them. They became the demons and devils who can wreak havoc in God's world. Because their intellectual and other powers remained intact, these permanently twisted beings could use those good powers for evil purposes.

In the human realm, Adam, tempted by Eve, who was tempted by the devil in the form of a serpent, chose to usurp his creator's place by turning his heart from God. He placed the created, rather than the creator, at the center of his universe. The prideful choice of his will permanently distorted human nature because all humans were seminally present in his loins. Since Adam, no human had the will power to avoid the evil of sin and the temporal suffering and destruction sin causes and the eternal punishment sin deserves. But God freely chose to save some from sin and its consequences through an unmerited gift of grace, preferring to bring good out of evil rather than to destroy the existent evils.

Hence, all evil in the world is a result of sin. Natural evils, including much human suffering, result from angelic sin, and moral and spiritual evils from human sin. Those who are damned deserve eternal punishment because they sinned. Their punishment restores order to the universe.

Modern critics of this theodicy recapitulate many charges made by Augustine's contemporaries. One critic charges that there is a "radical incoherence" in this theodicy, especially with regard to the "inexplicably perverse misuse of their God-given freedom" by good, free creatures (Hick 1978:62). Another resorts to an explanation that is a nonexplanation in writing that the "first manifestations of evil, then, were chance events—the fall of Satan and the fall of Man" (G. Evans 1982:94-95). Numerous skeptics have challenged the coherence of this theodicy, some biblical theologians have argued it is unfaithful to the New Testament,[1] and many social historians and feminists have catalogued its ill effects in human history (cf. Pagels 1988:98-154).

Obviously, numerous further questions could be raised about the coherence and credibility of this 'Augustinian account.' However, this account is not Augustine's.[2] Rather, subsequent theologians built this theodicy by amalgamating "relevant" texts out of Augustine's various writings. They have attributed to Augustine a system of 'theodicy' which goes far beyond what he actually claimed and said.

A fine summary of this account can be found in John Hick's magisterial theodicy, *Evil and the God of Love*. Hick synthesizes what he calls Augustine's "characteristic teaching" by drawing themes and claims found "not only in the great works of his maturity, *The City of God*, the *Confessions*, and the *Enchiridion*, but also in a succession of earlier books going back to his controversies with the

Manichaeans" into an Augustinian theodicy (Hick 1978:37). Hick then proposes to evaluate this amalgamation as "Augustine's doctrine" (1978:53).

But it is not Augustine's doctrine. Augustine did not write a theodicy. He wrote numerous works to various audiences, for various purposes, and with various illocutionary forces which touch on God and evils at various points and in various ways. Theologians amalgamate Augustinian "themes," "doctrines," "teaching," etc., into a single theodicy constructed from Augustine's various works, a sort of Augustinian "diatessaron" (cf. Tilley 1985:74-75). This practice is malpractice.[3]

Such amalgamations abstract "content" from early and late texts. But Augustine radically shifted his positions from his early works to his later works. Moreover, to attend only to the "content" of these varied communicative actions without noticing the different illocutionary points of those actions also distorts the significance of that content. If one fails to notice the differences among those texts as communicative/strategic acts, e.g., the different illocutionary forces of bishops' instructions to laypeople, theologians' arguments against heretics or apologies to outsiders, ecclesial politicians' letters to the pope, etc., one can misunderstand them. It is easy to misinterpret the precise force of speech acts in texts. Many readers of Augustine take some of his proposals of hypothetical possibilities as nonhypothetical claims about actualities.

In the four sections Hick (1978) devotes to Augustine, Hick (like most theological interpreters of Augustine) never adverts to the differences among these communicative actions. In fact, other than noticing that some works are earlier than others, all are simply taken as a vein from which useful nuggets of content can be mined. Moreover, when one correlates Hick's discussion of the 'Augustinian' theodicy with the range of his references and cross-references, an interesting picture appears. He weaves notions from other Augustinian and non-Augustinian writings into the basic framework he builds from parts of *City of God*, which is not a theodicy, but a highly politicized apologetic theology of history. Not only many of Augustine's works, but also numerous other ancient texts, provide "content" which Hick can mine, refine, and mold into an 'Augustinian theodicy' (compare Burns 1988 for a similar account on evil's origin, but drawn only from Augustine's works).

For instance, although Hick construes the principle of plenitude as a major theme in Augustine's theodicy, he makes only one citation to Augustine's works to buttress that claim. He develops this notion primarily from Plotinus and secondary sources. Although

Augustine himself may have accepted the principle, it is not clear that his specific speech acts presume it. Further, although sin is construed as the basic evil, and the effects of sin on the will are catalogued (Hick 1978:64-65), nothing is said about the effects of sin on the mind, e.g., deceptions and self-deceptions (cf. G. Evans 1982:52-90). Moreover, Hick treats an early polemic, *On Free Will*, which Pelagians later used against Augustine and about which Augustine had second thoughts (*Retractationes* VIII/3), and another early treatise written against the Manichees, *On the Nature of the Good*, as if the polemical context in which he wrote and the communicative actions he performed in writing had no bearing on the reliability or meaning of their "content." Indeed, even if one finds fault with Pagels' overall thesis, one cannot neglect the insight that ecclesiastical power politics shapes the anti-Pelagian writings (122-26). In sum, amalgamations which theodicists like Hick traditionally construct represent their view of an imagined perfect or ideal theodicy; but *it is not Augustine's theodicy*; it is an amalgamation.

What theodicists treat as 'Augustinian theodicy' is part of a discourse system for dealing with evil that arose in the Constantinian church. Its central concept is the bondage of the will in Original Sin brought about by the Fall of humanity, a concept Augustine moved to the center of the Christian story. Its acceptance means that humans radically need ultimately to be redeemed by Christ, to be restrained forcibly by political and ecclesial authorities, and to be retrained completely to overcome the evil that has infected them. The latter proximate implications of the bondage of will theologically legitimate the political and spiritual domination of established (male) authorities. Augustine, even as a master of ecclesial power politics, is not responsible for this system, although he contributed mightily to it by giving it one of its central intellectual pillars, the concept of the "will." The "Augustinian theodicy" is part of the justification of this ecclesio-political system, an explanation devised not by Augustine but propagated, in part, by the authorities who would keep that system intact. But it is not clear that such a theodicy is either necessary or appropriate in the absence of allegiance to that system.

If the Augustinian theodicy is not Augustine's own authoritative position, what is? His theological position? But his theological position varied markedly. For instance, although the will was a constant problem in his theology, Augustine's resolution of that problem shifted as he battled new opponents. Against the Manichees, he argued the freedom of the will. Against the Donatists, he argued the shaping of the will by habit. Against the Pelagians, he argued the bondage of the will. As a polemical theologian, Augustine's positions are too inconsistent to yield a coherent position.[4]

The text least constrained by polemics would be one addressed to Christians as an instruction, rather than a text that presents Augustine's speculations, apologies, reflections, polemics, etc. *Enchiridion* (421/423) is a "little handbook" of Christian faith and practice, based on the Nicene Creed and the Lord's Prayer, written in response to an appeal from Laurentius, a Roman layman. Its purpose was to instruct its reader on the essentials of Christianity. Its audience was an ordinary Christian. Augustine wrote it as a bishop for a believing layman (or for laypeople generally), thus taking the position of a religious authority vis-à-vis his audience.

*Enchiridion* is an institutionally bound assertive, an instruction. It was not shaped by the needs of polemic or apology or ecclesial politics, but by the needs of a Christian for religious (intellectual and practical) guidance. Because Augustine as bishop and polemicist legitimated the ecclesio-political system of late antiquity when he chose to do so does not mean that he always did so. *Enchiridion* does not defend that system. Its point is to convey the essentials of the Christian creed. The man who was asked to write it had to have a position of leadership within the institution: it is a "manual," a "guide to faith and practice" written by a bishop for a layperson to use. Were he not bishop, Augustine might have written the words of the *Enchiridion*, but he could not have written *Enchiridion*![5] Odd as that sounds, it is no more odd than the fact that a person as a general can command a private, but as a civilian could say the same words without issuing a command. *Enchiridion* is an instruction; to neglect its illocutionary force is to neglect the act Augustine performed in issuing it.

Hence, what follows takes *Enchiridion* as a central statement of belief from an authoritative source. This is precisely what Augustine has claimed for it. It is a book "bringing together the necessities": what must be followed, what heresies must be fled, what is based in faith, what supported by reason, what is primary, what is ultimate, "which would be a summary of all definitions; what is the certain and particular foundation of the catholic faith" (4).[6] He notes that a full defense of his teaching against the claims of heretics (that they have Christ among them and have the right view of things) is not possible. Such a disputation "is of so many volumes that it would seem infinite" (5). Rather, in writing this handbook, he says he is doing something else: "it is easy to *state* what must be believed, what must be hoped, what must be loved" (6). He then continues by saying what he is not doing: "but how this is to be defended against the calumnies of those who feel differently is a more laborious and lengthy instruction. In order to have that defense it is not the hand which ought to be filled with a short enchiridion, but the heart which ought to be inflamed by intense application [*studio*]" (6). *Enchiridion* is a statement of the faith.

Hence, rather than making an amalgam of Augustine's views and evaluating that amalgam, the next two sections focus on this text as a communicative action, because in it Augustine claims authority in the Christian community, in a way Augustine's other texts which deal with evil in a significant way do not. Then we can say what Augustine the bishop's instruction for the Christian community is with regard to God and evil, and whether this instruction is radically incoherent in its treatment of God and evil in light of its purpose as a guide to faith and practice. Most importantly, we shall see that it does not contain a theodicy.

## Enchiridion *as an Instruction on the Nature of Evil*

For the *Enchiridion* to be an instruction, an institutionally bound assertive, certain conditions must obtain.[7] To be a success it must be coherent; if it is not, it is self-defeating. As the most important charge against its content is that it is incoherent when it deals with "the problem of evil," we will focus on the claims Augustine makes in *Enchiridion* first about the nature, origin, and effects of evil and then about the redemption of evil. The first question is the nature of evil.

"Whatever is, is good, because God made it." Never, after his conversion to Christianity, did Augustine deny the fundamental equation of being with goodness, uncreated being with uncreated goodness, created being with created goodness. But then, why do we call some things "evil"? In *Enchiridion*, Augustine writes of the nature of evils (*mala*) in two distinct ways, as the following shows:

> In this world, what is called evil, well ordered and properly placed, more highly commends good things so that they may be more pleasing and laudable when compared with evil things. For the omnipotent God, who . . . is the greatest good, would not allow anything evil in his works, unless he were so omnipotent and good as to make good out of evil. But what is that which is called evil but the privation of good? (11)

Illustrations of evils as defects, corruptions, or deprivations of naturally good things then follow.

In the first sentence, "evil" applies to one of two or more entities compared to each other. Augustine gives no examples here. Perhaps one might think of the dull plants in a garden setting off the brilliant flowers, or of the plain framing which sets off the brilliance of a complex mosaic, or of the "blue collar" athletes on a team without whom the "star" could not be brilliant. We might call *mala* some things that are not very interesting or complex if they are out of place, or some supporting athletes who are not skilled if they are expected to star. However, in their proper places, these are not in themselves *mala*, but have their proper roles as setting off or enhancing the greater. Each is called *malum* when it is misplaced or compared with the greater. This first comparative use of "evil" undergirds what Hick (1978:82-85) has called the "aesthetic" theme in Augustine, especially as one finds such comparative "goods" and "evils" in the rhythms of nature. However, it is not an important motif in *Enchiridion*.

In the last sentence of the quotation, evil applies to an actual entity *in comparison to what it should be/is by nature*. This second comparative use of the term, as Augustine's illustrations show, is much different. Here the evil is seen not by comparing two things (legitimately or illegitimately), but by comparing a thing to its nature. It is less than it should be, deprived of its full measure of goodness. "Therefore, every entity [*natura*], even if it is defective, is good insofar as it is an entity and evil insofar as it is defective" (13).

It is important to keep these uses of *malum* separate. Distinguishing prima facie and genuine evil (Griffin 1976:22) serves this purpose well. The first use of *malum* is ambiguous. It may indicate that an entity is corrupted or it may indicate that an entity appears evil from certain perspectives or in certain roles or places. This is prima facie evil. For example, the sufferings which animals undergo as they are attacked for food by other animals as part of the natural food chain are prima facie evil. However, these animals are not certainly corrupted. Their natures may be such that it is part of their proper place in the natural environment to eat and to be eaten by others. If it be part of an animal's (or plant's) nature to be eaten by other animals, then the prima facie evils of their sufferings and deaths are not genuine evils, for these prima facie deprivations are not losses of goods which are natural to them. The second use of *malum* is not ambiguous. It indicates that an entity *is* corrupted, no matter how it may appear. This is *genuine* evil. If animals suffer because their natures have been corrupted, then such prima facie evil is genuine evil, because these prima facie deprivations are losses of goods which are natural to them. Unfortunately, commentators do not always seem to keep these separate (cf. Hick 1978:87-89); but then, it seems neither did Augustine in other places (cf. *Civ. Dei* XI/18,23).

Moreover, Augustine implied that an ability to disambiguate prima facie evils in the natural realm is irrelevant to religious belief. "Therefore, when it is asked what is to be believed with regard to religion, the nature of things need not be investigated as it is by those the Greeks call *physikos* [natural scientists]" (9). This includes not being concerned with the "origins and natures of animals." Yet if knowing the natures of animals is irrelevant to religion, then knowing if animals' natures have been or have not been corrupted must be irrelevant to religion. Thus, knowing whether evil in the natural realm is genuine or merely apparent is irrelevant to religious belief (cf. 16). And, indeed, Augustine makes this plain. After commenting on the multiple opinions of the *physikoi*, he concludes: "It is sufficient for a Christian to believe that the cause of created things, whether celestial or terrestrial, whether visible or invisible, is nothing but the goodness of the creator, who is the one true God; that there is no entity [*natura*] which is neither he nor from him; and that he is the Trinity, namely the Father and the Son generated from that same Father, and the Holy Spirit proceeding from the Father, but the very one and same Spirit of Father and Son" (9). In sum, Augustine teaches that the nature of evil is the privation of a good natural to an entity; but whether what appears to be evil in the rhythm of nature is actually evil is irrelevant to religious belief.

The second question is how evil originates. But the religious question must be limited to the realm of what Augustine calls the "rational creation," the realms of the angelic and the human. The origin of "evil" in nature is irrelevant to religious belief. So the question must be limited to how did the loss of goods natural to humans and angels occur? How did such evils originate? Augustine's answer is explicit: "Therefore, from good things evils originate, and there are no evils, save in various good things, nor was there any other place from which any entity [*natura*] of evil arose" (14).

But this naturally raises the objection that saying evil comes from good seems to contradict the obviously true teaching of the Lord that good cannot give rise to evil (15). His response to that objection seems oblique. He begins a long (for *Enchiridion*) discussion of cases of errors, mistakes, and lying. "But we are bound to recognize the causes of good and evil things insofar as it is given to people in this life full of errors and hardships to know how to avoid those errors and hardships" (16). For each of the examples, the causes can be recognized as simply luck (Augustine's getting lost and avoiding an ambush set up by an armed band of Donatists), ignorance (when one thinks one knows what one does not), or the will (when one chooses to lie, whether to benefit oneself or another). Yet bad luck can befall good people, and it is difficult to see how anyone can avoid bad luck. Ignorance is not necessarily bad, but ignorance can lead good people to make mistakes. And even "fellow-heirs of Christ" have to request forgiveness for the sin of lying (22). This last case suggests that even good people can do evil.

The structure of this section is obscure and Augustine makes his point elliptically. Because of the importance of Augustine's view, the embedded speech acts must be unpacked. First, Augustine asserts that evil arises from good. Second, he interjects the objection. Third, he responds to the objection by (a) giving examples in which evil can arise from or befall good people; and (b) distinguishing the varied causes of evil in these examples. Once he has distinguished luck, ignorance, and an evil will as causes, he can conclude his response to the objection by asserting his view of the cause of evil insofar as it is relevant to the present instruction:

> Therefore, having handled these matters with the brevity appropriate to this book, so far as the causes of good and evil things are to be known, to the degree sufficient for the way which would lead us to that kingdom where there will be life without death, truth without error, happiness without disquiet, we should never doubt that about things which pertain to us: of the good, that the cause is nothing but the goodness of God; of the evil, that the cause is indeed the will of changeable goods (first angels, later humans) falling short of the unchangeable good" (23).

Augustine has not here made an argument for his view, but responded to an objection by showing how his view that evil arises from the will of naturally good angels and humans fits with what we know about the evils people do.

As an argument for his position, eliminating luck and ignorance as the means by which good entities gave rise to evil would be rather weak—even if he had spelled out the structure of the argument in the text. However, *Enchiridion* is not an argument, but an instruction. It is not a theoretical discussion, but a guide "to show what is sufficient for the way . . ." Augustine does not bear a burden of proof, as he might in a situation, e.g., a debate, in which his assertives were institutionally free speech acts.

Rhetorically, because he is instructing, both he and his audience properly presume that his claims are correct—unless they can be shown to be wrong (as tennis players presume line judges' calls to be correct). Logically, Augustine is not committed to asserting the truth of his response to an objection, but only its possible truth. These rhetorical and logical points are usually overlooked. But their significance is crucial.

Rhetorically, the hypothetical objector bears the burden of proof in these circumstances. To mount a successful argument against Augustine's instruction, the objector would have to show either that Augustine misrepresented the Christian tradition or that Augustine's view was incoherent (and could not be true) or that an alternative account was a better expression of the tradition than Augustine's. Augustine, the presumed authority, does not have to prove the objection false or his own position true or legitimate. All he must do to respond to this objection in this context (whether it was raised by Laurentius as one of the questions he needed answered or was one that Augustine thought needed treatment) is to demonstrate that the objector has failed to show that Augustine's teaching is incoherent, i.e., that it is possible his view is true. And he attempts to do that by illustrating that for a good reason a good, but not perfect, person might sin. So, by extension, a good, but not perfect, being might perform an act that falls short of the immutable good. Augustine dispenses with the objection by invoking an analogy.

Logically, Augustine's analogy, if possibly true, shows that the objection does not give sufficient reason to reject his account of the origin of evil in the rational creation. Now one might not accept his analogy. But why not? One might object to analogical argument as a method of proving the truth of a claim. But given the institutional status presumed by the specific speech act he is performing, Augustine is not required to prove any claim true. All he has to do to respond to the objection is to show that his teaching is *possibly* true. There are, so far, three key items to his teaching:

(1)   All that is, is good, created by God, all-good and all-powerful.

(2)   Evil is the privation of good.

(3)   Evil originates from good entities.

Additionally, he has developed an explanatory thesis.

(3a)   Evil originates from naturally good, but changeable, angels' and humans' will falling short of the unchangeable good.

The force of the analogy is to show that (1), (2), and (3) can all be true, i.e., they are not incoherent as a set. He shows this by invoking a possibly true claim (3a) which, if asserted with (1) and (2), entails (3). Logically, if a possibly true proposition (such as (3a)) were asserted with another proposition or set of propositions which it did not contradict (such as (1) and (2)), and if their conjunction entails another proposition (such as (3)), then (1), (2), and (3) are compatible. Hence, his analogy needs to prove nothing, but only to be a possibly good analogy because (3a) needs only to be possibly, not actually, true. Rhetorically and logically, the point is this: both the interposed objection and the response to it "factor out." Propositions (1-3) remain standing: they are not incoherent.[8]

Augustine teaches that all the evil with which Christians are to be concerned originates from good entities. Good beings sin. His position in the community enables him to teach with authority. He defends the coherence of his teaching with an analogy. To reject his teaching on the origin of evil requires rejecting either his authority or his analogy.

The key point here is often obscured. Whatever position Augustine took in other contexts, when giving an authoritative instruction about the content of the faith, he did *not* here, in his instruction, propound a truth claim about his view of the origin of evil in the will. As an authoritative teacher, his assertion of (3a) needs only be hypothetical. If one takes Augustine as asserting the evil will as the cause of evil in authoritatively stating the content of Christian faith, then one could find that he was imposing an "idiosyncratic" account of the faith on a layperson. But here he does not assert, but hypothesizes, the cause of evil. The key question may be why this "teaching" became dominant in Christianity (cf. Pagels 1988:99-100); but that question does not apply to *Enchiridion*, because Augustine literally does not teach it here. Within the context of the instruction in the faith, finding the origin of evil in the will is hypothetical—as one might expect from a bishop who as a theologian did not conclusively resolve the problem of the will.

The third question is what the effects of evil are. First, there are the results of evil choice, the effects intrinsically connected with evil choice. These results affect human nature in itself, warping and twisting it from what it was when God created it. Augustine lists a number of privations humans suffer (24). The first privation is the deficiency of the human will. The second is ignorance of things to be done, which leads to error. The third is desire for noxious things, which leads to sorrow. These lead to "all the miseries of our rational nature" (24). However, rational nature did not lose its desire for blessedness (25). Second, there are the consequences of evil choice, the effects brought about by evil choice, though not intrinsically connected with that choice. The difference is that such consequences affect human beings, rather than human nature *per se*, and bring humans sorrow and misery. These include the penalty of death and damnation (25) and the extension of this penalty to "all the children" of Adam and Eve, born of carnal desire and thus infected with original sin (26). He concludes by quoting the version of Romans 5:12 which is this chapter's epigraph.

Then Augustine suddenly shifts gears: "Ita ergo se res habebat" (27). "And so, therefore, this was the way things were going." Whether *ita* refers to the previous or to the following discussion is unclear. This simple sentence separates two realms of Ciceronian rhethoric. What follows is not more philosophical discussion of the nature, the causes, or the effects of evil. Now appears a concrete "empirical description" of the human situation as Augustine saw it. This portrayal of the "damned mass of the whole human race" rolling in evils and being thrown down to worse evils is not a metaphysical theory about the effects or consequences of evil. It is the summary of Augustine's vision of the misery which afflicts all of humanity.

He follows this summary with a theological claim that in these circumstances, God "judged it better to make good from evils than to permit evils to be [come to] nothing." After a digression in which he explains why some angels could remain good after the Fall (in contrast to humanity) and God's purpose of bringing humans into heaven (to replace the lost angels), Augustine returns to the theological. The human plight is such that neither allegedly good works nor allegedly free choice can stop the destruction. How can works generated by an evil will be good? How can choice fixed on evil be good? Since human nature is distorted by evil, neither works nor will can be good. He concludes with his analysis of the situation: "For one freely serves who freely does the will of his master. By this, who is the servant of sin is free only for sinning. Wherefore the servant will not be free to act justly unless, freed from sin, will begin to be the servant of justice" (30). Given this plight, humans cannot free themselves, but need to be freed.

Augustine's teaching on the effects of evil can be summarized in the following:

(4)   Evil effects a distortion of human nature and brings ills and sufferings to human beings.

His claim is that evil has become "second nature" to humanity. Hence, people cannot straighten out their natures naturally or overcome their ills and sufferings by their own efforts. Is the situation then hopeless? Obviously not. God makes good from evil. There is redemption.

## Enchiridion *as an Instruction*
## *on the Redemption of Evil*

For Augustine the bishop, the problem of evil is primarily a human problem. Evil is not merely the affliction of suffering and death, but the corruption of human wills and intellects. He has explained the nature, cause, and effects of evil. In so doing, Augustine has offered the *Enchiridion* as an instruction to guide the reader's intellect and will. He notes that when Christians' perceptions of the body or intelligence of the mind fall short of defending "what must be believed, what must be hoped, what must be loved," they are to accept the testimony of the writers of Scripture: who "either through the body or through the mind [*animum*] by divine help were enabled to see or foresee" what is to be followed in religion (4). In short, *Enchiridion* assembles all the available authorities into an authoritative teaching which functions as a direct attempt to overcome part of the effects of evil: the weakness of the Christians' minds and wills.

But this is not the real solution of the problem of evil. That solution lies elsewhere. *Enchiridion* is an instruction, a set of reminders of that solution. Augustine's key theological claim about 'solving' the real problem of evil centers on the redemption of and from evil. It can be summarized as:

(5) Evil is overcome by the free gift of God's grace through Jesus Christ.

That this is Augustine's resolution can be shown by two reflections on the text.

First, Augustine's theological claim that God "judged it better to make good [*benefacere*] from evils than to permit evils to be [come to] nothing" should be understood as a claim about the redemption of humanity. The "evils" (neuter plural) in this claim that are to be made good could be anything. But if the primary result of evil is the distortion of human nature and the primary consequence the twistedness and suffering of humanity, then the primary thing that needs benefaction is humanity. As shown above, in *Enchiridion* Augustine is concerned only with genuine evils in the rational creation. Moreover, his main focus is on the evil that afflicts the human condition. Hence, it is in this area that the key problem to be solved lies.

Second, Augustine sees the key problem as practical and historical: the loss of humans' freedom to be and to do good. This loss is redescribed as being servant of or enslaved to evil. But if this is the problem, what is the solution? "But whence will be the freedom to do good [*bene faciendum*] for an enslaved and sold human unless he whose voice this is redeems: 'If the son shall free you, then you will be truly freed'" (30). If human nature is twisted, then humans cannot untwist it. Something from beyond human nature is required. That is the redemption of humanity: "Therefore we are reconciled to God through a mediator and we accept the Holy Spirit so that we are transformed from enemies to sons . . . this is the grace of God through Jesus Christ our Lord" (33).

Hence, Augustine's discussion of the nature, causes, and effects of evil is brought to a conclusion by introducing the doctrine of the redemption. Augustine the bishop teaches not so much that a "problem of evil" is solved as that the *redemption of evil* is effected by the gift of divine grace through Christ.

But an obvious objection can be raised. By Augustine's own description of the way things have gone in the world, not all people are redeemed. Why aren't some redeemed? Does this mean that God could not fully solve the problem? That would deny God's omnipotence. Does it mean that God did not will all to be saved? That would deny God's benevolence. Here is a perplexity similar to the problem theodicies are designed to solve. How did Augustine the bishop deal with this perplexity?

Augustine does not undertake a discussion of this nexus of topics constituting the central part of the modern problem of evil until he initiates his discussion of the resurrection of the flesh in the last third of *Enchiridion*. The manner in which *Enchiridion* deals with these issues suggests that this is not a problem for Augustine's authoritative teaching. He begins the discussion as follows:

> I do not see how I could briefly discuss [*disputare*] and resolve [*satisfacere*] all the questions usually raised under this topic of the resurrection of the flesh. . . . Yet in no way is a Christian obliged to doubt the resurrection of the flesh of all who have been or are to be born human and who have or are to die (84).

Again, to make this clear, we need to unpack the embedded speech acts in these sections.

First, Augustine teaches the resurrection of the flesh:

(6)   All people are resurrected.

He then begins a response to various implied questions concerning specific topics about the resurrection of those who were miscarried, deformed, had their bodies dissolved, or deviated significantly from the norm in height or girth, etc. Only then does he return to offering his teaching on the general resurrection. He first discusses the resurrection of the bodies of the saints:

> Therefore, the bodies of the saints rise without any defect, without any deformity, without any corruption, burden, or difficulty, in which so much ease [facilitas] will be so much happiness [felicitas]. . . . Moreover, the apostle affirms, "An animal body is sown, a spiritual body arises" [cf. 1 Cor. 15:44], for such will then be harmony of flesh and spirit, the spirit (without need of any sustenance) quickening the subdued flesh, that nothing from inside us would resist us; so we ourselves would not suffer enemies from without, nor any from within (91).

This teaching can be summarized as:

(6a)   We will rise in our bodies without internal or external defect to ease and happiness.

Augustine then turns to the resurrection of the bodies of the damned:

> Whosoever, then, are not liberated from that mass of perdition which was brought about by the first human, through the one mediator between God and the human, rise again indeed each with their own flesh to be punished with the devil and his angels. What need is there to labor finding out whether they would really rise with the defects and deformities of their bodies, whichever defective and deformed members they would bear in themselves? And uncertainty about their condition or appearance does not oblige us to worry. Certain will be their endless damnation (92).

This teaching can be summarized as follows:

(6b)   Those who are not liberated by Christ will be raised to endless damnation.

The contrast between the "us" of (6a) and the "those" of (6b) may be merely incidental if one is intent upon amalgamating Augustine's system or "personal view." But it might be used to ground the politics of repression where the "other" is marginalized, forcibly restrained, or coercively retrained. But if one is sensitive to the rhetoric of and audience for Enchiridion, the contrast is essential, yet does not support political and ecclesiastical repression.

Augustine writes for believers. He includes among his audience only those who will be raised to felicity. Whosoever is not liberated by Christ is "them," outside his audience. Whatever Augustine may have written for other audiences, in this instruction, the audience's redemption is presumed. Hence, Augustine dismisses out of hand the importance of many of the speculative issues, especially those which have nothing to do with "us." They need not worry "us." However such thinking was used by the ecclesio-political system, Augustine never materially identifies "them." Implicitly, all who read *Enchiridion* as an instruction are "us."

After further dismissals of other uncertainties and speculation on the intensity of punishments, which vary according to the depths of sin to which each of the nonsaved had fallen, Augustine concludes:

> Therefore, if reprobate angels and humans remain in eternal punishment, then saints will know more fully what goods grace will have conferred on them. Then what is written in the psalm will appear more obvious, "I will sing to you, O Lord, of mercy and judgment," for no one is freed except through unobliged mercy and no one is damned except through obligatory judgment. Then shall be uncovered what is now hidden (94-95).[9]

The title the English translator gives to section 94 indicates the way this section is usually read: "By contrast the saints will the better appreciate the benefits of God's grace." But *what* are contrasted here? The knowledge two groups of resurrected people had or the saints' temporal and eschatological understandings (the latter enhanced by seeing the sufferings of the others) of God's mercy and judgment? *When* is this contrast occurring? Now or in the resurrected life? And *who* is doing the contrasting? The resurrected saints or Augustine? The traditional amalgamating approach to Augustine has taken the second of each of the oppositions as determinative.

However, if we are sensitive to the speech acts embedded and to the contrast between the "us" of (6a) and the "them" of (6b), the first option in each pair is correct. What Augustine is teaching here is not how things *will be*, but that *now* we saints, grateful for God's mercy, don't see clearly enough to be properly grateful, for much is hidden. But *then* we will see clearly, for the hidden will be uncovered for us. *They* don't see clearly now, either. But they will never understand—their mind and will remain enslaved by sin and darkness, and what is hidden will remain covered for them. In this passage, Augustine is deconstructing any attempt which construes him as teaching clearly now what no one can see until after the resurrection. He cannot assert that he has seen clearly—he is not in the proper position, a postresurrectional position, to do so. He is not a bishop of the "church triumphant" in heaven, but of the "church militant" on earth! In short, a traditional reading of this passage takes Augustine as teaching *now* about what the future will be, but close analysis of the passage shows this is scarcely possible; Augustine is teaching the contrast of the limited knowledge "we" have *now* on earth and the fuller knowledge "we" will have *then* in glory.

What follows this teaching is Augustine's responses to more implied questions, some repeated or restated. *Why does God save some and not others?* We don't know (95). *Why does God permit evil to exist?* For some purpose, not discussed (96). *What does it mean when the Scripture says God wills all humans to become saved when obviously so many are not being saved? Are human wills blocking God?* No (97). *Then why does God grace some and not others?* If one doesn't know, who is he to ask God? If one does know, why ask? (98-99) *What does the Scriptural saying mean?* Evil acts are permitted by God, some good acts don't coincide with God's will, and sometimes God uses evil for good. So it can be understood in various ways (*alio modo*)—so long as the understanding does not contradict God's omnipotence (100-103).

What usual accounts of Augustine's work often ignore is that all these issues are not central to Augustine's teaching. Augustine did not write *Enchiridion* to answer these questions. He is not necessarily teaching them or their answers. In fact, he is only providing *possible* answers to these questions, especially to the question about the meaning of Scripture which can be understood in various ways. As the analysis of 94-95 above showed, by his own admission he could not now be in position to give definitive answers to them. Moreover, giving possible answers is all he needs to do. As in his discussion of the causes of evil, he only needed to show his analogy *possibly* true, so in discussing the relation between God's will to save all and the damnation of some, he only needs to show that there are some possibly true ways to resolve the problems. All he has to do to respond to these problems in this context is to show that there can be an answer to the questions raised, not to say definitively what that answer must be. If he has shown that there can be answers to these questions, then both the questions and the answers "factor out" from his teaching, whatever role these claims might play in his apologetics or speculations or politics. In short, *Enchiridion* does not teach an Augustinian theodicy.

After discussing various points—that God foreknew (*praesciebat*) Adam's sin which enabled him to prepare (*praeparavit*) his will to deal with it (104), that we have no reason to complain that our wills are unfree because we have no capability of being inclined to wretchedness (105), that humans have no good deserts apart from the gift of grace (106-7)—Augustine returns to the theme of the Mediator and Redeemer, reiterating the teaching summarized in (5). He concludes with another reiteration of (6a) and (6b), now using the language of the two cities (111-13), but does so in a way which undercuts any certainty about what hell is like. He claims that hell is beyond our imagination: "so great is the penalty that no torments which we invent [*novimus*] could be compared to them, as it would be [*sit*] eternal, while these would be many ages long" (112). He only claims that it is alienation from the life of God and permanent (113). In sum, what "endless damnation" in (6b) is like is beyond our imagination.

## *The Logic of* Enchiridion

I have shown elsewhere (Tilley 1984) the crucial logical and rhetorical differences between constructing defenses of religious faith in the face of challenges and constructing theodicies.[10] Each has a different purpose, burden of proof, and structure of argument. Being clear about the differences is crucial for properly evaluating *Enchiridion*.

In constructing a *defense*, a defender of religious belief is not trying to warrant a claim that God exists. The defender believes in God on other grounds, e.g., religious experience, authority, etc. Nor is the defender trying to warrant a claim that any given event or class of events is not genuinely evil. The defender may admit that there are genuine evils in the world, and may even recognize as evil all the states of affairs that an opponent recognizes as evil. Rather, the defender seeks to show that an attack against the religious believers' claims attempted by the opponent does not affect, and should not affect, the quality of assent religious believers give to their beliefs. The defender does this by showing that the set of beliefs is coherent. A defender need only find a possibly true proposition which, when conjoined with belief in God, entails that evil exists. That shows belief in God compatible with belief that evil exists.

The opponent bears the burden of proof in attempting to overthrow an established belief which the believer accepts. To be successful, this opponent must show that the believer cannot rationally hold both beliefs: that God is omnipotent, omniscient, and omnibenevolent, and that evil exists. To show this, the opponent must show that there is no proposition which, when conjoined with belief in God, entails that evil exists. Hence, a defense succeeds if it rebuffs the attack. Because a defense is not used to show those beliefs true, but to defend them from an attack of incompatibility, a defender does not have to demonstrate that the set of challenged beliefs is true, or that the conjoined belief is true, but only that all are possibly jointly true, that is, that they are not contradictory and do not entail propositions which would contradict what else the believer accepts. A successful defense is the rebuttal of a challenge.

In constructing a *theodicy*, the theodicist tries to show "what God's reason is for permitting evil. At bottom, he [sic] says, it's that God can create a more perfect universe by permitting evil" in it (Plantinga 1974b:27). The purpose of a theodicy is not to defeat an opponent's attempt to show that believers' claims about God and evil are incompatible. Rather, the theodicist seeks to show that the warrants for her or his own beliefs are reliable. Here the theodicist must make the argument. Here the burden of proof is not on the attacker, but on the theodicist who attempts to show that "the facts which give rise to the problem of evil" do not truly count against belief in God. "Accordingly, theodicies proceed by bringing other facts and theories into account so as to build up a wider picture which includes the fact of evil but which is such that it is no longer more natural to infer from it that there is no God than that there is" (Hick 1978:371).

A successful theodicy demonstrates either that a person can justly move from the data of the actual world, including its evils, to the claim that an omniscient, omnibenevolent, omnipotent deity created it; or that the actual world is as good as or better than any other possible world; or that its picture of the world is at least as plausible as other available alternatives. In contrast to a defense, which only attempts to show the compatibility of a set of beliefs, a theodicy has the more difficult task of warranting the set of beliefs which comprise it.

The key point can now be made simply: With regard to God and evil, the logical structure of *Enchiridion*, an instruction of Augustine the bishop for the layman Laurentius and others in his position, is not a theodicy, an explanation of why God permits evil, but a statement of faith (claims (1-6) above) and a defense of its coherence. The usual accounts of Augustine's work not only treat the assertions embedded *in* his works as if all had equal and identical assertive illocutionary force, but also fail to distinguish the various illocutionary forces *of* his works and to distinguish the logical forms and rhetorical purposes of these works as Augustine's linguistic actions. The traditional objections to Augustine's work are to the amalgamated theodicy traditionally presented as Augustine's view. They show that the beliefs which go to form the theodicy are not all warranted (cf. Hick 1978:169-98). But that is irrelevant. The important question is to what extent such objections are cogent as objections to Augustine's defense of faith in his authoritative teaching in the *Enchiridion*.

There are two main loci for objections to Augustine's defense. The first is the origin of evil (3,3a). As Hick put it, "The basic and inevitable criticism is that the idea of an unqualifiedly good creature committing sin is self-contradictory and unintelligible" (1978:63). In response to a later defense of this claim which construes evil as a necessary consequence of contingency, he writes, "we must insist that the fact that created beings exist contingently does not entail that they *must* fail. It would be possible for God to create contingent beings which, though in principle capable of failing, are in fact so constituted and sustained that they never fail" (1978:191).

However, this objection fails. Augustine does not construe creatures as "unqualifiedly" good. They are mutably, not immutably, good. Moreover, it is just the point of the contemporary Free Will Defense (cf. Plantinga 1974a:170-84) that it is not logically possible that there are beings such that they always *freely* choose the good and that God *makes* them choose the good. The logical possibilities are that God makes beings choose the good, or allows them to choose. Hence, Hick's conclusion, quoted above, is false. That, however, leaves intact the objection that because contingent beings *can* fail does not mean they *must* fail. Yet this doesn't count against Augustine's defense. Augustine's introduction of analogies to suggest how the good will can err (15-22) introduces possibly true propositions which show how it is possible that good wills could will and do evil. Using modern terms, one could argue, in a way similar to Plantinga, that it is possible that either some or all contingent rational creatures with the ability to will and to do both good and evil will (perhaps angels and certainly Adam) choose to do evil (1974a:184-90). Happily, some of the angels didn't. Sadly, Adam did, and involved all humanity in his fall. But if these claims are logically possible, then (3) is possibly true given (1,2). In sum, it is true that Augustine does not show how evil arises from good entities, but he doesn't have to do so to sustain his defense. He only needs to show that it is *possible* that evil arises from good entities.

The second objection is to (6b). The notion that apparently a majority of humanity will be subject to endless punishment is not only morally repugnant, but is a blot on God's good creation, a testimony that God did not or could not redeem all evil and a reintroduction of the philosophical problem of evil (cf. Hick 1978:89).

However, given that Augustine allows that damnation is more tolerable the less one has sinned (93), that sacrifices for the dead who were not very bad could be propitiations (110), and that the penalties of the damned are sometimes eased (112), it is clear that there is some flexibility in the doctrine. Moreover, some recent philosophers (e.g., Swinburne 1983; Stump 1985:399-402) have defended versions of the doctrine of hell which avoid its moral repugnance, but construe "hell" as the varied ultimate destinies appropriate for the kind of person each has become in this life. So it is clear that not every doctrine of hell is necessarily morally repugnant.

Whether Augustine's teaching on hell in *Enchiridion* must be construed as morally repugnant is the issue. Clearly, Augustine does not use hell as a threat or warning to terrify or to repress people. *Enchiridion* is addressed to true believers who are bound for glory. So he is not performing directive speech acts which might be morally repugnant. And because he has in 112-13 deconstructed all the images which might be used to specify what "endless damnation" is, there is no reason to understand his teaching on "hell" in morally repugnant terms. At worst, he marginalizes outsiders in *Enchiridion*. But it is Augustine in other roles, and others who take authoritative positions in the ecclesio-political structure of late antiquity, who violently repress others. In sum, *Enchiridion* is an instruction which successfully defends the compatibility of belief that God exists and that there is evil in the world (compare G. Evans 1982:168).

## *Reading* Enchiridion

Surin and Evans have pointed out that Augustine did not share the "modern" problem of evil familiar since the emergence of theodicy, nor its solutions. For him, the key problem was not one of reconciling belief in God with recognition of the sin and suffering in the world. The central problem was the terrible condition all humanity wallows in. For him, the real solution is not the construction of theodicies or defenses, but the redemption of the creation by the gift of grace given in the redemption effected by Jesus Christ.

The main columns in Augustine's intellectual edifice are not philosophical theories, but those credal pillars of a traditional Christian story of the world: Creation, Fall, Redemption, Resurrection. Philosophical excursus and speculations serve not as a "foundation" for this edifice, but as tools to clear out the intellectual rubbish that obscures its beauty. If one believes that credal story told that way, then *Enchiridion* is a successful authoritative instruction, a reminder of the shape of that story.

However, *Enchiridion*, like every communicative act, is of limited significance. It proves nothing but the coherence of the position it defends (basically the story summarized in propositions (1-6)).[11] The Christian story is warranted on other grounds. That *Enchiridion* contains a successful defense does not mean that it provides moral warrants for performing any other actions. Nor does Augustine provide warrants to accept as true the possibly true hypotheses he uses to defend that position. Thus, it licenses neither hellfire and brimstone preaching nor theodicy nor any speech acts which assert just what heaven is like, just what hell is like, just how evil arose, etc. It licenses no practices such as forced baptism or violent repression of heretics. If such actions were thought to be licensed by *Enchiridion* or positions entailed by the statement of faith in it, then Augustine's communicative action did not fully meet the perlocutionary conditions necessary for *Enchiridion* to be a fully successful communicative act (cf. note 7). If his audience did not notice the difference between teaching and hypothesizing in *Enchiridion*, then that oversight would explain why Christians might claim Augustine's authority as a warrant for performing such epistemically and morally dubious actions.

Perhaps Augustine's other actions led to the flaw. Perhaps the audience beyond Laurentius could not or did not distinguish his roles as authoritative teacher and speculative theologian and ecclesial politician. Perhaps they simply assumed that all of his texts were actions in an ongoing theoretical conversation about God and evil. Perhaps conflating Augustine's actions as bishop and as philosophical theologian created a context for hearing him as authorizing those acts. Perhaps the theological context of the misogynism of early Christian theology (see the summary in Noddings 1989:51-57 and the literature she cites) and the ecclesio-political context in which the Catholic church and its famous bishop of Hippo Regius tried to insure Catholic domination by "consolidating its identification with the imperial rule" (Pagels 1988:123) made it impossible for readers to separate instruction in religious faith from exercises in political action. Or perhaps people would warrant such morally dubious acts on other grounds. But *Enchiridion*, as an instruction in faith and Augustine's central and distinctive authoritative teaching, provides no independent moral license for performing communicative or political actions.

But why should one accept the present account over the traditional view transmitted by the theodicists that "Augustinian" theodicy is Augustine's view? The answer to that question depends upon which practice of reading has better preconceptions and purposes. Rather than accepting every claim he made as an assertion of neutral strength, a statement of the facts independent of any contextual determination, of relatively equal worth in amalgamating his "real view," the present approach comes to his texts as the record of communicative actions he performed in specific contexts for specific audiences, of varying worth and uttered with varying illocutionary forces for varying purposes, and finds his authoritative teaching for and to the church central for seeing what the tradition is. Rather than wanting to build a systematic response to "the problem of evil," this approach has sought to unearth the communicative actions that constitute his text and the logical structure embedded in it. Rather than using only a "logic" or "grammar" of statements, this approach has used a logic of speech actions and the necessary logical distinction between theodicies and defenses, unused in traditional accounts.

The present reading is preferable to the traditional approach of the theodicists because it can account for their strategies of reading or processes of interpretation and "misinterpretation," as in the previous paragraph, while the traditional theodicy can account for the present strategy only by dismissing it. It is preferable to the radically historicizing approach because it can retrieve Augustine's voice, while a radically historicizing approach silences Augustine's voice in the present conversation.[12] Both ahistorical theodicists and radically historical antitheodicists provide inadequate readings of Augustine.

The strongest challenge to the present reading comes from those who would argue that Augustine's voice ought to be silenced. Because he supported not only the use of coercive political force to suppress enemies but also the politics of patriarchy, and because his religious notions have been long used to legitimate the suppression of difference in the Western Christian traditions, and because he reshaped traditional Christian doctrine, his position should be abandoned. Surely, what needs to be abandoned is disseminating the discourse system of patriarchy, loathing the body, and construing lust as the primary evidence of evil. But that does not mean abandoning the teaching in *Enchiridion*, for it neither implies nor asserts any of these. Augustine's instructing voice may not necessarily be sounded only in the discourse of patriarchy, although its author was embedded in the system. The *Enchiridion* can be salvaged as an instruction to preserve a voice which enables Christians to speak out about their faith knowing that its central pillars are coherent.

While theodicists did not originate this distortion of Augustine's voice, they have carried on a tradition of systematization which has forced the theological analysis of his communicative actions into the dead end of analyzing their content without regard to their force (see p. 28). Those who practice theodicy obscure the rhetoric and logic of other texts about God and evil. They participate in the practice of legitimating the coercive and marginalizing ecclesio-political structure which is the heritage of Constantinian Christianity.

As the practice of theodicy effaces Job, so it continues the distortion of the meaning of Augustine's instruction. Job is a silenced warning. By defending the believer's right to believe in Christian doctrine, Augustine empowered the believer to speak (see p. 40). His authoritative reminder to the believer of the convictions of Christian faith showed how those beliefs could fit together. The believing readers could then speak on his authority. Obscuring his communicative action may disable those readers who properly depend on his authoritative voice. That is a problem which those who engage in the discourse practice of theodicy are at least responsible for transmitting.

While much of Augustine's theology should be abandoned or reformed, the *Enchiridion*, properly understood, should be recovered. But it is not the only voice of late antiquity which sounded influentially through the ages on God and evil. Although theodicists tend to ignore him because he allegedly simply recapitulates the central themes of the Augustinian "theodicy," Anicius Manlius Severinus Boethius provided a profoundly non-Augustinian understanding of suffering and evil, a countervoice to the "Augustinian theodicy." For him, the problem was not the condition of humanity. The disease was the suffering and misfortune of the innocent. The solution was not "redemption," but the *Consolation of Philosophy*.

## NOTES

1.   Although in the Hebrew Scriptures, the joys and sufferings people experience are sometimes explained by construing them as reward for good deeds and punishment for evil deeds, that view is not only undermined by Job, but is not a constant in the New Testament. The blessings and cursings of Deuteronomy 28 suggest that such a view is part and parcel of one strand of Jewish thought. The view is summarized in Isaiah: "Tell the righteous that it shall be well with them, for they shall eat the fruit of their deeds. Woe to the wicked! It shall be ill with him, for what his hands have done shall be done to him" (Is. 3:9-10).

In the New Testament, Jesus is portrayed as responding to accepted connections of present suffering and death with earlier sin by disconnecting suffering from retribution. He does this, for instance, when his disciples ask him if a man is blind because of his own sin or his parents' sin. Jesus responds that the man is blind so that the "works of God might be made manifest in him" and then gives the blind man sight by rubbing the man's eyes with spit and clay and sending him to wash in the pool of Siloam (John 9:1-12). His comments on the stories he was told of the sufferings of Galileans and the people killed when the tower of Siloam fell (Luke 13:1-5) also undermine a doctrine of retribution.

This disconnecting of suffering from sin can be reliably attributed to the actual (historical) Jesus. (1) It is multiply attested, not only to two different sources (Special Luke, John), but also to two different types (forms) of narrative (miracle story, transitional material). (2) It is also dissimilar enough from the "common sense" of both Palestinian Judaism and post-Jesus Christian belief, which tend to a retributive view, that it is unlikely it was 'interjected' or 'retrojected' by the early Christian communities into the teaching of Jesus. If the argument made in Tilley 1985:101-4, is correct, what we can reliably attribute to the actual Jesus must be a 'touchstone' for Christian theology. Contemporary Christian philosophers and theologians must at least take account of this when dealing with the topics of sin and suffering. Theologians who would differ from what historians reliably attribute to Jesus bear a burden of proof to show why they advocate a position as Christian which prima facie differs significantly from what we warrantably claim to be Jesus'.

The tensions between Luke 13:1-5, John 9:1-12, Romans 5:12 and 6:20-23, and other texts dealing with the connections between sin, suffering, death, Jesus' death, and atonement theory make it plain that there is no single "New Testament" account of the problems of and solutions for suffering and sin. The significance of this is that there is no single Christian "solution" for "*the* problem of evil," a point developed in chapter 9. Even if retrospective explanations of suffering and death can find some warrant in the New Testament, refusals to accept such explanations also find support in the New Testament traditions.

2.     Even if it were, it would certainly not be Augustine's *whole* account. As G. Evans (1982:x-xi) notes, there are both "man-centered" [sic] and "God-centered" views of the problem of evil. Besides Augustine's God-centered, 'metaphysical' approach, he offers a human-centered, 'psychological' approach, e.g., in the *Confessions*. Yet it is typically ignored by theodicists as irrelevant to "the problem of evil." Nonetheless, confession provides a resolution of a problem of evil, the suffering of the guilty—a resolution which all people need, if Augustine's account of sin is correct. The importance of confession appears in chapter 8 and the problems theodicists create by ignoring confession are brought out in chapter 9.

3.     The process of constructing an amalgamation is not always malpractice. Once one recognizes that reconstructing an author's view is authoring a novel text, not retrieving some hidden ideal system of which mundane writings are only traces, one can avoid the malpractice of amalgamation. We have no direct access to Augustine's "system" or "personal beliefs." We know of Augustine (or any past author) *only* in his time-bound roles as apologist, instructor, debater, confessor, etc.

Especially for an author who did not write systematically, reconstructing a "system" is often taken to be finding out what the author's system would be independent of all the contexts in which the author wrote and roles the author assumed in writing. But once we abstract a text completely from any determinate context, its meaning becomes indeterminate (cf. Fish 1982). We cannot say what Augustine's "ideal system" was without assuming some context and purpose for articulating that view. Even for authors who did create a philosophical or theological system, these were created in contexts and for purposes which may not be ours. When we "infer" what the author's system would have been, we do so for our purposes and in our contexts. The problem is that amalgamators often not only obscure their own interests in their efforts to present the authority's "real view," but also simply neglect the forces of the texts they amalgamate.

Now the practice of amalgamation can be legitimate, especially if it resolves problems in one text by expanding it judiciously with arguments and discussions from others, or if the novel amalgamation makes more sense than the individual texts taken one by one. But that does not apply to 'Augustinian theodicy.' Even Hick judges his amalgamation radically incoherent, leaving an impression that Augustine is radically incoherent. But is Augustine radically inconsistent? Are his assertive communicative actions incoherent and self-defeating? That has not been shown.

Augustine made his points in a political and intellectual climate different enough from ours that his texts cannot be presented as part of the contemporary conversation (Surin 1986:12-15). Augustine's critics tend to take Augustine as dealing with "our" problems and then to evaluate his amalgamated answers. The scotomata of Augustinian amalgamations undermine the claim that evaluating an amalgamation is the best way to evaluate what Augustine taught about God and evil.

4. As an alternative, one might try to consider him as an apologetic theologian and center on the *City of God*. Augustine composed the *City of God* (416-426 C.E.) for a Christian audience. But it was evidently directed primarily to a literate, aristocratic audience who had fled to Carthage when Alaric advanced on Rome in 410. Although readers can excerpt political theory, ecclesiology, etc., from it, the *City of God* was directed to the pagans in the audience (or against the attractive paganism which had infected the Christian reader). It grew from traditional Roman and Greek philosophical roots in Augustine's own experience—paralleled in his audience—into an argument that his final step into the *civitas dei* was a step they could also rationally take for this city would endure, even though Rome fell (cf. G. Evans 1982:57). To convince his audience, Augustine could not write as an ecclesial authority who could catechize them, but had to write as a literary equal who could walk their path with them and lead them into truth by the persuasive power of his arguments. While less controlled by polemical purposes than Augustine's other writings, *City of God* remains a communicative action intended primarily for outsiders (but which may be read by insiders as an aid in confronting either outsiders or the "outsider" in themselves). In speech act terms, *City of God* is not Augustine's authoritative teaching for Christians. Leaving aside the problems that most Christians have with Augustine's treatment of grace and predestination in that book, as a speech act it is polemical.

5. Unlike the case with *Enchiridion*, were Augustine not bishop of Hippo Regius, he still could have written *City of God*. As a communicative action, it is an institutionally free speculation and/or apology. Augustine was not writing as a bishop guiding his fellow Christians, but as a rhetorician "defending the City of God against those who prefer their own gods to the Founder of that City" (*Civ. Dei*, I/1). As a speech act, *City of God* can be classified as an institutionally free assertive. Obviously, no one else was as capable as Augustine of writing it. Marcellinus asked the most capable man he could find not merely for a letter, but for a more extensive work (*Ep.* 136). But the man who wrote that work did not have to occupy a specific place in the ecclesial institution to write it.

6. Parenthetical references are to sections of *Enchiridion*. Translations are the author's from the text in Barbel. I have consulted E. Evans (1953), but have sought to be more literal.

7. Unlike the previous chapter, the task here is not to figure out what sort of speech act is being performed, but to show the significance of a speech act with a specific force. Hence, I chart the conditions explicitly because they are important for understanding the empowerment institutionally bound assertive speech acts give to the hearer.

*Contextual Conditions*

(1a)   A bishop can instruct other Christians on Christian teaching with regard to faith and practice.

(1b)   Audience recognizes the speaker as a bishop.

Both these conditions obtain. Augustine is a bishop and Laurentius' request to him implies Laurentius recognizes Augustine's authority to teach.

*Illocutionary Conditions*

(2a)   Augustine represents Christian teaching, with sufficient accuracy, given the topic and occasion, in issuing the instruction.

(2b)   Augustine and his audience can and do recognize the speech act as having the illocutionary force of an instruction.

Presumably, both these conditions obtain. Condition (2a) will be evaluated in the next section, assuming for present purposes that only Augustine's discussions of God and evil need be analyzed. If (2a) obtains and Augustine is incoherent, then this form of Christian teaching is incoherent (leaving open the question whether there can be other forms of Christian teaching). Condition (2b) does not obtain for every reading of *Enchiridion*. Those who read it from outside the tradition can take it as a *portrayal* of Christian doctrine for them, but not as an *instruction* to them.

*Perlocutionary Conditions*

(3a)   Augustine presumes that his audience can understand the content of his instruction.

(3b)   The audience presumes that Augustine's instruction adequately and accurately represents Christian teaching. The audience can report the instruction to others as Christian teaching on Augustine's authority.

(3c)   Christians can claim Augustine's authority as a warrant for their accepting the instruction as Christian doctrine and act on the basis of that instruction. Non-Christians cannot claim Augustine's authority for their own beliefs or acts, save to report the content on Augustine's authority.

(3d)   It is not obvious to either Augustine or Laurentius that Laurentius is currently aware of the content of the instruction.

Condition (3a) must obtain if there is to be communication of doctrine to the audience. Presumably it obtained, at least on some occasions when the *Enchiridion* was read. Condition (3b) notes the audience's recognition of Augustine's authority. Without that recognition, he could not instruct them. Condition (3b) also notes that the audience may not be authorized in church to give instruction, but that they are in position to "pass on" the teaching on Augustine's authority. Condition (3c) adds that Christians can follow their leaders. Neither of these is immediately relevant to the present discussion. Condition (3d) must obtain for the speech act not to be redundant. Even if Laurentius were a fictitious character introduced by Augustine to stand in for many ordinary laypeople, Laurentius' questions indicate a need for the instruction. The importance of clarity about these conditions will emerge in the conclusion of the chapter.

Given the text as it has been transmitted, the context in which it was issued, and the audience for which it was composed, I see no reason to doubt that when Laurentius (or other Christians with a similar standing in the Christian community vis-à-vis Augustine) read *Enchiridion*, Augustine instructed the audience. It was a successful communicative act. The question of whether it is a fully successful speech act centers around condition (2a): whether Augustine misled the audience either by authoritatively representing as Christian teaching what was not Christian teaching or by presenting Christian teaching as true when as a whole it could not be true, i.e., if it were incoherent.

8.     What one must do to warrant rejecting his analogy, if one accepts his authority as a teacher, is to show why it cannot be a good analogy, that is, why (3a) is not possibly true. But it is difficult to see how one could show this analogy impossible. Alternatively, one could reject his authority as a teacher. But then one has placed oneself outside the intended audience for *Enchiridion*, outside the community seeking the kingdom of God which recognizes Augustine the bishop as an authority. Then one would not be taking instruction from Augustine. Surely, one can object to Christian teaching on various grounds from a vantage point outside the Christian community. But Augustine did not write *Enchiridion* to address those objections.

9.     Although the standard Latin text places the final sentence of this quotation in the next section and appends a long relative clause to it, both Evans and Barbel separate the relative clause from this sentence. Because of the *tunc* found here as in several previous sentences in the section, I see this sentence as the conclusion of a series. What follows then is an illustration—Barbel's translation introduces it *Zum Beispiel*.

10.     These paragraphs develop the discussion in Tilley 1984:307-9. At that point I argued that neglecting the distinction between theodicies and defenses has led to confusions in critiques of the work of Alvin Plantinga; such mistakes are still found in the literature, e.g., in the discussion of Plantinga's work in Surin 1986. I then accepted Hick's critique of the "Augustinian theodicy" (cf. 310, fn. 23), and still do. But there I did not clearly distinguish, as I have here, between an 'Augustinian theodicy' and Augustine's authoritative teaching.

11.     The epistemic warrants for accepting its central teaching are finally the scriptures and traditions of the Christian community. If a hearer accepts Scripture and tradition as valid sources of knowledge, and accepts Augustine's authority as a teacher in the community formed in and through those vehicles, then Augustine's instruction may be a successful defense. However, if one does not accept Scripture and tradition, if one seeks other epistemic warrants, *Enchiridion* finally provides none. If one accepts Scripture and tradition, but not Augustine's authority, one could seek other ways of defending the coherence of the central teachings of Christianity. One might seek such warrants even in Augustine's other writings, but one would encounter problems involved with both Augustine's biblical literalism and the traditional Augustinian theodicy. In short, *Enchiridion* is "preaching to the converted."

12.     Hence, Surin cannot be allowed the last word. Surin rightly warns that Augustine cannot be taken as a voice in the contemporary conversation. But Surin's radical historicism suggests that Augustine has nothing to say in the present. Yet Augustine is an authoritative teacher in an institution and community which endures to the present. Recognizing *Enchiridion* as an institutionally bound assertion from an authoritative teacher in the tradition provides a way for again hearing his voice, which has been drowned out by those who speak for him by 'systematizing' and 'totalizing' his view (see pp. 250-51 below).

*Chapter 6*


# PHILOSOPHY AS CONSOLATION IN MISFORTUNE: BOETHIUS' SCRIPT FOR REINSCRIBING A SELF


*Who let these sluts of the theater come to this sickbed?*
*They cannot offer medicine for sufferings;*
*their sweet poisons only make things worse.*
*They kill the fruitful harvest of reason*
*with the barren thorns of passion;*
*they do not free human minds from disease,*
*but merely make them accustomed to disease.*
—Boethius, *The Consolation of Philosophy* (I pr 1)[1]


These are the very first words uttered by Lady Philosophy to an innocent prisoner in one of the most influential books in Europe from the early Middle Ages through the Renaissance: Anicius Manlius Severinus Boethius's *Consolation of Philosophy*. This Christian humanist, an active intellectual and politician, wrote while exiled from Rome to Pavia, an exile which ended with his execution in 524 or 525. Lady Philosophy's initial speech of the dialogue, addressed to a man exiled from power and awaiting execution (as was Boethius in life), is as shocking and dramatic as the second act entrance of the Queen of the Night in *The Magic Flute*. Both are designed to clue in the audience to the fact that a character they thought they knew was not at all what she appeared to be.

But this clue is rarely followed up in the analysis of the *Consolation*. The book's influence is usually attributed to its resolution of the perennial problem of the innocent person suffering unjustly from misfortune. This "remedy against desolation of spirit . . . has never lost its curative power" (Green 1962:ix). Yet beyond these admiring words, scholars rarely say how it cures or where it gets its power. Moreover, theodicists have consistently ignored this remedy and deprived it of its power by silencing the voice of Boethius. Hick, for instance, consigns him to a footnote (1978:11) as a possible source for a "Latin tag." If Boethius provided such a powerful remedy, modern theodicists fail to recognize it. How can Boethius' text have such power?

This chapter argues that its power can be understood only when one accounts both for the content and the illocutionary force of this text as a communicative action, a strategy neither historians nor theodicists use. To reclaim the power of this text, we need first to understand the structure of the *Consolation* and the progress of its argument. Second, we need to notice a key anomaly in the text and a rarely noticed prisoner's regress—a loss of his voice—which undermine the typical accounts of the *Consolation* in the literature. Then we can see why the illocutionary point of the text is directive. Its force is to be understood neither as asserting truths nor as assuaging feelings nor as autobiographically confessing, but quite literally as a script—a dramatic script to be performed, a text for enactment—a script for reinscribing a self (although it is *not* a script for every person). The enactment of this text is one resolution for the problem of the suffering of the virtuous.

## The Prisoner's Progress: The Therapy of Philosophy

The "philosophical therapy" in the *Consolation* combines dialectical and logical forms of argument. One is first apprised of this by the oft-noted portrayal of Lady Philosophy's garment near the beginning of the text when she appears before a distraught prisoner (I pr 1): the lower margin has a *pi* for practical philosophy and the upper has a *theta* for theory. Between them are the *gradus*, the steps of argument, ascending from the lowest concern of philosophy to the highest. The dialogue seems to progress up those steps, beginning with dialectical establishment of first principles and ending in abstract, logical reasoning which resolves the problem of the virtuous sufferer. In ascending this way the argument depends formally on Plato and Aristotle, but materially as much on the Stoics and Augustine as the earlier writers (cf. Watts 1969:23).

There are four series of arguments which constitute the ascent of the argument in the text. First, in the first two of the *Consolation's* five books, Lady Philosophy's arguments are dialectical. Most are valid arguments *ad hominem* against the prisoner, of the form, if you believe $p$ and $q$, and upon examination $p$ entails *not-q*, then you cannot consistently hold both $p$ and $q$, for one or the other must be false. So which will you drop? And if $p$ is your deeply held conviction, and $q$ less important, you will probably be wiser to drop $q$. These preliminary dialectical arguments are, of course, effective only if one holds both $p$ and $q$.

What is the prisoner's problem? The prisoner believes that God is in control of the world, that virtue is rewarded and that vice is punished. He knows that he is innocent of crimes against the state, and yet wicked men have succeeded in having him punished, depriving him of the goods of fortune, i.e., wealth, honor, power, fame, and pleasure, which he deserves. How can this be?

Had comforters like Job's been around, they might have tried to show the prisoner that he was not really innocent, that he deserved his punishment. But the prisoner, like Job, would properly resist the imputation of guilt. Had Philo from Hume's *Dialogues* been around, he might have attempted to show the prisoner that the course of nature and society shows that "the original source of all things is entirely indifferent . . . and has no more regard to good above ill than to heat above cold, or to drought above moisture or to light above heavy" (1779:212). But the prisoner would resist the temptation to render the world's creator as indifferent to order; that would be a temptation to abandon a conviction that the cosmos is ordered and to construe the cosmos as chaotic merely in order to hold onto a belief about what happened to oneself. While such deconstruction might explain how the prisoner's problem arose, abandoning all belief in an orderly world would not solve the prisoner's problem, but compound it.

Lady Philosophy takes a different path. She proposes to begin by getting the prisoner to see that he has become confused about what is truly good, that he has forgotten who he is, and that his confused forgetfulness has deprived him of the good (I pr 6, II pr 1). She acknowledges that these elucidations and arguments are merely preliminary and temporary (I pr 5,6 and II pr 3). They are first aid against the poisons of falsehood and confusion, but not the medicine of truth needed for deep healing.

Throughout Book II, Lady Philosophy argues that the goods of fortune cannot be constitutive of human happiness. Fortuna's gifts are fleeting and found even among the wicked. But human happiness by its nature must be enduring and good. So these cannot constitute happiness. Thus the prisoner has not been deprived of happiness just because he has been deprived of the goods of fortune. He is confused: he construes the goods of fortune, the marks or symptoms of a truly and perfectly happy person ("sufficient, powerful, revered, famous and joyous" [III pr 8]), with the substance of happiness. Having these goods does not relieve one from further desires. But attaining the true Good relieves one from further desires (III pr 2). So these cannot themselves be the Good which brings happiness. The first eight prose sections of Book III rehearse and summarize this dialectical argument.

If the various goods of fortune do not in themselves constitute happiness, then what *does*?[2] This is the topic of Philosophy's second series of arguments. The prisoner himself recognizes the strength of her arguments:

> "You are playing with me," I said, "by weaving a labyrinthine argument from which I cannot escape. You seem to begin where you ended and to end where you began. Are you perhaps making a marvelous circle of the divine simplicity? A little while ago you began with happiness, declared it to be the highest good, and located its dwelling in almighty God. You said that God himself is the highest good and perfect happiness. From this you inferred that no one could be happy unless he too were a god. Then you went on to say that the very form of the good is the essence of God and of happiness; and you said further that unity is identical with the good which is sought by everything in nature. You also affirmed that God rules the universe by the exercise of His goodness, that all things willingly obey Him, and that there is no evil in nature. And you proved all this without outside assumptions and used only internal proofs which drew their force from one another" (III pr 11; Green 1962:72-73).

Only in the eternal unity of or with the divine is true happiness possible.

This second series of arguments about true happiness is the crown of Lady Philosophy's dialectic. Her argument amounts to the following: Either one can see the world as chaos, with a random distribution of goods and evils without regard to virtue and vice. Or one can see the world as orderly, where the virtuous are happy and the vicious unhappy. But in an orderly world, happiness is simple; for if it were multiple, disorder could occur. But if happiness is simple, then it is indefeasible; for something defeasible could be disordered. But if happiness is indefeasible, it must be divine, for only God is indefeasible. Therefore, one can either figure the world as ordered by God, or one can live in a world disfigured by chaos.

But, as she will later show, to believe in chaos is not rational (V pr 1,2). And if the world is chaos, if whirl is king, then true happiness is also impossible.

The conclusion to be drawn from this argument is that if the prisoner has been virtuous and has lost the goods of fortune, and if the world is orderly, then the lost goods of fortune cannot *constitute* happiness for a virtuous person. Happiness is finally constituted by virtue. The next question the text details is whether such an understanding as Lady Philosophy's is not itself defeated by the chaos of incoherence, especially by the problem of how God can allow evil in the world.

The third series of arguments (in the second half of Book III and Book IV) explores the Augustinian hypothesis that evil is nothing. As Lady Philosophy puts it:

> For if our previous conclusions are valid, and with the help of Him whose kingdom we are now speaking of, you will discover that the good are always powerful and the evil always weak and futile, that vice never goes unpunished nor virtue unrewarded, that the good prosper and the evil suffer misfortune, and much else which will remove the causes of your complaint and strengthen your convictions (IV pr 1; Green 1962:75).

Those who give themselves to evil by sin punish themselves by weakening who they truly are: they replace their good substance with the nothingness of evil. And if they choose to incorporate enough evil into themselves, they even lose their human nature (IV pr 3). Watts, following Campenhausen, remarks (1969:23) that the discussion of evil as nothing in Book III gives the appearance of being implausible word games—only to be superseded by a more useful theodicy in IV. However, Book III is not word games (as we shall see below) and Book IV is no more a theodicy than is *Enchiridion*.

The prisoner summarizes the central pillars of Lady Philosophy's claim in his recapitulation of her labyrinthine argument. The claims made there are about God and the divine governance of the world. In elaborating this, Lady Philosophy parallels the Christian writer who apparently had most influence on Boethius, Augustine of Hippo, by endorsing the hypothesis that evil is nothing. However, as in *Enchiridion*, this hypothesis is not a constituent in a theodicy, but in a defense of the coherence of the notions which form Lady Philosophy's vision: the simplicity of providence, the course of fate, unforeseeable chance, divine knowledge and predestination, and free will (IV pr 6).

That her argument is a defense rather than a theodicy is indicated in the conclusion of her sketch of this vision:

> For it is not fitting for people to comprehend intellectually or to explain verbally all the devices of divine works. It suffices to understand that God, the Creator of all natural things, directing them to the good, guides them. And as God preserves everything made in God's own likeness, God eliminates all evil from God's dominion by the necessity of fate. But if you could see disposing providence, you would see that the evil which is thought to fill the world to be nothing (IV pr 6).

The key is that people do not comprehend intellectually (*comprehendere ingenio*) or explain verbally (*explicare sermone*) the ways of God. But this is just what theodicy requires: the explanation of why God allows evil in the world. To assert this explanation successfully, one needs to be able to give or have warrants for one's claims about God (cf. Tilley 1984:308-12). But here Lady Philosophy eschews that. Thus, she cannot be offering a theodicy.

Instead, she offers a defense. By placing the last sentence in the quotation in the subjunctive, Lady Philosophy does not assert a claim that evil is nothing, but rather utters a counterfactual ("if you could see"). This does not *assert* that evil is nothing. Indeed, there is no way a person reading Lady Philosophy's claim at this point could say anything to count against it. If the reader had a God's eye view, if she could see, she would not be in a position to read the *Consolation* seriously. She would know the answers and thus not be one to whom Boethius addressed the text. And if he did not have that view, if he could not see, then he would not be in position to warrant a claim against Lady Philosophy's point. The only possible way to undermine her claim is to show that *no one* could get into position to see it by demonstrating that her claim that evil is nothing is incoherent.

Lady Philosophy must mount a defense against such a charge by showing that her overall vision is coherent and thus possibly true. To do so she must demonstrate the coherence of its central elements: providence, fate, divine knowledge, and human freedom. And that is just the project for her fourth series of arguments, the final heights to which she seems to lead the prisoner.

Lady Philosophy handles the issues of fate and providence quite facilely. Fate is simple, eternal providence unfolded in time. Providence is multiple, temporal fate enfolded in eternity. And all fortune is good, a position derived by Lady Philosophy from the common views of humanity, the first principles, voiced by the prisoner in response to her dialectical arguments. Hence, whatever the fortune of the virtuous or of one on the road to virtue be, it is good fortune. Whatever the fortune of those who persevere in wickedness be, it is very bad fortune. The virtuous person neither despairs in the face of misfortune nor becomes corrupted by the enjoyment of good fortune. The wicked person despairs in the face of misfortune and is corrupted by the delights of good fortune. She concludes:

> Hold fast to the middle ground [of virtue] with courage. Those who fall short or go too far are scornful of happiness and are deprived of the reward of labor. You can make of your fortune what you will; for any fortune which seems difficult either tests virtue or corrects and punishes vice (IV pr 7).

The quality of one's fortune is based on the quality of one's character. And one's fortune is under the control of fate/providence.

But how is one's character formed? If human character results from the habit of the will (the propensity to choose good, virtue; or evil, vice), and if the human will is under divine control, then humans are not truly responsible for their character and thus for their ability to accept their fortune. Yet if they are not under divine control, they are free and responsible, but then God is not in control of everything. Here the dilemma of accepting both human freedom and divine power arises.

The substance of Lady Philosophy's resolution of the dilemma is in the Augustinian tradition. She responds to the prisoner's question that when individuals freely choose to give themselves over to their passions and to vice, they lose their reason and become captive of their vices. When individuals freely choose to contemplate the divine, they become more free. God does not control free choice, but seeing (*prospiciens*) everything from eternity, disposes everything predestined according to its merits (V pr 2). So God knows what happens (including what humans freely choose) and disposes things to go rightly (fate/providence). But this then leads to the dilemma of divine foreknowledge and human freedom, for if God knows how one's character will be formed and deploys fortune accordingly, then how can one be free to form one's character and deserve one's fortune?

Lady Philosophy's solution is that God knows all that happens in the world, but God's necessary knowledge of what happens does not imply that those things happen necessarily. Although Boethius is influenced by Augustine, at this point he has Lady Philosophy steer clear of Augustinian tactics and vocabulary.[3]

Lady Philosophy's argument is that God knows and sees eternally and simply, not temporally and multiply. So neither "foreknowledge" nor "postknowledge" is properly predicated of God; God's knowledge is eternal because God is eternal, that is, God perfectly possesses "completely simultaneous endless life" (V pr 6). God's simple and simultaneous 'vision' of every event implies no necessity in the events. The events happen according to their natures. Some are contingent. Some are necessary. God knows them according to his nature. God's knowledge is necessary. The prisoner has erred by presuming that what is known is known by its capacity to be known, whereas what is known is known by the capacity of the knower. God's necessary and time-encompassing knowing can include knowing contingent events. God's capacity to know is different from humans': what we know as fate, God knows and enacts as providence.

Lady Philosophy weaves all the loose ends into her philosophical labyrinth. All we can know is that we are responsible for our character. We choose and we are responsible. God knows what we choose and deploys fate/providence appropriately. Our choices which determine our characters which determine how we take our fate are not necessary even though God's knowledge of them is. Her vision is thus vindicated.

Commentators often take a description of the prisoner's progress up the *gradus* of philosophy as the key to the rhetoric of the text, whether the text be construed as confessional or fictional. Philosophy's consolation is seen as enabling the distraught prisoner to ascend to and assent to true knowledge. The arguments of the philosophers provide the path of ascent which the prisoner walks by assenting to what is relevant from Plato, Aristotle, the Stoics, and Augustine, woven together by Lady Philosophy into the seamless garment of True Philosophy. However, such interpretations ignore the prisoner's simultaneous regress: his loss of voice.

## The Prisoner's Regress: The Loss of Voice

The plot of the *Consolation* begins with an uncanny therapeutic engagement. A patient, a prisoner, has an initial complaint of unhappiness, which he attributes to the misfortune of having been accused falsely and convicted fraudulently. He presents himself as an innocent, suffering victim. Yet, unlike what one might expect in a therapeutic engagement, the sufferer neither sends for nor presents himself to the physician. Rather, an unexpected physician makes a shocking entrance, dismisses the muses of poetry who gave voice to his laments, and presents herself to the sufferer.

Despite this unusual beginning, once the social relationship of physician and patient is established, they are in position to communicate. The physician is in the proper position to diagnose the patient's disease. But then the text again upsets the 'normal' plot. Here is the crucial anomaly: The 'wrong' voice speaks. The narrator, not therapist Lady Philosophy, gives voice to the diagnosis: ". . . she saw me not as silent, but rather speechless and muted . . ." (I pr 2). Why have the narrator report the diagnosis rather than portray Lady Philosophy as performing it?

The reason is that the diagnosis could not have been voiced by a character in the text because the person who had to give it had no voice. The act of diagnosis is described, rather than performed, because the prisoner, not Lady Philosophy, must render the diagnosis. But the prisoner could not perform the speech act of diagnosing himself because it could not be done: the prisoner would have had to vocalize his problem as one of having no voice, an illocutionary act that he literally could not perform.

Before prescribing a remedy, a physician must render a diagnosis. But Lady Philosophy does not do so. For in this therapeutic engagement, she is properly neither diagnostician nor therapist. The therapeutic prescription is philosophy. But such a prescription cannot be merely compounded by a pharmacist and dispensed to a patient. The patient himself must both render his own diagnosis and compound his own prescription to remember himself, recall his true country, and recover his voice (I pr 6). Philosophical therapy, thus, does not mimic the dependency relationship often found between patient and physician, but demands that the diseased person become the agent of her or his own healing. Indeed, had the rendering of the diagnosis not been an impossibility, the proper therapist would have given the diagnosis. For the diagnostician and therapist is the patient himself, the prisoner.

The specific shape of philosophical therapy becomes clear in the *Consolation* when Lady Philosophy tells the prisoner how a reader is to take a text.[4] The text is not to script the reader. The reader must enact the script in reading it. Lady Philosophy rejects the prisoner's reception of the Poetic Muses' "dictating words for my complaints" (I pr 1). Instead of tolerating such passivity in which the prisoner is merely a vehicle for the Poetic Muses' text, she requires the prisoner to *act*.

The medicine of philosophy works only if the patient performs the script. Quoting the *Iliad* (I 163) in Greek, Philosophy commands the prisoner: "SPEAK OUT! DON'T HIDE IN YOUR MIND! If you seek a work of healing [*medicantis*], you must reveal the wound" (I pr 4).[5] Whether speaking out is preparation for, ingredient in, or constitutive of a healing revelation, the suffering prisoner must act. He must perform his own speech acts, not hide himself and merely take dictation to parrot the verbal acts of others. Philosophy's therapy has "patients" cure their own diseases.[6]

An understanding of the plot in the text requires explaining not only the progress of the philosophical argument, as voiced by Lady Philosophy, but also accounting for the prisoner's first startlingly finding his voice and then his progressively losing it.[7] Had it been possible, he would have begun by vocally complaining of voicelessness. Under her encouragement in I pr 4, he is enabled to voice a "prisoner's defense" structured by the *Insitutio oratoria* of Quintillian.[8] He then engages in dialectical explications of his own belief in response to Lady Philosophy's prompting, questioning, and inferring in Books II and III. He listens to Lady Philosophy's building a theological edifice out of his beliefs and accuses her of mocking him in III pr 12, a charge she denies. To this point the prisoner has a voice and performs speech acts.

But then he loses his voice. He merely expresses his grief one last time in IV pr 1. After this, he only expresses amazement at what Lady Philosophy has inferred from his own and common beliefs. By IV pr 5, he is only a foil for Lady Philosophy, merely voicing stock difficulties with her position. Finally, save for one to three (depending on how one construes the Latin text) purely stylistic interjections, the prisoner is silent from his question (a stock dilemma which the prisoner could mouth as he once mouthed what the Muses of poetry dictated) which initiates V pr 3 until the end of the text.

Commentators rarely notice that Lady Philosophy first encourages the prisoner to speak and then silences the prisoner's voice.[9] Her rhetoric and logic seduce him into speech and then reduce him to a silent shadow. At the end, he has been deprived of his voice. He cannot respond to her injunction, "SPEAK OUT! DON'T HIDE IN YOUR MIND!" Such a progress hardly seems consonant with the *Consolation*'s supposed content of "moral truths, and their implications, which [Boethius] held to be valid for all men" (Green 1962:xiv). If we take the text as the descriptive record of a real or imaginary oral dialogue, it records a dialogue of repression, of Philosophy overwhelming the prisoner by taking away his voice and substituting her own. It is hard to imagine that a dialogue of repression is so powerful a conveyer of "moral truths." A more likely account is needed.

## A Script for Reinscribing a Self

To account for both the ascent of argument and the prisoner's finding and losing his voice, the *Consolation* must be understood not as an assertive record of truths or a declarative autobiography or therapy, but as a prescription for healing.[10] It is a script for replacing the imprisoned man's voice with the free woman's voice of Lady Philosophy. It is not that the prisoner is healed. By the end of the text the prisoner no longer speaks. The prisoner disappears. Rather, any healing occurs in the readers' performing, enacting, the text. If the reader enacts the text, the reader effects a self-cure by making his own prison voice disappear and her own philosophical voice sound out.

Notice that a reader of the *Consolation* is not in position to take either the role of the despondent prisoner or of Lady Philosophy in enacting this text. The prisoner is ground down by his wallowing in misfortune. He can't *act* to get out of his dilemma. He needs someone to come to him to empower him to escape. The serious reader cannot take the prisoner's role, for playing that role requires taking a position of inaction, a position a reader presumably is acting to escape—otherwise why read the *Consolation* for consolation? The reader also can't be in position to play the role of Lady Philosophy, who is perfect in wisdom and virtue, for that requires taking a position a reader presumably wants to reach. Such a reader who is already there has no need for the consolation of the *Consolation*. In short, a reader cannot get into position to play either part in the text.

However, one can read both roles, for echoes of both voices can be found in the reader's soul. In this sense, the dialogue can be construed as an internal one, but only if a reader internalizes it by enacting it in her soul. The serious reader is inclined to say both that he has bad fortune (as does the prisoner) and that all fortune is good because it is in God's hands (as Lady Philosophy argues). Although the reader is in no position to play either role in the dialogue, the reader can take the text as a prescription, a script which can enable a serious reader to make progress in developing her own philosophical voice while silencing his melodramatic voice. This prescription gives the reader directions for compounding the medicine of consolation: the proper disciplining of both voices in the soul. In short, the therapy of the text is its prescription of a way of learning how to perform proper speech acts.

The voice of the prisoner is self-dramatizing. The voice of Lady Philosophy is self-actualizing. The former is bathed in pathos, the latter exercises rationality. The former descends to pity, the latter ascends to wisdom. For one to read the *Consolation* as a script and to perform the actions it portrays in both roles is a way to overcome one's own voice of passion with one's own voice of reason. To read the *Consolation* properly is to engage in an active struggle to leave the debilitating realm of pure emotional expressive speech acts scripted by the Poetic Muses and to ascend to the invigorating realm of declaiming and even declaring the truth.

One may come to the text to be consoled by philosophy. But if one is attentive to Lady Philosophy's shockingly vulgar first words, to the text's disordering of the therapeutic engagement, to the progress of her voice and the regress of the prisoner's voice, then a reader afflicted with misfortune and believing that the universe is orderly may learn the practice which constitutes the consolation of doing philosophy. In short, the practice is speaking this text in order to learn how to overcome one's self-dramatizing voice which snares one in grief and despair, and simultaneously to learn how to develop one's self-actualizing voice that frees one to contemplate the Good.[11]

But not everyone can perform those actions. Not everyone oppressed by evils and suffering has the ability to get into position to perform the therapeutic actions the text prescribes. For some readers, the medicine of the *Consolation* would be pure poison, self-therapy as inappropriate as any debilitating opiate silencing the voice of the suffering.

But Boethius was aware of this. Consider the chapter's epigraph. In it, the medicine of philosophy (associated with reason and freedom) is opposed to the poison of the theater (associated with passion and bondage). But what is medicine and what poison is not eternally given. Depending on circumstances, what is medicine for one is poison for another. The opposition—and linkage—of these is hardly new to Boethius. It is as ancient as Philosophy herself. However, Boethius's pharmacology is rather different from earlier authors.

Derrida's exploration of Plato's writings has 'exposed' a 'pharmaco-logical' link between poison (*pharmakon*) and medicine (*pharmakon*) in philosophy. He finds a paradoxical link between the poison (*pharmakon*) of writing and the medicine (*pharmakon*) of speaking, as ancient endorsements of therapeutic speaking survive only in 'poisonous' written texts. Derrida suggests this generates a tradition of philosophical writing which both undercuts and advocates good speaking:

> According to a pattern that will dominate all of Western philosophy, good writing (natural, living, knowledgeable, intelligible, internal, speaking) is opposed to bad writing (a moribund, ignorant, external, mute artifice for the senses). And the good one can be designated only through the metaphor of the bad one. Metaphoricity is the logic of contamination and the contamination of logic. . . . [P]hilosophy is played out in the play between two kinds of writing. Whereas all it wanted to do was to distinguish between writing and speech (1981:149; also cf. 108).

However, Boethius evidently deviates from the "pattern that will dominate all of Western philosophy." He gives it an interesting twist.

In the *Consolation*, Boethius not only distinguishes writing from speech, but also contrasts poisonous and therapeutic speaking. Lady Philosophy must prescribe an antidote not only for the prisoner's poisonous writing of his complaints in response to the dictation of the Muses (I pr 1), but also for his destructive speaking (in I pr 4 and I m 4). The Muses' dictation dulls the mind. The prisoner's turbulent anger and sorrow poison his speech. Her therapy begins by getting the prisoner to bare his wound by speaking out. Although his speech does not declare who he really is, his speaking does provide an entry for therapy. Here writing does not oppose speaking, nor do two kinds of writing contradict each other. Rather, Boethius contrasts poisonous with therapeutic speech acts.

Indeed, the power of Boethius's writing comes from his performing a therapeutic linguistic act. His act undermines destructive, emotive, and sickly communicative actions and valorizes liberating, rational, healthy communicating. Even if the philosophical tradition is "played out in the play between two kinds of writing," as Derrida put it, Boethius deviates from this tradition by distinguishing medicinal and poisonous expression, whether spoken or written.

Lady Philosophy's opposition to poetry is also not new. Plato had banned tragic poetry from the ideal city because its mimesis would corrupt those who do not possess the medicine of knowledge (cf. *Republic* X; Derrida 1981:137). As Plato banned the poets, so, after labeling the Muses of poetry "sluts of the theater" in her first sentence in the *Consolation*, Lady Philosophy exorcises them. Yet in doing so, and in bringing the prisoner to understanding, Lady Philosophy, like Plato, used all the rhetorical tricks of the trade. Her speaking passionately excoriates passion, rhetorically attacks rhetoric, and metaphorically derides metaphor. Indeed, immediately after banishing the Muses of poetry, Lady Philosophy begins a poem to soothe the prisoner (I pr 2). If contemporary deconstruction is "the most recent invasion of grammar by rhetoric, more exactly the destabilizing rhetoric of the tropes" (Tracy 1987:56), then 'postmodern' deconstructionism simply offers new variations on tactics as ancient as philosophy herself. Philosophy may denounce poetry, but she does so poetically. Boethius's use of the Menippean satire form, alternating prose and poetry through the text, "allows Boethius to compose a kind of metapoem, that is, a poem freed from the conventional constraints of traditional literary genres, able to subordinate those genres to the demands of philosophy . . ."(Curley

1986:253). Boethius has philosophy use therapeutic poetry to undercut the poisonous power of amusing and distracting theater and poetry.

In the script, Lady Philosophy expels the theatrical Muses and introduces her own Muses to cure and sanitize (*curandum sanandumque*; I pr 1) a prisoner educated by the Eleatics and Academics. Yet her directives rejecting theatricality and demanding the prisoner to perform (I pr 4) are in some tension with each other. Moreover, if the *Consolation* is a script, how does Boethius, the author of a text to be performed in the real world, differ from the dictating Muses rejected in the world he creates? Both prescribe scripts to be performed. Is it not paradoxical and even self-contradictory to inscribe a text which both proscribes and prescribes such performance?

The way to resolve this apparent contradiction is to take the text as the content of a communicative action. The directives *in* the text are key to understanding the force *of* the text. The *Consolation of Philosophy* is a most complex prescription. It is not addressed to everyone, but only to specific addressees: those who, like the prisoner, suffer misfortune unjustly and who want to leave the prison created by the fickle fortunes and enjoy the freedom to contemplate divine providence.

What is remarkable about Boethius's text is that it prescribes for a reader in bondage a way to reach the goal of freedom. But to complete our understanding of this 'pharmaco-logical' text, we need to consider the status of the patient for whom this inscription is prescribed, the reader who responds to the directive to enact or perform the script. For some readers, this medicine of philosophy would be poison.

## *The Performer of the* Consolation

The *Consolation* is not a panacea. It does not prescribe a therapy for every evil or every victim. It is prescription for those with the disease of being unable to see that whatever fate has brought them is good for them. It is therapy for those who are not fully virtuous, but who seek to be virtuous and thus to be happy. Two passages show who would be poisoned by the medicine of the *Consolation*.

First, the *Consolation* is not prescribed for those who lack what is proper to humans. Lady Philosophy makes this clear in the context of a passage on beauty:

> You are, of course, delighted by the beauty of the open fields. And why not, since this is a beautiful part of a very beautiful creation. In the

same way we are pleased by a serene sea, we admire the sky, the stars, the sun and the moon; but do any of these things belong to you? How then can you glory in their splendor? You are not adorned with spring flowers, nor are you laden with summer fruit. When you act as though such external goods are your own, you are deluded by foolish satisfaction. Fortune can never make things yours which nature made foreign to you. No doubt the fruits of the earth are given to animals and men for their food; but, if you simply wish to satisfy the demands of nature, there is no reason why you should struggle for the superfluities of Fortune. For nature's needs are few and small; if you try to glut yourself with too many things, you will find your excesses either unpleasant or positively harmful (II pr 5; Green 1962:31-32).

What is crucial about this passage is the distinction between what belongs to a person by nature, what is not of human nature, and what is superfluous to nature. The goods of fortune, which the prisoner mistakes for satisfying his desire for happiness, are superfluities. The beauties of the creation may entertain one, but they do not satisfy one's human needs—and if they are "possessed," perhaps they become like goods of fortune. And there is a veiled warning against being corrupted by excess. But basic human needs are part of human nature. These are distinguished from the goods of fortune.

Hence, *Consolation* is poison for those whose basic needs are not fulfilled. It is not medicine for those who have no food, clothing, and shelter. For those with such dis-eases, the *Consolation* is a poisonous opiate. Now Boethius does not directly claim that a person whose basic needs are not met cannot be happy. It is, however, consistent with Boethius's argument; and given his discussion of the needs of nature, and the claim that the fruits of the earth are given to people for food, it may be an unspoken presumption that a person who is in position to perform the text must have her basic needs met before philosophy is possible or appropriate. Without them she is deprived of the material conditions which make therapeutic enacting of the text possible. Moreover, Aristotle's description of the happy person notes that the eudaemon will bear misfortune nobly (1100b20), but must be furnished with sufficient goods to live (1101a16, 1179a1-5). Hence, prescribing philosophical consolation does presume that the patient's basic needs are met. If that presumption does not obtain, prescribing the medicine of *Consolation* is dispensing a poison, truly opiating those suffering from evils other than misfortune.

Second, the *Consolation* cannot be therapy for the wicked. They are beyond hope. In a powerful passage, Lady Philosophy claims that the truly wicked are so evil that they "de-nature" themselves, that is, they lose their human nature:

> See the punishment which afflicts the wicked as compared with the rewards of the good. You learned earlier that whatever is, is one; whatever is one, is good; it follows then that whatever is must also be seen to be good. And it follows from this that whatever loses its goodness ceases to be. Thus the wicked cease to be what they were; but the appearance of their human bodies, which they keep, shows that they once were human. To give oneself to evil, therefore, is to lose one's human nature. Just as virtue can raise one above the human, it must be that vice lowers beneath human nature those whom it has dethroned from the human condition. For this reason, anyone whom you find transformed by vice you cannot count a human.
>
> The violent thief of others' wealth burns with avarice. You would say he is like a wolf. The wild and restless one wags his tongue in lawsuits. You will compare him to a dog. The secret trickster rejoices over success in frauds. Let him be like a little fox. Someone overcome by anger? He is believed to grow the spirit of a lion. The timid and fearful one fears the unthreatening? Let him be reckoned like a deer. The stupid sluggard is numb: an ass lives! The fickle and inconstant changes his pursuits. Nothing separates him from birds. One wallows in foul and impure lusts: He is gripped by the pleasures of a sow. Thus whoever has deserted goodness has abandoned being human, and since he cannot pass into the divine condition, becomes a beast (IV pr 3).

Lady Philosophy advocates their punishment, as that is better for them than letting them continue in the wickednesses which render them inhuman.

Those who are so far gone on the road to wickedness that they can no longer recollect what it is to be human are beyond philosophical therapy. They need forceful restraint, even punishment. They should give themselves up to their judges to cure this disease of their souls. For them, the medicine of consolation is neither opiate nor poison, but a waste of time. They are not candidates for philosophical therapy. The violence they have done to their human natures requires forceful remedy.

Thus, attempting to enact the *Consolation*, to struggle to ascend to philosophical truth, is therapy only for the person afflicted with misfortune, not for the depraved or the deprived. Those who would prescribe such *Consolation* for them engage in malpractice. Those who prescribe "counting your blessings" or "nonattachment" to necessities for the deprived collapse two diseases into one. Those suffering material deprivation need other help. Those who prescribe only philosophical therapy for the wicked may even endanger those on whom the wicked would prey by not treating them properly. Such malpractice is immoral. Indeed, it is just these sorts of malpractice which are the proper targets of Marxian critiques of religion and philosophy.

As Boethius merely mentions the deprived and the wicked in passing, it is not clear that he has thought out prescriptions for their misery. Nor does he offer proofs to provide a justification for his contention that the option of belief in an orderly universe is preferable to belief that the universe is chaos. Hence, the *Consolation* cannot be a panacea.

Whether one finds this specific exercise in philosophical therapy sound will depend on whether one accepts the basic beliefs the prisoner has and the validity of the arguments Lady Philosophy makes along the way. For those whose basic beliefs bear little similarity to the prisoner's, this sort of exercise may be useless. For those whose basic beliefs overlap with the prisoner's, a rescripting of the text may be needed. For instance, Boethius argued that the truly wicked cannot harm the truly good person. However, he neglects to mention their bad example and to evaluate the damage they do if they deprive others of the goods (food, etc.) proper to their nature. While they may be in God's providence, the evil they do creates more than misfortune for others. The contemporary Boethian may still be sanguine about the virtuous person's fortune always being good, but should be worried about the possibility that the thoughtless and the wicked have destroyed the conditions necessary to engage in the practices needed for making people good. A Boethian after Auschwitz and Nagasaki may need to pay more attention to the malignant forces the wicked and thoughtless unloose.

The *Consolation of Philosophy* carries on a great tradition of philosophical texts.[12] The *Consolation* is as mimetic a text as those excoriated by, yet also written by, Plato. It is an exercise in "figurative praxis" (Schweiker 1988:34), an act in which an author renders a meaningful world. The 'pharmaco-logic' of philosophical consolation is the reader's enacting, or even rewriting, the script Boethius prescribed. It is a prescription for re-educating the voices of the soul. Thus, Boethius has inscribed a text that is not only a script to be played, but also a prescription to be taken by certain sufferers. Like any inscription, it is always vulnerable to conscription as philosophical dogma, or, alas, to reinscription as panacea. But it does not pretend to be a description of the indescribable, whether the processes of thought or of God. In short, Boethius's script conscripts its readers who suffer from misfortune and reinscribes them (as they act it out) into readers who embrace their fate because it is good for them. It is a script for reinscribing a self, a prescription that is an antidote for the virtuous who are poisoned by forgetting who they truly are, a solution for resolving *a* problem of evil!

But philosophy does not only provide consolation. It also challenges. Chapter 7 explores one of the key challenges from the philosopher who put the Enlightenment problem of evil most clearly, David Hume.

## NOTES

1.    Citations to *The Consolation of Philosophy* are to book and either prose (pr) or poetic (m) sections within the book. Unless a specific translation is cited, I have retranslated the texts (in light of the translations of Watts, Tester, and/or Green).

2.    Because this is a major topic in Aristotle's *Nicomachean Ethics* and because Boethius was familiar with Aristotle's works, in the second half of Book III of the *Consolation* where Boethius deals with happiness, one would expect some similarities between them. While Boethius parallels some of Aristotle's doctrines, he also deviates from them.

In the *Ethics*, Aristotle had claimed that a happy person "realizes complete goodness in action, and is adequately furnished with external goods" (1101a15). Although external disasters might distress a happy person, a truly happy person's happiness would not be undermined by external losses. Moreover, the highest happiness for Aristotle was the act of contemplation—and even if the prisoner could not engage in other actions, at least he could actively contemplate. In this sense, the prisoner seems to have been an Aristotelian eudaemon, a happy or satisfied person, despite everything, save that he had forgotten himself. A task of Lady Philosophy is to get him to remember this. Yet Boethius's resolution differs from Aristotle's at two key points.

First, Boethian happiness requires no friends, whereas Aristotle finds that friends are necessary for a person to be truly happy (1170a2; but compare 1177a30). Boethius and Aristotle both claim that the happy person is self-sufficient. However, for Boethius this means a person whose character and virtuousness are independent of other people and dependent only upon God/the good. For Aristotle this means a person whose character and virtuousness, although genetically and developmentally dependent on other people, is now dependent only on herself, although usually blessed with friends.

One of the reasons why Boethius differs from Aristotle on this issue is that between the two Stoicism emerged as a philosophical movement. Stoicism encouraged cultivation of a self-sufficiency in which the presence or absence of the goods of Fortuna does not enable or upset a person's disposition. Much of the argument in the first half of the *Consolation* is akin to Stoic arguments, and probably is indebted to Seneca. The Stoics' notion of happiness was not ability to act well, but apatheia—passionlessness, or euthymia—spiritual peace and well-being. It was enjoined on people in two ways: by studying physics and by becoming morally wise—that is, valuing only virtue, for that is the only valuable thing. Boethius's prisoner was perturbed and confused and came, by philosophy, to equanimity and self-sufficiency in solitude. While Boethius was not a Stoic, Stoicism influenced Boethius and the form and content of the arguments in the *Consolation*. (Cf. Hallie 1967:22 on Stoicism and Wright 1967:406-7 on Seneca).

Boethius is not a Stoic. Reiss (1982:148) claims that there is little of Stoicism in the *Consolation*, citing Boethius's not accepting its epistemology, materialism, pantheism, and fatalism. But this is overstated. Boethius clearly does not reject the Stoics' substantial account of what virtue consists in; he may accept the basic structure of the argument that happiness comes from becoming morally wise; and he may not be 'fatalistic' only because he is a Christian and construes fate as the way providence operates (as discussed on p. 145).

Second, near the end of Book III, Boethius finally pins his hope for the reality of true happiness on God, whereas Aristotle made no such connection. For Aristotle, the truly happy person may be above the human level, but this does not depend on the gods or God, but on something divine (theion) within him (1177b31). For Boethius, apparently influenced by Christian doctrine and/or Neoplatonic authors, true happiness had to be eternally indefeasible; for Aristotle, true happiness was apparently indefeasible only so long as a person who had achieved eudaemonia remained alive (1101a16-23).

3.   Augustine did not clearly separate philosophical from theological work. In many ways Augustine is difficult not because his ideas are more difficult than other people's, but because he does not always distinguish explicating the received truths of divine revelation (one way of doing theology) and investigating to find truth by dialectical and philosophical argument (one way of describing philosophy). This especially affects Augustine's approach to divine foreknowledge and the human choice for evil (cf. Green 1962:xix).

Augustine had asserted both divine foreknowledge of every event, including what humans will to do, and human freedom to act. The problem is that if God foreknows that person $p$ will do act $a$, how can the act be free? If $p$ performs $a$ freely, how could God foreknow what will freely be done in the future? How could God, who created that person, know that the person would freely perform the act, for if God knew the act would occur, how could anything else possibly happen? Thus if God knows, then no other act could be performed. So how can the act be free? Does this not void humans of moral responsibility for the act? If God does not know what the act would be, then the act might be free and a human properly held responsible for it, but then God would not be perfect because God would not know everything.

Augustine did not resolve this apparent logical difficulty. Asserting apparently inconsistent claims may be tolerable for some theologians in some circumstances. However, Lady Philosophy is laying out an argument with the point of showing the coherence of the claims that God orders the world, that it is good, and that people are free. Hence, if her argument is to be successful, she must show that the claims are not incompatible, that the vision is not necessarily incoherent, that there is a possible solution to the problem (see V m 3).

4.   Reading is an institutionally free practice or set of practices. However, I argue elsewhere (1989) that, with regard to reading the Bible, the social context in which one performs acts of reading affects the specific illocutionary force of reading. Reading is essentially a communicative practice in which the reader takes different roles, depending upon the context in which and purposes for which a text is read.

5.   This suggests that, despite his translation of and familiarity with Aristotle's works, Boethius's notion of dialectic is more akin to Plato's. Cf. Plato, *Sophist* 263E and Aristotle, *De Sophisticis Elenchis* 169a37 (R. Hall 1967:386-87).

6.   One of Wittgenstein's aphorisms reflects this: "The philosopher treats a question—as an illness"(1958: §255). Philosophers do not treat patients, but illness. Indeed, philosophers themselves are patients. In philosophical therapy, the healer is the unhealed becoming healed. The dependency relationship of patient on physician does not apply. The person with the problem must be able to diagnose the disease

and compound the medicinal solution. The "real discovery is one that enables me to stop doing philosophy when I want to—the one that gives philosophy peace, so that it is no longer tormented by questions which bring *itself* into question" (Wittgenstein 1958: §133).

Lady Philosophy's act of presenting herself unbidden to the sufferer and the sufferer's apparently rendering his own diagnosis suggests that Boethius's view of philosophical therapy, like Wittgenstein's, breaks the form of conventional therapeutics.

7.    This is paralleled by the minimalization of the narrator's voice. Whereas in Book I the narrator not only sets the scene, but speaks for the prisoner, by Books IV and V, the narrator has nothing important to say. This may be a reflection of the tension between time and eternity in the *Consolation*. But it may simply be that as the philosophical dialogue ascends, the narrator's voice is less important. As her argument begins to move up the *gradus* under its own power, the narrator is literarily superfluous.

8.    In the Loeb edition, lines 7-33 form an exordium preparing the audience; 34-88 form a narration of the facts; 89-134 is a *probatio*, a proof of the account; 135-154a are a refutation of the accusers' case; and 154b-174, a peroration with final plea. Reiss has suggested (1982:132-33) that the five-part division of the book has this same structure, but this cannot account for the variety of philosophical argument involved nor for the other literary elements in the text.

9.    More esoteric analyses like Lerer's simply obscure the development of voice in the text. The text gives no warrant to assume that the prisoner ascends to prayer or contemplation, save that the prisoner is silent. Silence alone proves nothing; its meaning must be determined by its context—and the progress of the text suggests that Lady Philosophy renders the prisoner incapable of speaking.

10.    Boethius wrote the *Consolation* adapting the genre of Menippean satire, placed arguments in an allegorical mode, and used the style of a dialogue. The dialogue style offers a flexible vehicle in which an author can reinscribe earlier texts (where the earlier 'text' can be rewritten in a 'teacher's' voice instructing a 'student'). The author can also raise problems in a 'student's' voice and resolve them in a 'teacher's' voice. Thus, some written dialogues, such as those of Plato and Cicero, invite a reader who wants to understand a classic text or needs to solve a problem to take the 'student's' voice in the dialogue. The author can then use the 'teacher's' voice to lead the reader to appropriate the point of an earlier text or to solve the problem. The philosophical dialogue draws the reader into the text (compare Nussbaum 1986:125ff).

The *Consolation* specifically induces readers to read themselves into the story. Its plot creates a passage of ascent from the perplexity of innocent suffering to the height of philosophical understanding. But the *Consolation* is neither a didactic dialogue where the 'student' is a mere foil for a 'teacher,' nor is it a dialogue exploring the strengths and weaknesses of concepts and practices. Rather, the *Consolation* is a dialogue of healing.

However, construing the text as a therapeutic and directive speech act clashes with a standard interpretation which takes this seeming dialogue of healing as an autobiographical report (cf. Green 1962:xiv; Curley 1986:253). In this view, the text describes the progress of Boethius's own self-consolation. They thus equate the prisoner *in* the text with the author *of* the text. Lady Philosophy is analogous to a divine power or angel who liberates the prisoner as Uriel does for Esdras in 2 Esdras 3 (Watts 1969:19). The *Consolation* is then a report which adapts the form of a sacred dialogue or literary consolation (cf. Watts 1969:19) which "represents certain moral truths, and their implications, which [Boethius] held to be valid for all men" (Green 1962:xiv).

Yet this interpretation is unpersuasive. If the *Consolation* is a report or treatise, an extended assertive speech act representing moral truths, why would the author use the genre, style, and form he does? If these are adopted arbitrarily, there is no answer for the question. If they are adopted strategically, e.g., to enhance the possibility that the text will be read after his death, then the use of these literary strategies is at least a weak directive to the reader on *how* to read the text. If they are part of the substance of the text, they are an essential part of the communicative action. So unless Boethius was arbitrary in adopting his literary devices, the *Consolation* cannot be a pure assertive.

Alternatively, it might be an autobiographical confession, a declarative speech act. This seems more promising. Indeed, Reiss has argued that the legend that the *Consolation* is autobiographical may have helped get the *Consolation* read through the ages. But Reiss claims such an approach can undermine our understanding of the text. He suggests that it is not necessarily Boethius's "last will and testament," and the absence of Christian theological themes in it does not imply, as some have argued, that Boethius turned to philosophy rather than to religion for his final consolation (1982:80-102). He claims that "the *Consolation* is more precisely a representative of the literary genre of *confessio* and should be linked to the various autobiographical confessions . . . that appeared in the fifth and sixth centuries, doubtless due to the influence of Augustine's own *Confessions*" (93). Of course, for Reiss, this is not an actual confession, but a fictional one (94-102), structured as a Neoplatonic ascent, from the concern with autobiographical material at the beginning of the text up to the general and universal at the end of the text—just as the last three chapters of Augustine's *Confessions* (so rarely read in the classroom) move away from the narration of a life to a story of the whole. Reiss thus saves the appearance of the text as autobiography by construing it as a fiction.

But if the *Consolation* is pure fiction, composed in a library and at perfect leisure, as Reiss suggests, it is necessarily a phony, for the act of writing a confession is not merely a writer's representing the truth, but an author's creatively making the truth by an assertive declaration, as shown in chapter 3. Although fictional characters can make confessions in fictional contexts, an actual person cannot successfully make a fictional confession in an appropriate actual context. To perform an assertive declaration whose purpose is to declare to be true what is not true is not merely a lie. Lying is merely asserting a falsehood. Such a declaration is either an illocutionary impossibility and necessarily fails or is the creation of a realm of falsehood which necessarily suppresses, distorts, or supplants what is true (compare Peck 1983:passim). The *Consolation* cannot be Boethius's fictional confession without being either a self-defeating or a diabolically vicious action.

As a variation on this theme, Lerer considers the *Consolation* as a portrayal of the *prisoner's* confession. In his meticulous and provocative study, Lerer recognizes that the prisoner begins mute and "tongueless," and finds a voice:

> The prisoner's move from lethargic silence, through oratory, rhetoric, dialectic, and philosophy represents the development of a mind traced through different levels of language use. At the top of this hierarchy is prayer. It is essential that Boethius reserve mention of this form of discourse for the *Consolation*'s end, for it is the last stage in the sequence of his education in the arts of expression. Significantly, Boethius does not transcribe whatever his concluding prayer might be, and in this he contrasts sharply with the lush, rhetorically assured Platonic hymn of III m. 9. . . . As a counterpoint to Philosophy's brilliantly executed hymn, there is only silence (1985:235).

This silence has three aspects, according to Lerer: There is the silence of the student listening to the teacher, the silence of the reader of the increasingly predominant texts of Lady Philosophy, and the silence of prayer (236).

However attractive Lerer's concern to differentiate levels of language use in the *Consolation*, his overall thesis about the structure of the *Consolation* is unconvincing. First, the text provides no context for reading anything the prisoner says as a confession. Not only is the crucial diagnosis of voicelessness, the closest thing to a confession in the text, not given in the prisoner's voice, but also by the final book of the text, the prisoner has been rendered practically voiceless again (a point developed on p. 150). As the prisoner inhabits the world created by Boethius in his text, and not the actual world in which Boethius created his text, the *Consolation* itself cannot be the prisoner's confession. Hence, the *Consolation* neither portrays nor can be the prisoner's confession.

Second, the conclusion of the prisoner's ascent is not necessarily the silence of prayer. At best, it might be construed as the silence of philosophical contemplation. For the Christian tradition in which Boethius wrote, a silent prayer is an adoring silence in front of God in which one can hear God or in which one can rest in awe over God's beauty or goodness. In contrast, philosophical contemplation is an active, awe-struck silence one reaches in harmony with whatever is ultimate. While the differences may seem trivial, the practices of prayer require presumptions different from those required for the practices of philosophical contemplation. Admittedly, a participant in a religious tradition *may* find that philosophical contemplation may be prayerful, but it need not be. Given that the context does not show that the silence is a prayer, it follows from Searle and Vanderveken's discussion of illocutionary denegation (1985:4), arguments *sola e silentio* cannot prove what authors said or meant, but only what authors did not say or mean in what they wrote.

Third, Lerer's reading of the *Consolation* takes the ascent of the prisoner as key to the text, a text which requires no "literal, biographical criticism. The *Consolation*'s close has its meaning within the structure of the text itself; within the tropes and patterns . . . through the work" (1985:236). While Lerer rightly rejects interpreting the *Consolation* as an autobiographical confession, he neither explains the prisoner's loss of voice nor does he show how a reading limited to literary intratextuality explains the illocutionary force with which the text was inscribed and read. The *Consolation* is not merely a naked text any more than *Enchiridion* is merely a naked text. To understand each requires understanding them not merely as texts, but as *read* and received texts, as communicative actions or interactions.

In view of the difficulties in construing the illocutionary point of the *Consolation* to be declarative or of taking it as having no illocutionary point, it seems preferable to take the *Consolation* as a directive, as a therapeutic script, a prescription directed to those who present themselves as imprisoned by the fickle fates. Its purpose is to enable that specific audience to see that they are really shackled by their own contradictory wishes and beliefs. But if a reader is to attain her freedom, she cannot merely 'recite' or 'mouth' the text, but must enact it or perform it. The sufferer must come to have a voice of his own.

A therapy for acquiring one's own voice makes it possible for one to free her mind from the disease engendered by incoherent wishes. Indeed, this strategy fits the therapeutic encounter which begins the dialogue. This section of the text explores the *Consolation* as prescriptive. If the analysis of the progress and regress of the dialogue between the prisoner and Lady Philosophy can account for both the literary strategy and the speech actions within the text, that will warrant a reading of the text as an inscription prescribing a medicine to heal the self by reinscribing the self.

However, the drama is not merely an internal dramatization or portrayal (Curley 1986:253). Nor are the specific themes of the *Consolation* especially new. A frequent accusation is that the *Consolation* contains no original philosophy, but is only a pastiche of earlier philosophers' doctrines. Boethius clearly synthesizes ideas from Plato, Aristotle, Augustine, the Neoplatonic and Stoic philosophers. But in our era, when the originality of any authorship is under severe challenge (Derrida 1978), and when a book or essay can be nothing but "a tissue of 'quotations'" (Derrida 1981:287; e.g., Taylor 1986: passim), such accusations become trivial. Moreover, Boethius is influenced by the secular and religious traditions of late antiquity which valued the writing of florilegia. Now, the *Consolation* is not a florilegium; nor does Boethius often refer directly to his sources; nor does a single authorial voice speak in the dialogues, even though the prisoner speaks in the first person. What is original and provocative is how Boethius deploys these resources in an "impressive effort to bring the pure order of logic into the variegated experience of life" (Whitman 1987:121). Boethius makes his sources available for his readers in a new way.

11.      Indeed, this reading also explains one of the classic problems with interpreting the *Consolation*. The absence of Christian theological themes, especially the redemption of sinful and suffering humanity in and through Christ, has led some to suggest that Boethius abandoned Christianity for Philosophy (cf. Reiss 1982:80-102). But rather than try to force Lady Philosophy into the mold of the logos-Christ, as Clebsch does (1979:103-4), one can explain the absence of an explicitly Christian voice because the therapy required is not to mimic an authoritative answer scripted for one, but to come to give that answer oneself. If a "Christian" voice were present, the text could not work: simple surrender to an already accomplished redemption is no therapy for anyone in the prisoner's condition. An authoritative Christian voice would drown out the possibility of enacting the voices which constitutes the therapy of the text. Appeal to religious claims would be too facile to resolve the actual problem.

12.      Nussbaum has demonstrated that Greek philosophical dialogues are not innocent of theatricality in form or content. They can be musings for mimesis even when their characters deride the amusements of the theater. Commentators have noticed the drama of the *Consolation* (e.g., Whitman 1987:121). For instance, Curley suggests that the multivocity of the dialogue "reflects the alienation of Boethius the author, master of the tradition at a time when the tradition was in danger of being forgotten; but it also enables him to dramatize the only interaction available to him, interaction with himself" (1986:240). He sees Boethius as accomplishing in a novel and systematic way "the dramatization of the process of thought" (241).

*Chapter 7*

# Hume's Challenges

*Epicurus's old questions are yet unanswered:*
*Is God willing to prevent evil, but not able?*
*Then, he is impotent.*
*Is he able, but not willing?*
*Then, he is malevolent.*
*Is he both able and willing?*
*Whence, then is evil?*
    —after Philo, in David Hume,
       *Dialogues Concerning Natural*
       *Religion*

David Hume's *Dialogues Concerning Natural Religion* is one of the greatest books ever written in the philosophy of religion (cf. Stroud 1977:15; Penelhum 1983a:131). This philosophical dialogue, "beyond dispute the most brilliant in the English language" (Mossner 1977:2), was loosely modeled on Cicero's *De Natura Deorum*. It was published posthumously in 1779. Three voices engage in the conversation. Demea supports the incomprehensibility of the Deity: God's ways are not human ways and human ways cannot get one to God. Cleanthes argues that the design of the world supports the reasonableness of belief in the God of traditional providential monotheism. Philo allies himself with Demea in the first eight parts against Cleanthes to argue against the design argument, and in Part IX with Cleanthes against Demea to undermine an a priori argument for the existence of God. The shifting alliances are particularly evident in Parts X and XI, where all three discuss the Enlightenment's problem of evil, as formulated in the epigraph for this chapter. Demea leaves the conversation at the end of Part XI and the other two conclude their discussion about religion in general and the design argument in particular in Part XII.

Most interpreters of the *Dialogues* "carry on a detailed discussion of the philosophical arguments in Hume's works without bothering about who said what and to whom and whether Hume himself would have agreed" (Gaskin 1978:159). Many see Hume's undermining the apologetic value of the design argument, so central to the philosophical theology of the Enlightenment, as the distinctive contribution of the *Dialogues* to the philosophy of religion (e.g., Morrisroe 1969b:966; 1969a:134; Tweyman 1986). Others focus on the philosophical arguments in Parts X and XI which explore the significance of evil in the world for belief in God (e.g., Pike 1964, Henze 1970). Both approaches tend to ignore the interactions between the participants and obscure the relations of their discussion of God and evil to the design argument.

This chapter approaches the *Dialogues* in a new way. It takes the speech acts in the conversation[1] about God and evil portrayed in the text as key to understanding the significance of the text. This approach reveals important elements in the Dialogues that both typical approaches obscure. The first section analyzes a standard account of the philosophical arguments in Parts X and XI of the *Dialogues*. This shows how analyzing only the arguments made without regard to who makes them and ignoring the illocutionary acts performed by speakers in the *Dialogues* obscures much of the significance of the conversation. The next section analyzes the speech acts performed in these parts of the conversation. It shows how attending to the remarkably subtle rhetoric Hume employs reveals the way in which penetrating points emerge in and through the conversation. The third section shows how the analysis sheds light on deciding the perennial issue of "who speaks for Hume" in the *Dialogues*. The final section offers an interpretation of the *Dialogues* as Hume's communicative action.

Most theodicists construe Hume as skeptically challenging religious belief. They then try to meet that challenge by constructing a theodicy. Yet just as theodicists obscure points made in and by classic texts because they ignore the force with which those texts are written, so they obscure Hume's challenges. Once those challenges are clarified, the practice of constructing theodicies will be seen—correctly—as inadequate and irrelevant responses to Hume's real challenges.

## On Analyzing an Argument in the Dialogues

In an influential article, Nelson Pike has argued that the *Dialogues* discusses the problem of evil in two different ways. The first way deals with the "logical problem of evil." In its sharpest form, it is a claim that there is a logical incompatibility between:

(1)   The world contains instances of suffering;

(2)   God exists—and is omniscient, omnipotent, and perfectly good creator of the world;

(3)   An omnipotent and omniscient being would have no morally sufficient reason for allowing instances of suffering.

That is, if any two of those are true, the third is necessarily false (Pike 1964:85-89). Pike then goes on to argue that Demea has out-lined a defense[2] sufficient to show that (1-2) are not logically incompatible. He enlarges the defense to show that it is "far from clear that God and evil could not exist together in the same universe" (1964:97).

Pike argues that the second argument Philo makes is a form of the "evidential problem of evil," i.e., that the mixture of good and evil, virtue and vice, joy and sorrow, delight and disgust, satisfaction and suffering, pain and pleasure in the world provides no evidence for belief in an omnipotent, omniscient, and perfectly good God. However, Pike concludes that the lack of evidence for belief in such a God does little to undermine a Christian theological position:

> Within most theological positions, the existence of God is taken as an item of faith or embraced on the basis of an a priori argument. Under these circumstances, where there is nothing to qualify as a "hypothesis" capable of having either negative or positive "evidence," the fact of evil in the world presents no special problem for theology. As Philo himself has suggested, when the existence of God is accepted prior to any rational consideration of the status of evil in the world, the traditional problem of evil reduces to a noncrucial perplexity of relatively minor importance (1964:102).

Yet if this be so, why does the evidential problem of evil remain a crucial difficulty of great importance—even for those who espouse a Christian theological position? Why do all theologians not follow Demea by abandoning the conversation and taking purely on faith what Philo and Cleanthes find worth discussing philosophically? Has Pike begged the question (cf. Henze 1970:377)?

As part of his analysis, Pike sees Philo as finding Demea's defense cogent, despite Philo's rhetorical jabs to the contrary. He writes, "At the end of Part X, Philo agrees to 'retire' from his first position. He now concedes that 'God exists' and 'There occur instances of suffering' are not logically incompatible statements" (1964:97). And indeed, Philo seems to concede: "I will allow, that pain or misery in man is *compatible* with infinite power and goodness in the Deity . . ." (Hume 1779:201; cf. 211). But this sentence continues, ". . . even in your sense of these attributes: What are you advanced by all these concessions? A mere possible compatibility is not sufficient. You must *prove* these pure, unmixed, and uncontrollable attributes from the present mixed and confused phenomena. . . ." However, the addressee of Philo's remarks is not Demea, who constructed the defense formalized by Pike, but Cleanthes, who is arguing from the design of the world to the existence of a providential deity.

Thus, *if* Philo concedes, he does not concede to Demea. Moreover, his "concession" to Cleanthes may be only for the sake of argument. Analyzing only logical issues at stake in the arguments of Part X of the *Dialogues*, while ignoring the communicative interactions between the participants who speak in the *Dialogues*, obscures the anomalies of this "concession." While approaches like Pike's and Gaskin's apparently clarify arguments about God and evil, they obscure the forces of the actions that constitute the conversation in the *Dialogues*. Philo's concession may be disingenuous or merely strategic. In either case, it cannot support Pike's analysis. As P cannot forgive C for D's having insulted P, so Philo cannot concede to Cleanthes what Demea claimed against Philo's argument—especially when Cleanthes himself has challenged Demea's claim. This problem gives good reason to think that the logical and evidential arguments from the reality of evil to the irrationality of belief in God may not be the only important issues in the conversation about suffering in the *Dialogues*. Analyzing the speech acts the characters perform shows what those other issues are.

## *Points in a Conversation about Misfortune, Suffering, and God*

The conversation in Part X can be analyzed in five phases. In the first phase, Demea begins by asserting his opinion that each feels "the truth of religion within his own breast, and from a consciousness of his imbecility and misery . . . is led to seek protection from that Being on whom he and all nature is dependent."[3] He goes on to ask whether religion does suggest "methods of atonement and appease those terrors, with which we are incessantly agitated and tormented." Philo admits "that the best and indeed the only method of bringing every one to a due sense of religion is by just representations of the misery and wickedness of man" (193). For that purpose, eloquence and imagery, not proof, is the way "to make us feel" that misery more deeply and lead us to religion. Demea catalogs the "miseries of life, the unhappiness of man, the general corruptions of our nature, the unsatisfactory enjoyment of pleasures, riches, honours; these phrases have become almost proverbial in all languages." Philo adds poets' testimony to life's misery (193). Demea claims that almost all writers on the human condition have written about human misery. Cleanthes objects (wrongly) that Leibniz is an exception to the rule. Demea counters rhetorically, "can any man hope by a simple denial (for the subject scarcely admits of reasoning) to bear down the united testimony of mankind founded on sense and consciousness?" (194)

At this point, Philo accepts, perhaps only for the sake of argument, Demea's comments about the misery of life and religion as a response to feeling that misery. They also agree on a way to deepen religious feeling (a perlocutionary result). Demea finally claims that all testify to this state of affairs. The evils are mostly complaints with which Boethius was familiar. They do not focus on pain, sin, or suffering, but on the loss of the goods of fortune. However, unlike Lady Philosophy and the prisoner, Demea and Philo do not analyze what causes such misery. No one answers Demea's early question and it never figures again in the conversation.

The second phase begins with Demea adding a list of sufferings engendered by physical ills. Philo submits the problem of animal evil and molestations, to which Demea responds that humans together in society can surmount the evils of the animal world. Philo objects that this is no solution, for man has recreated in his imagination "daemons of his fancy, who haunt him with superstitious terrors, and blast every enjoyment of life? His pleasure, as he imagines, becomes, in their eyes, a crime . . ." Beyond this, fear of hell inflicts much harm, as do the crimes people perpetrate against each other. "Man is the greatest enemy of man." Society would be dissolved, were not the state of nature more feared (195).

What is odd about this section of the dialogue is the incongruity of the positions each takes. Demea, characterized by Pamphilus, the narrator, in the introduction as a man of "rigid, inflexible orthodoxy" (128), is usually taken as the representative of traditional religion. But he suggests society, not prayer or meditation or religious resignation, as a remedy for some natural evils. Philo, the skeptic, points out the psychological and social evils humans perpetrate against each other, especially the 'sin' of moralizing preaching (one of Hume's bêtes noires). This is the only time in the *Dialogues* where the evils people do, rather than those they suffer, are featured. But given that Philo is not directly asserting that society is evil, but responding to Demea's claim that society is an improvement on the state of nature, Philo's critique is not of society per se, but of the evils possible only because humans are social. Philo's final comment suggests that human life without society may be unthinkable. Combined with his concession in the previous section of Part X, Philo sees both religion and society as similar in one way: both are reactions or responses to fears and physical miseries. This section of the conversation serves notice that the characters do not merely assume stereotypical positions.

In the third phase, Demea returns to the problem of pain and suffering by reciting a list of bodily ailments drawn from *Paradise Lost*. He also adds a list of mental ills. After recounting the inequalities of wealth in society, he then returns to the Boethian problem: "All the goods of life united would not make a very happy man: But all the ills united would make a wretch indeed . . ." (196). He then continues with language borrowed from what Morrisroe (1969b:973) has called the "ready-made imagery of the churchmen":

> Were a stranger to drop, in a sudden, into this world, I would show him, as a specimen of its ills, an hospital full of diseases, a prison crowded with malefactors and debtors, a field of battle strowed with carcases, a fleet floundering [sic] in the ocean, a nation languishing under tyranny, famine, or pestilence. To turn the gay side of life to him, and give him a notion of its pleasures; whither should I conduct him? to a ball, to an opera, to court? He might justly think, that I was only showing him a diversity of distress and sorrow (196).

Philo then adverts that there "is no evading such striking instances, . . . but by apologies, which still farther aggravate the charge." (However, no charge has yet been made—that comes a bit later and is made against Cleanthes' position, not Demea's). Philo also recollects humans' frequent complaints of their misery. Cleanthes remarks that he doesn't feel such misery. Demea cites examples of Charles V, Cicero, and Cato, who claimed never to have been happy. Philo then cites "all these reflections, and infinitely more which might be suggested" (197), and challenges Cleanthes to show in what respect divine benevolence and mercy resemble human benevolence and mercy; he summarizes the challenge with Epicurus's Old Questions (the epigraph for this chapter); and he asks Cleanthes to show how the divine benevolence can be seen in the morally mixed phenomena of nature. Cleanthes then concedes the following to Philo: "If you can make out the present point, and prove mankind to be unhappy or corrupted, there is an end of all religion. For to what purposes establish the natural attributes of the Deity, while the moral are still doubtful and uncertain?" (199) Cleanthes then charges that Philo's agreement with Demea has been only a ruse for constructing arguments against Cleanthes' view.

Although it is rarely noted, Part X makes it obvious that Demea differs from Cleanthes on the nature of religion. Cleanthes is a foundationalist. For him religion is based in reason: it is belief in the providential guidance of God and is worthless if the design argument could not establish God's intelligence and goodness. Without it, religion is at an end. For Demea religion is based in feeling: it is a natural response or reaction to awareness of threat and to adversity.[4] This also brings into focus the significance of the rarely discussed first conversation in Part I of the *Dialogues* (130-31). There Demea separated the principles of religion from natural theology. He claimed it proper to season the minds of the young with the principles of religion, while he reserved natural theology to the end of one's studies. For Demea, being religious does not require that one be able to justify one's religious practices. Nor is it clear than these practices need any justification. Demea represents an "antifoundationalist" view of religious belief. And at this point in the conversation, Philo agrees with Demea, although this agreement may be merely strategic, as Philo will apparently agree with Cleanthes in Part XII.

Hence, Cleanthes and Demea do not mean the same thing by "religion." Using Hume's distinctions in *The Natural History of Religion*, Cleanthes advocates the foundation for, but not the content of, "true religion," and Demea takes religion as "superstition" or "vulgar religion." Philo's skeptical arrows puncture the design argument of Cleanthes, but miss the "vulgar" view of Demea. Cleanthes' charge, then, is well founded: Philo has joined with Demea to attack his position.

Cleanthes recognizes the problem Demea and Philo have shown in his position. His providential theism, like all versions of the design argument, is vulnerable to the "evidential problem of evil." But what problem has Philo raised for Demea's view? To this point, none. The only "challenge" he has made, to show how the divine benevolence can be seen in the morally mixed phenomena of nature, has nothing to do with Demea's claims or with his religion, but only with Cleanthes'.

The fourth phase begins with Demea citing a solution to the difficulties evil presents for belief in God:

> Have not all pious divines and preachers, who have *indulged their rhetoric* on so fertile a subject; have they not easily, I say, given a solution of any difficulties which may attend it? This world is but a point in comparison of the universe: This life but a moment in comparison of eternity. The present evil phenomena are rectified in other regions and in some future period of existence. And the eyes of men, being *then* opened to larger views of things see the whole connection of general laws, and trace, with adoration, the benevolence and rectitude of the Deity through all the mazes and intricacies of his providence (199; emphasis added).

Demea need not be construed as asserting the solution. Rather, he cites the rhetoric of pious divines and claims that in the future humans will see the solution. Demea does not necessarily endorse the illocutionary force of their preaching or accept its content. He need only have the content they preach be possibly true. Moreover, his way of citing them implies that the truth of their claims is not now known. Hence, he can be read as citing as possible, not asserting as true, the preachers' claims.

Cleanthes' next speech (199-200) is important for two reasons. First, he concedes that Demea has established only the "bare possibility of our opinion." But then he continues by claiming, "but never can we, upon such terms establish its reality" (200). He then asserts: "The only method of supporting divine benevolence (and it is what I willingly embrace) is to deny absolutely the misery and wickedness of man." He continues by contradicting Philo's and Demea's view: "Your representations are exaggerated: Your melancholy views mostly fictitious: Your inferences contrary to fact and experience." He concludes his speech by asserting: "Health is more common than sickness: Pleasure than pain: Happiness than misery. And for one vexation which we meet with, we attain, upon computation, a hundred enjoyments" (200).

What is crucial about this pair of speeches is that Cleanthes says nothing substantial against Demea's position. His concession gives Demea all he needs, for Demea does not seek to provide an evidential foundation for his view, but merely to show that it is not incoherent. Moreover, just as Cleanthes has misunderstood the scope of Philo's skepticism in Part I, here he mistakes the status of Demea's claims. It is not at all clear what opinion Demea shares with Cleanthes. Certainly they do not share a doctrine of God—Demea has fought Cleanthes over both the foundation for and the content of this doctrine in Parts II-VIII as strongly as Philo did, and

Cleanthes refuted Demea's listless a priori argument in Part IX. Hence, Cleanthes' subsequent methodological claims about showing the goodness of the deity and his factual claims about the extent of human misery which deny the reality of any genuine evils in the world are irrelevant to Demea's view. Thus, Philo's subsequent attacks can be aimed only at Cleanthes.

The fifth phase begins with Philo conceding to Cleanthes the bare possibility of his view (and only by extension, Demea's view, which he has not attacked), and asserts the excess intensity of pain over pleasure. He attacks Cleanthes' foundationalist method for establishing religious truth on the happiness of human life by a *tu quoque* argument: "And thus by your resting the whole system of religion on a point, which, from its very nature, must for ever be uncertain, you tacitly confess, that that system is equally uncertain" (201). He then reiterates his concession to Cleanthes of the bare possibility of his view, but argues again that on Cleanthes' own principles, Cleanthes must establish the goodness of God: "Here I triumph. Formerly, when we argued concerning the natural attributes of intelligence, I needed all my sceptical and metaphysical subtilty to elude your grasp. . . ." The objections to a creator are "mere cavils and sophisms" when considering the beauty of the natural world. But no view of the human world in which moral values are found can be a foundation for providential monotheism. So it is Cleanthes' "turn now to tug the labouring oar, and to support your philosophical subtilties against the dictates of plain reason and experience" (201-2).

Part X of the *Dialogues* concludes with Philo having shown that the evidentialist Cleanthes bears the burden of proof for establishing providential theism against plain reason and experience. Cleanthes has not met his challenge, reiterated in Philo's showing that the human world is morally ambivalent. Demea's responsive reverence is basically unscathed.[5] Philo has admitted that people respond religiously to misfortune and suffering, but neither he nor Demea has explored a Boethian resolution for the problem of misfortune. Philo and Demea have implicitly agreed that society can resolve some of the problems individuals have with molestations, but Philo has claimed that humans recreate the terrors of the state of nature, especially when enthusiasts preach. Philo has claimed that this "imaginary" evil is a real social evil, a claim which stands uncontroverted by either Demea or Cleanthes.

Part XI begins with Cleanthes proposing a possible understanding: "benevolence, regulated by wisdom, and limited by necessity, may produce just such a world as the present" (203). He requests Philo's "opinion of this new theory," which Philo gives at length.

Philo responds with arguments which reach three conclusions that undermine the proposal that either wisdom or necessity may have constrained God to produce a world with as much pain and suffering as the present. First, the greatest part of natural evil depends on animals' having a sense of pain, and the world not being run by "particular volitions," animals being skimpily endowed by nature, and the principles of the universe being not "so accurately framed as to preserve always the just temperament and medium" (210). The world may be run by natural laws, but they are not a necessity constraining a providential God. Philo implies that Cleanthes' God could run the world in a way that attenuated its misery. Second, there is no ground for inference to the goodness of the deity from the evidently amoral course of nature, although Philo is "sceptic enough to allow, that the bad appearances, notwithstanding all my reasonings, may be compatible with such attributes as you suppose . . ." (211). Nature does not license an inference of God's moral wisdom. Third, from an examination of nature and society the "true conclusion is, that the original source of all things is entirely indifferent to all these principles, and has no more regard to good above ill than heat above cold, or to drought above moisture, or to light above heavy" (212). Here Philo seems to draw a conclusion from the actual morally indifferent states of affairs in the world—to a morally indifferent creator of the world.

At this point, the interactions between the speakers again are odd. Philo then challenges Cleanthes to find a cause for evil other than the deity, a challenge to which Cleanthes does not respond. Demea expresses amazement that Philo, with whom he allied himself to prove the incomprehensibility of God, is now "running into all the topics of the greatest libertines and infidels, and betraying that holy cause, which [he] seemingly espoused." He asks, "Are you secretly, then, a more dangerous enemy than Cleanthes himself?" (213) But Philo doesn't answer: Cleanthes does. He chides Demea for being slow in recognizing Philo's tactics, and then he admits that "the injudicious reasoning of our vulgar theology has given him but too just a handle of ridicule." After some remarks by Cleanthes and Philo about popular divines trimming the sails of their theology and their preaching to the changing winds of each age, Demea withdraws.

Perhaps more than any other, the complexity of this section of the conversation shows the need to pay attention to Hume's artistry by attending to the specific force of each speaker's utterances. Neglecting either Philo's or Demea's speech acts, as many interpreters do, can lead one to an interpretation of their positions that is at variance with what they actually say.

First, some commentators have read Philo as asserting his own position when he says "that the original source of all things is indifferent to all these principles . . ." But that neglects the fact that Philo is responding to Cleanthes' request to examine Cleanthes' proposal.[6] Throughout this part, Philo speaks presuming Cleanthes' method. He brings out "facts" visible to common sense to show that if one accepts them (which all of common sense must, unless they have good reason to reject them), and uses Cleanthes' method, one does not reach Cleanthes' conclusions. But Philo's displaying an argument presuming Cleanthes' method does not mean that Philo makes that argument, accepts that method, or draws that conclusion himself. Because Philo is responding to a request, the precise illocutionary forces of his "assertions" and "conclusions" are ambiguous at best. Hence, Philo's position cannot be reliably inferred from his long response to Cleanthes—for he may be merely exploring Cleanthes' approach with a view to undermining it.

Second, Philo undermines only Cleanthes' evidentialism. Nothing he says counts against Demea's responsive reverence. Yet, incongruously, Demea speaks up when Philo challenges Cleanthes. Demea expresses amazement and questions Philo, but then Cleanthes unexpectedly responds (but does not answer his question) with an insult and his hang-dog admission about "our" theology. This "our" cannot include Demea, but must refer to Cleanthes' foundationalist fellow travelers. Cleanthes cannot coopt Demea's views. First, they hold incompatible views about the nature of religion. Second, they evidently disagree about the nature of God. Third, Demea has unceasingly opposed Cleanthes' evidence-based theology. So how could Cleanthes get into position to perform the speech act of admitting the weakness of Demea's, his erstwhile opponent's, views? In a three-way wrestling match where C, D, and P all oppose each other, and C is beaten by P, C cannot be in position properly to admit to P that C and D are defeated. Only D—or his delegate—can concede his own defeat. Cleanthes cannot properly admit Demea's defeat here. Hence, Philo's challenge remains unmet, Demea's question is not answered, and Cleanthes' admission cannot encompass Demea's position without evacuating Demea's view of any determinate meaning. Then why does Demea leave the conversation?

One "obvious" view is that Demea has been betrayed by Philo, defeated by his opponents' arguments, and left as these have rendered him speechless. But this presupposes that his question to Philo is either rhetorical or adequately answered by Cleanthes, that Cleanthes' admission covers them both, and that Philo's or Cleanthes' arguments have undermined his position. But Demea's question cannot be rhetorical, for that would presume that Philo has been laying out his own position, a point which the text does not warrant. We have also seen that Cleanthes didn't answer his question and that Cleanthes could not admit Demea's injudicious reasoning. Finally, both Philo and Cleanthes have conceded that a position like Demea's is possibly true, and have given him no reason to abandon his religion. So the final condition does not obtain. This "obvious" view simply ignores the fact that the conditions for its interpretive adequacy are contradicted by the text it interprets. It cannot account for Demea's leaving.

Morrisroe has suggested that Demea "leaves the scene in anger" (1970:106). But he sees Demea as "an essentially comic character" (105), violent, passionate, generally weak of mind, and introduced "to direct the attention of the audience away from Philo" (106). But this simply won't hold water. While Demea's speeches often read as if they were an enthusiast's, he never allies morality with religion, an essential characteristic of the enthusiasts Hume opposed. And although part of Demea's literary function is clearly to direct attention away from Philo, and the argument he mounts in Part IX is a disaster, Demea (in alliance with Philo) undermines Cleanthes' evidential foundationalism, and against Cleanthes (and presumably Philo) he shows that his position is possibly true and not undermined by skeptical arguments. This is hardly the work of a purely comic character of weak mind. Moreover, Pamphilus never clearly specifies the reason for Demea's departure, and Demea cannot properly be angry at being defeated, since he hasn't been defeated. This leaves only the possibility that he is angry at the snide comments about clergymen. While such comments are congruent with Hume's views expressed in other places, they are at best incidental to the main points of the *Dialogues*. If he does leave "in anger," it is with his position intact, and for either a trivial or dramatic reason.[7]

Yet it is as likely that he simply has nothing more to say not because he was defeated or miffed, but because he has established his view. Despite the minimal amount of space Hume gave Demea (only 12% of the text; Mossner 1977:5-6), he is not merely a foil for the others. He shows the strengths and weaknesses of an antifoundationalist position in religion. In Part XII Philo and Cleanthes come to agree that philosophical theism is true religion and Philo then claims that the real difference between providential monotheism and attenuated deism is merely verbal. Philo and Cleanthes disagree on the proper effect of this religion or theology on morality. But then Demea doesn't share their position in Part XII on the nature of religion, not because he does not believe in providence, but because he finds their conflation of religion and theology alien to his own view.[8] Demea may or may not have something left to say, but given his nonfoundationalist view of the nature of religion, he has nothing to contribute to the discussion of religion's foundations in the design of the universe in Part XII. In sum, from the perspective of Parts X and XI, if there is a real loser in the *Dialogues*, it is Cleanthes, for both Demea and Philo appear to warrant the essential aspects of their respective positions as well as they must in order to maintain them.

But this internal analysis of the dialogue in the *Dialogues* does not address what many see as the crucial question for interpreting their meaning and for understanding Hume's view of religion. As Gaskin put it, it is "essential to decide which characters speak for Hume himself" (1978:160). The standard interpretation accepts Philo as Hume's mouthpiece and Philo as victor over the other two in argument. However, deciding that a character speaks for Hume presumes that a character in a literary piece voices the position of the author—a dubious presumption in light not only of recent literary criticism but also of the above investigations into *Job* and *The Consolation of Philosophy*. The following section argues for a different answer to the question of who speaks for Hume in the *Dialogues*.

## On Hearing Hume's Voices

One of the perennially discussed puzzles about the *Dialogues* is the question of "who speaks for Hume" in the *Dialogues* (cf. Noxon 1966, Gaskin 1978:159-66). At the conclusion of the work, Pamphilus, the usually silent student who "recorded" the dialogues, says with apparent irony, "so I confess, that, upon a serious review of the whole, I cannot but think, that Philo's principles are more probable than Demea's; but that those of Cleanthes approach still nearer to the truth" (Hume 1779:228). Some scholars took this as evidence that Cleanthes is Hume's mouthpiece which he uses to defeat the other two voices. Beyond the problematical conflation of narrator's voice with author's voice, and the fact that Philo has undermined all of Cleanthes' arguments, Cleanthes' own student who was a "mere auditor of their disputes" (128-29) cannot be in position to render a verdict on the cogency of these arguments. Surely a student can assert an opinion or evaluate a teacher's ability to communicate. But a student does not occupy a position in which making this assertive declaration, that is, rendering a verdict on his own teacher's contested principles, is an illocutionary possibility. Pamphilus's opinion can hardly be evidence for the author's verdict (compare Battersby 1979:244-45 and Mossner 1977).

Pamphilus called Demea a person of "rigid inflexible orthodoxy." Cleanthes chided him for being a "mystic" for maintaining the absolute incomprehensibility of God (128, 158). Demea did not relish Philo's "spirit of opposition and his censure of established opinions" (213; also see Cleanthes' remark:199). Few have even considered the possibility that Demea could speak for Hume: his withdrawing from the conversation, his anti-empirical positions, his apparent congruence with popular orthodoxy, and the similarity of his religion to the popular religion Hume sought to undermine in *The Natural History of Religion*, render him an unlikely candidate.

Philo appears to undermine both Cleanthes' arguments and Demea's views. He shows that Cleanthes' attempt to construct analogical arguments for the existence of God from the design of the universe at best "prove" the reality of a deity too ambiguous to be worthy of worship by Christians. Given Hume's empiricism, his arguments against the probity of miracles, and his other positions on religious subjects, many have found Philo's position most compatible with Hume's known views. Thus, they have suggested that Philo articulates Hume's position (cf. Penelhum 1979:270).[9]

However, Philo doesn't *have* much of a position throughout the *Dialogues*. He rarely constructs an argument or asserts a view of his own, save that he apparently espouses an "attenuated deism" (Gaskin 1978:168) with no practical implications in Part XII. He prefers to play the role of philosophical gadfly, taking others' principles as given and showing their arguments inconsistent or unable to support the conclusions they derive. So if this is Hume's position, it is far less substantial and definitive than those he asserted in his other writings on religion.

Yet friends had frequently urged Hume not to publish the *Dialogues*, as they would evidently give offense (Kemp Smith 1947:88). Since the only 'offensive' character in the *Dialogues* is Philo, his friends must have read Philo as speaking for Hume. Additionally, in correspondence dating from the period of the initial drafts (1751) he acknowledged that he needed help with Cleanthes and could himself play the role of Philo (Kemp Smith: 1947:87-88; cf. Battersby 1979:247). Finally, in Philo's last speech, quoted below, the phrase "man of letters" is interposed as a qualifier. Hume made his final revisions to the *Dialogues*, including this speech, in the early summer of 1776. In April of the same year he had used the same title to characterize himself in his brief autobiography, *My Own Life* (cf. Kemp Smith 1947:87-96 and Hume 1777:236). All this suggests that the skeptical Philo is the most likely candidate for being Hume's mouthpiece.

Only in his last speech, added in the final revision of the manuscript, does Philo unambiguously urge a position. He says:

> But *believe* me, Cleanthes, the most natural sentiment, which a well-disposed mind will feel on this occasion, is a longing desire and expectation, that Heaven would be pleased to dissipate, at least alleviate, this profound ignorance, by affording some more particular revelation to mankind, and making discoveries of the nature, attributes, and operations of the divine object of our Faith. A person, seasoned with a just sense of the imperfections of natural reason, will fly to revealed truth with the greatest avidity: While the haughty dogmatist, persuaded that he can erect a complete system of theology by the mere help of philosophy, disdains any farther aid, and rejects this adventitious instructor. To be a philosophical sceptic is, in a man of letters, the first and most essential step towards being a sound, believing Christian; a proposition which I would willingly *recommend* to the attention of Pamphilus (Hume 1779:227-28).

Here, Philo urges Cleanthes and recommends Pamphilus to believe something: as speech acts, these are directives. But what he urges Cleanthes to believe is that when one is left in the frustrating position of being unable to resolve the problem of the nature of the divine, it is 'natural' to long for a revelation.

Mossner sees this speech as a dissimulatingly ironic prayer (1977:14-15). But Philo is not praying—he never performs *that* speech act. Nor does Philo suggest any reason to believe that he expects such a 'natural' longing to be fulfilled. Nor does he imply that *he* longs for revelation. This speech is not "ironic," but has the precise illocutionary point of directing Pamphilus (and, by extension, the reader) merely to accept a proposition. He does not urge Pamphilus to become either a skeptic or a Christian. Reading "irony" here is unnecessarily reading dissimulation into the text by ignoring the illocutionary force of Philo's speaking. Further, Philo's directive does not strictly imply that he is either a skeptic or Christian. What Philo says here does not imply anything about what Philo (much less Hume) believes about the divine, but only what Philo recommends believing about human psychology and (perhaps ironically) about skepticism and religious faith.[10]

If one took this final speech as a series of assertions, one might, like Kierkegaard, read this late addition Hume made to the *Dialogues* as endorsing a position much like Demea's. Demea is skeptical about the ability of philosophy to arrive at truth about the divine. He is literally a philosophical skeptic.[11] So if this speech were assertive, it could possibly be read as Hume endorsing a position like that of the departed Demea. But as these "claims" occur as part of directive, not assertive, illocutionary acts, they offer no reason to believe that the speaker is committing himself to any specific actions or beliefs other than a hypothetical acceptance of a skeptical 'foundation' for faith.

Hume's own position cannot be readily inferred from the content of the *Dialogues*. Hume himself wrote to Adam Smith that he found "nothing can be more cautiously and more artfully written" (Kemp Smith 1947:91) than the *Dialogues*. Part of his art may have been not only the irony many (e.g., Mossner) find in the *Dialogues*, but also a careful construction of the speeches his characters gave. Hence, it is unwarranted to infer hypothetical commissives from directives within the text, or the necessity of their speaker's holding positive representational claims about the way things are (rather than negative representational presumptions about the way things are not, which is all that is required to perform directive speech acts), especially in reading an author "one of whose most original discoveries is that of the performative use of language" (Livingston 1984:333). So, even if Philo spoke with Hume's voice, that voice rarely asserts an unambiguous position, but undermines others' arguments.

It has been suggested that the unambiguous voice of Hume could be found in the notes to the *Dialogues*. There Hume's claim that the only differences between believers and unbelievers were merely verbal was stated in his own voice, without the complications of dialogue (Tilley 1978:7-9; cf. Noxon 1966:379, Tweyman 1986:xv). Moreover, his psychological-genetic account of the differences between dogmatists and skeptics (Hume 1779:219) was compatible with his other writings. This view takes the *Dialogues* as simply an exercise in deconstruction of the arguments which supposedly provided foundations for religious claims. Kemp Smith draws out the conclusions of such a view:

> What Hume has achieved in the *Dialogues*, considered by themselves, is, at most, to show that the traditional arguments which he has been considering have in fact the defects which he asserts. The reader, should he approve of Hume's criticisms, has still the alternatives before him either to follow Hume in his thorough-going skepticism, or, should he so choose, to look to the *Dialogues* for instruction only in the *via negativa*—a discipline upon which theology, thanks to the mystics no less than to the sceptics, has found reason to insist (1947:75; also cf. Penelhum 1983a:143).

However, the conclusion that the *Dialogues* is an exercise in philosophical skepticism is only partly right. There are three points which provide reason to rethink this conclusion.

First, the argument which supports that conclusion presumes that the voice in the notes "speaks for Hume." Yet the status of the crucial note is unclear. It may be an authorial comment on the point then at issue. Or Hume may have written it as an addition to a speech of Philo. Or it may be a summary of Hume's view. But it is ambiguous enough to provide no support for any conclusions about Hume's own position (cf. Battersby 1979:245).

Second, within the *Dialogues* no voice carries the author's unambiguous imprimatur. Further, no speech acts performed by voices within a text determine the communicative action performed by its author in writing the text.

Third, this view neglects any consideration of the rhetorical structure of the work as a dialogue. This view hardly accounts for the fact that Hume wrote a *dialogue*, not a dry philosophical treatise in which he raised his opponents' arguments and refuted them seriatim without seeking to establish any claims of his own. However, Hume did not essay another *Treatise* or *Enquiry* or *Natural History*, but a conversation among three distinctive voices.

Hence, as none of the characters nor the narrator nor the possible authorial voice has credentials to speak exclusively for Hume, the answer to the perennial question posed by historians of philosophy is that the Dialogues as a whole "speak for Hume."[12] As with Augustine's *Enchiridion* and Boethius's *Consolation of Philosophy*, what sort of communicative action he has performed in writing the text cannot be determined by the content of what the text 'teaches' alone. One must consider the illocutionary forces with which the text is communicated. The present question is *how* the text speaks for Hume.

## *The Reality of Evil and Faith in God*

From the perspective which takes the *Dialogues* as a dialogue, the text is a narrative whole, not a "timeless" series of arguments. In this way, the question of "who speaks for Hume" *in the text* is unimportant compared to the question of how the text speaks for Hume. The text is not merely an arbitrary context for Philo's—or Hume's—arguments and assertions. If Philo is the main character—a contention hard to controvert, as his speeches take 67% of the space in the text (Mossner 1977:6)—the narrative can be seen as a story of

"Philo's progress." He begins in the *Dialogues* by testing both Cleanthes' and Demea's approaches in Parts I-XI, sometimes siding with one against the other as a way of exploring their views. Then, in Part XII, he lays out his own conclusions. He comes to prefer Cleanthes' view of the nature of true religion as philosophical theism over Demea's view of true religion as a response or reaction. But then if one applies Cleanthes' methods, one must evacuate religion of almost any determinate doctrinal content, including the inculcation of superstition and moral sanction—a position to which Demea raises no objection. Philo mounts no telling arguments against the "vulgar religion" or "superstition" of Demea as a *kind* of religion. But he does not accept it. His probing and Demea's leaving combine to display the philosophical limits of that position. Philo may not speak for Hume, but he may represent the journey of a mitigated skeptic through relatively coherent accounts of religion.[13]

This outline of the structure of the *Dialogues* as a narrative portrayal of a conversation, rather than as an argument disguised in a dialogue form, includes accounting for the argumentative strategies the characters use, especially with regard to the design argument and the evidential and logical problems of evil. It can also explain the "inconsistencies" in Philo's view as an outcome of a developing position. But this approach can also show the other contributions of the *Dialogues*.

First, in the *Dialogues*, Hume offers a sophisticated view of the relations between the reality of evil and faith in God. Philo shows that for an evidential theist like Cleanthes, human pain, suffering, and misfortune undermine the evidential foundation for theism. But Demea also shows that one 'natural' response to a sense of inadequacy, to misfortunes, and to ills is to turn to God and that a 'natural' belief in the worship-worthiness of the god to whom one turns neither can be established nor has been shown incoherent by the arguments of the philosophers. Philo and Demea see forming a society as another 'natural' response to natural evils, but Philo also points out that humans themselves can and do recreate many of the terrors of nature—the only reference to the evils people do, rather than those they suffer, in the *Dialogues*.

Second, the *Dialogues* also show a most important corollary of a religious position for which the existence and nature of God cannot be at issue. Although for such a view "the traditional problem of evil reduces to a noncrucial perplexity of relatively minor importance" (Pike 1964:102), it is also the case that those who take that position have nothing to say to and nothing constructive to learn theologically from those who do not share that view. If experienced evil can be an occasion for deepening religious faith and the logical problem of evil has been defanged, then 'natural' religious belief in God may be rendered safe from attack. However, theological explication of the presumptions and implications of that belief may be undermined. While Demea participates in many of Philo's attacks on evidential foundationalism, and uses Philo's strategies to undermine Cleanthes' position, nothing Philo says changes, enlarges, explicates, or clarifies Demea's religious position. And although his partners have not shown that Demea's view is incoherent, the question of whether his approach is wise remains unasked. Had Hume had his characters return to the issue of the relationship of religious practice and natural theology with which the *Dialogues* began, for instance, by discussing whether Demea's 'natural' response should be impressed upon one's children, perhaps he would have had to continue the conversation and defend his position. But Hume did not take that path. Hence, Demea could leave the conversation unscathed.

Third, moral evils are not at issue for Hume. Moral evils, e.g., social injustice, may be a cause of some persons' 'naturally' turning to God (193). Philo mentions the real but *"imaginary"* evils of superstitious terror and fear. These recreate the fears the natural world evokes in even deeper ways—especially when death is presented as a possible beginning of endless and innumerable woes, rather than as a release from "every other ill" (195). Society apparently should provide some relief from misery, but in practice too often fails to do so. The implication is that moral evil as the re-creation of natural evil counts *mutatis mutandis* against the evidentialist theism of Cleanthes. However, sin is not a problem for the attenuated deism of Philo; it is simply further evidence of the ambiguity or indifference of the natural and human world to good and evil. As for Demea, evil as the *result* of others' sin may bring people to turn to God, but sin as a *cause* of evils is simply ignored. The *Dialogues* has nothing new to say about the problems of sin, but by its silence may insinuate Hume's view of the irrelevance of moral evil to the two viable religious positions the *Dialogues* presents.

In sum, the *Dialogues* has properly been taken as Hume's successful challenge to the credibility and foundations of evidentialist, providential monotheism. But to read it as merely a challenge is to underread it. And to read it as asserting Hume's own views is to overread it. It has forces beyond that of a man of letters' instruction in a *via negativa*: Hume also coincidentally *challenges* the reader to become aware of some of the weaknesses and strengths of nonfoundationalist faith. He *warns* about the perils of evidential foundationalism as a rational account of the nature of religion by showing the vulnerability of Cleanthes' position. He *displays*, but does not advocate, the significance of 'natural' responsive faith. He may condemn the inculcation of superstition and support separating religion, either vulgarly reactive or philosophically attenuated, from moral sanctions. To read the *Dialogues* as only undermining theodicy is to ignore the full range of illocutionary forces the *Dialogues* has. To read it as staking out intellectual turf for Hume to defend is to attribute far too much strength to the minimal assertions made in and through the text.

The enduring significance of the *Dialogues* lies in its showing how the Enlightenment theodicy project in particular and the Enlightenment design argument in general are untenable. Yet people do "turn to God" in response to those imaginary terrors Philo mentions. They engage in the practice of confession. But it is not easy to confess. Chapter 8 examines the relationships and the process which enable a truly terrorized and horrified person to have a voice in which to confess.

# NOTES

1.    Some recent writers have taken steps in this direction. Morrisroe's series of articles helpfully focus on the rhetorical force *of* the *Dialogues*, but never get clear of the rhetorical forces of the speeches *in* the *Dialogues*. Rurak sees the *Dialogues* as a drama, but then takes all the speeches as assertives and neglects to note any of the subtle interactions among the characters. Vink also neglects the speech acts the characters perform, but helpfully describes the characters and notices Demea's dramatic departure, often unacknowledged by critics.

2.    Pike writes of Demea's "theodicy," but, as with Augustine's *Enchiridion*, the argument is logically a defense. Demea introduces a possibly true claim to the effect that (4) the present evils are rectified "in other regions," and that in eternity people will see the reasons for present suffering (cf. Pike 1964:199). Proposition (4) is compatible with proposition (2) and taken jointly with (2) entails proposition (1). This shows the set of propositions (1-2) compatible and proposition (3) not necessarily true.

3.    Because of Hume's linguistic usages, I have found it impossible to write all of what follows in inclusive language. I beg the readers' patience.

4.    The debate over whether Hume considered religious belief natural is extensive. Among recent writers, Williams claims that "While Hume did not regard religious belief as natural, in his special sense of that term—that is, as something which human nature, by its very constitution must embrace,—there are certain obscurities in his account of it" (1963:81). Gaskin also argues that belief in God does not meet the criteria for being a natural belief in Hume's sense (1978:132-39). But Yandell (1979) argues that there are different senses of natural belief in Hume's works; he seeks to show how Hume could reject some natural beliefs but not others. Harris (1987) points out that natural beliefs are socially conditioned, so the failure of a religious belief to be universal in human nature may not count against its being

natural. Penelhum (1983b) also notes the social context for recognizing a natural belief (180) and suggests that Philo's confession in Part XII expresses something like a natural belief, a point Phillips also endorses (1985:102-3). Penelhum has most clearly shown the similarities and differences between religious 'natural' beliefs and secular *natural* beliefs. Those similarities are sufficient to call religious belief at least 'natural.'

Thus, Demea's speeches at the beginning of Part X represent 'natural' religious belief in at least one sense, but a belief which Hume would disdain. Yet as Williams suggests (1963:83-84) and Livingston points out (1984:315-16,329-34), Hume was not completely disparaging of vulgar religion. What he clearly opposed was both vulgar and sophisticated theologies, the systematizations and illegitimate extensions of popular, 'natural' religious beliefs.

5. The "a priori" argument Demea mounts in Part IX is irrelevant. Both Demea's mounting of and Cleanthes' attack on the argument are the weakest parts of the *Dialogues*. Kemp Smith justly labels the part a "digression" (1947:114; cf. Morrisroe 1969b:966). The argument is not needed to provide a 'foundation' for Demea's position, as both his complete lack of response to Cleanthes' attack and his initial speech in Part X attributing the cause of religion to the human heart indicate.

6. The strongest argument against my account would adapt the arguments Morrisroe applies to Demea (1969b and 1970). Cleanthes' literary function here would simply be to direct the audience's attention away from Philo by making Philo seem to be only responding to Cleanthes' request and not presenting a position of his own. However, other commentators have pointed out that this is the only place in the *Dialogues* before Part XII in which Philo draws a conclusion, and that his argument here does not square well with the position he takes in Part XII. Nor does it square well with Philo's usual tactics, best articulated at the end of Part VI, where he says he wants to show Cleanthes the error of his ways. Nor does Demea have the minimal role Morrisroe attributes to him (as I argue below). Either Philo is inconsistent or he is not drawing a conclusion. As the former requires explaining how or why Philo shifts positions and the latter only requires taking Cleanthes' request for Philo's opinion at face value, the latter explanation is to be preferred.

7. Vink has argued that Demea's departure is crucial for the drama of the *Dialogues*. Demea's departure changes the *"way* the discussion is carried on . . ." (1986:391). Without Demea's presence, the two friends can come to a rapprochement. Philo can make his "confession" in Part XII without Demea there supplying the "revelation" he "desires." However, Vink follows Mossner in overstating Philo's irony because he also doesn't notice Philo's speech acts; hence, he doesn't notice that Philo does not request a revelation (as I show in discussing Part XII). Further, Vink finds "when present Demea is of little consequence" (391), a contention which is simply wrong. Demea's departure is crucial for the drama; but Vink doesn't see the full significance of that departure.

8. Demea, like Philo, never associates religion with the regulation of morality. For a representative of traditional religion, identified by many commentators as a clergyman, it seems odd that Demea never mentions sin or attributes human evil to human sin (although Philo does).

9. Gaskin (1978:159-66) reviews the major positions in the dispute, with a focus on Kemp Smith and Noxon. There are, however, problems with the view that Philo speaks for Hume. Mossner has added to the "evidence" for this view, but his essay also brings out the problems in that "evidence."

He cites a letter about an earlier published dialogue in which Hume asserts that no more than one speaker in a dialogue can be assumed to be speaking for the author(Mossner 1977:4). This supposedly cements the argument for Philo as Hume's mouthpiece. However, Mossner must then introduce "irony" as an explanation for the fact that Cleanthes, not Philo, refutes Demea. It must also be "ironic" that Demea supports Philo in Parts I-VIII. So if one argument is 'transferred' to Cleanthes, why not others, especially the argument in Part XI? Moreover, how does one account for the apparent shift in position that Philo undertakes in Part XII? If Philo alone speaks for Hume, then Hume already must articulate more than one position. Why not the other views? Moreover, Hume must be mischievously engaging in "dissimulation" (6) when *he* declares Cleanthes the victor in some correspondence, as well as when he has Pamphilus do so. But why accept that Hume is dissimulating in private correspondence, unless one already believes Philo the victor? Hume may have been dissimulating, but if Cleanthes' coming to agreement with Philo in Part XII is neither blind nor ironic, but an authentic agreement about the minimal success of the design argument, is that not a victory—at least of Cleanthes over his credulous approach and of Philo over his former skeptical attacks? Does their agreement not in fact support the "attenuated deism" (Gaskin 1978:168) usually conceded to be Hume's own 'religious' view?

"Dissimulation" and "irony" are two-edged hermeneutical swords. They often rhetorically support a reader's own view and conceal the multiple possibilities for interpretation a text offers. If other speakers are sometimes Hume's mouthpiece, as even Mossner claims, the issue is *when* they are his mouthpiece. Mossner does not address this issue. Clearly, when they are mounting arguments refuted by Philo or incompatible with Philo's position, they are foils and not speaking for Hume. But that allows far more that may be Hume's in their positions than Mossner suggests, especially if one views the *Dialogues* as a narrative and a dialogue, rather than as merely a set of arguments. In short, despite some similarities between Philo's skepticism and Hume's own mitigated skepticism displayed in other works, the ambiguity of the internal and external evidence suggests that the *Dialogues* is too artful a composition to be read as having one voice within the *Dialogues* alone speak as the author's voice.

10.  For present purposes, we do not need to delineate the precise form of Hume's skepticism and whether Philo matches it. Among recent writers, Stove argues that Hume consistently claims that the propositions supported by nonanalytic arguments are less conclusively warranted than most folk think and that Hume consistently supports the most minimal conclusions that arguments entail. Penelhum (1983a) and Gaskin (1978) disagree about how pyrrhonic Hume's skepticism was, but conclude with relatively similar views about his severance of religion from the common and practical life. Battersby's conclusions are similar to Stove's, but she goes on to suggest that Hume thought change in religious opinion occurred by shifts in passion. She also writes that "Philo's admission of the inadequacy of his position means that he and Cleanthes are equal adversaries. We cannot doubt that Hume inclined more toward Philo's position than Cleanthes'. . ." (1979:251). Nonetheless, that inclination was not rationally demonstrable.

11.  Demea might be expected to be open to revelation as a foundation for his position (Vink thinks he would, although Demea never makes such a claim in the *Dialogues*; if the present reading of Demea as an antifoundationalist is correct, Vink must be wrong at this point). Reading him this way would make Demea a forebear of Karl Barth and T. F. Torrance. However, it is more congruent with the text to read him as anticipating Schleiermacher, especially given his first speech in Part X (193).

12.  This view is supported by Gaskin's analysis of Noxon's rejection of Kemp Smith's view (Gaskin 1978:162-66), which shows that Noxon's conclusion, that "In one way, Hume was all or two of his characters; in another he was none or neither," is actually compatible with Kemp Smith's view. However, no simple view that Philo alone "speaks for Hume" can remain intact (cf. note 9, above). Surely, Hume's personal views were roughly in line with Philo's, but that does not make Philo alone

his mouthpiece, any more than Lady Philosophy alone was Boethius's mouthpiece. Also see Morrisroe 1969b:974 for another argument in support of this conclusion.

13.    This view of the significance of the *Dialogues* is supported by Morrisroe's analyses of Hume's rhetorical strategies. In short, Hume saw the design argument as a rhetorical, not demonstrative, argument and used rhetorical strategies in the *Dialogues* with the purpose of having the *Dialogues* undermine the argument's persuasive influence on his audience (Morrisroe 1969a:964ff). However, Morrisroe sees the discussion of the problem of evil merely as contributing to Philo's attack on the design argument. He unfortunately construes Demea as merely contributing powerful images useful for undermining the persuasiveness of Cleanthes' argument (972-73) and thus neglects Demea's own independent stand. Hume did attack the vulgar religion Demea represents more straightforwardly in *The Natural History of Religion*, but omits that attack in the *Dialogues*. While one reading is that such an attack would be redundant in the *Dialogues*, it is equally plausible to read that omission as admitting that vulgar religionists who do not draw unwarranted inferences from their religious experiences and convictions (as Demea usually does not) have occupied a battery impregnable to the sort of assault a skeptic can mount.

*Chapter 8*

## GIVING VOICE TO THE VICTIM: CONSOLATION WITHOUT FALSIFICATION

*Evil's evil, and sorrow's sorrow;*
*and you can't alter its natur'*
*by wrapping it up in other words.*
—George Eliot, *Adam Bede*

Repentance and confession, forgiveness and reconciliation: these are often prescribed for the guilty. Eliot's *Adam Bede* is a classic text which connects clear-eyed realism about sin and suffering with an account of the possibility of these practices.

However, classic texts generate multiple readings.[1] Eliot's first full-length novel is no exception. These readings differ on how the plot is shaped and centered, which character (if any) is the subject of the book, what problems Eliot had to resolve to complete the text, and what the significance of the book is. Yet construing *Adam Bede* as a communicative action makes possible a reading which goes beyond these interpretations. Its "happy ending," alleged to disfigure the text, is necessary to show the depths of unacknowledged, unconfessed, unforgiven, and permanent evil. Its author, a brilliant woman who had 'retired from' the evangelical religion of her youth, has insights not only into misery and evil, suffering and sin, but also into a way to the good of reconciliation. Or so this chapter argues.

## The Methodist and the Murderess

Hetty Sorrel is a farm girl, living with the family of her Uncle Poyser on the Donnithorne estate in Hayslope, supervised in her dairy by an incessantly grousing aunt for whom even a sunny day is an ill omen.[2] Eliot describes Hetty's extraordinary beauty: "There are various orders of beauty, causing men to make fools of themselves in various styles, from the desperate to the sheepish; but here is one order of beauty which seems made to turn the heads not only of men, but of all intelligent mammals, even of women . . . a beauty with which you can never be angry, but that you feel ready to crush for inability to comprehend the state of mind into which it throws you. Hetty Sorrel's was that sort of beauty" (1859:90). Her professed aim in life is to become a lady's maid, so she leaves the house to take lessons in darning. Her fantasy is to become a lady—which to her means to be waited upon in carefree splendor, to wear fine clothes all the time, and not to work under her Aunt Poyser's nagging direction. Eliot draws Hetty in a way that does not evoke the reader's sympathy. She highlights the fact that Hetty's temptations are not sexual. Hetty wants at least the imagined soft and luxurious life of a lady or possibly "social glamour and power" (Auerbach 1982:174).

Arthur Donnithorne, the son and heir, is one of the many whom Hetty has smitten with a half-coquettish glance. He makes her promise to give him two dances at his upcoming twenty-first birthday celebration, when all classes from gentry to peasantry from throughout the fertile valley will come together for a fête. His attention has churned "Hetty's little, silly imagination" (105). She comes to hope that Arthur will marry her. But Arthur *is* smitten—and knows that he must not see her again, or he will fall fully in love (136). He thinks of going away, but meets her the next time she is alone in the wood. He responds to her crying:

> "You little frightened bird! little tearful rose! silly pet! You won't cry again, now I'm with you, will you?" Ah, he does not know in the least what he is saying. This is not what he meant to say. His arm is stealing round the waist again, it is tightening its clasp; he is bending his face nearer and nearer to the round cheek, his lips are meeting those pouting child-lips, and for a long moment time has vanished. He may be a shepherd in Arcadia, for aught he knows; he may be the first youth kissing the first maiden; he may be Eros himself, sipping the lips of Psyche,—it is all one (139).

Arthur flies homeward, appalled with himself for being so possessed as to give in to the madness of flirting with a dairymaid on his estate.

Hetty flutters back to the Poysers. While readying herself for bed, she admires herself in the mirror, places an old lace scarf on her shoulders and large earrings in her ears, and allows her fantasies and vanities free rein in the privacy of her room. A knock on the door jolts her to reality. She fears it is her aunt Poyser who castigates her vanity and knows her self-centeredness (159). But it is her aunt's niece, Dinah Morris.

Dinah is a "Methody." She is visiting Hayslope from neighboring (and less prosperous) Snowfield, that June of 1799, to preach repentance, not like a "Ranter," but from her own deep emotions and her own "simple faith" (38). She is a comely redhead, sensitive to the feelings of everyone she meets. Her eyes had "no peculiar beauty, beyond that of expression; they looked so simple, so candid, so gravely loving, that no accusing scowl, no light sneer could help melting away before their glance" (34). When a simple journeyman carpenter, Seth Bede, proposes gallantly to her after her preaching, she responds that if there were any she were called to marry, it would be he, but she cannot. "I seem to have no room in my soul for wants and fears of my own, it has pleased God to fill my heart so full with the wants and suffering of his poor people" (45). Dinah can make no home in this world. They part, after Seth has walked her to the Poysers, with Seth saying, "'There's no knowing but what you may see things different after a while. There may be a new leading.' 'Let us leave that, Seth. It's good to live only a moment at a time, as I've read in one of Mr. Wesley's books. It isn't for you and me to lay plans; we've nothing to do but to obey and to trust. Farewell.'" (46) Both Dinah and Seth seem credulous. Yet each has sublime feelings of faith, hope, and charity (48). Both Seth and the Anglican pluralist, Parson Irwine, accept her goodness fully and are reconciled to her preaching—which might vex each of them for rather different reasons—because of her powerful sense of vocation and her ability.

Dinah is a riddle to Hetty. Nonetheless, Hetty likes Dinah because Dinah does much of Hetty's work when Dinah visits the Poysers' house. Yet Hetty never listens when Dinah talks in a "serious way" to her. "Hetty looked at her in the same way as one might imagine a little, perching bird that could only flutter from bough to bough, to look at the swoop of the swallow or the mounting of the lark; but she did not care to solve such riddles" (143).

Dinah's meditations lead her to believe that God is calling her to Hetty, whose self-devotion and shallowness she clearly sees and whose loneliness and distress she sympathetically imagines. When she enters Hetty's room, Hetty appears "confused and vexed" (159).

Dinah tells Hetty that she had a feeling that Hetty would some day be in trouble. If Hetty would "need a friend that will always feel for you and love you, you have got that friend in Dinah Morris at Snowfield; and if you come to her or send for her, she'll never forget this night and the words she is speaking to you now" (160). At this remarkable pledge, Hetty feels only fear: "Why do you come to frighten me? I've never done anything to you. Why can't you let me be?" (161)

Eventually, the inappropriate 'flirtation' between the son of the manse and the dairymaid is discovered by Arthur's longtime friend, the master carpenter Adam Bede. All admit that Adam is the best man in the neighborhood. But Adam is a "hard" man, uncompromising in principle, who has been infatuated with Hetty since her arrival. Arthur, called out and beaten unconscious by Adam, 'repents' of his erring ways and joins the army.[3] Hetty acquiesces to the love-blinded Adam's proposal of marriage. Her passions and fantasies had been her life, and when they were drowned by Arthur's departure, a dreary life of marriage to a 'mere' country craftsman seemed all that was left for her. But to her friends' and relatives' consternation, she disappears.

Hetty is obsessed with seeking Arthur. She begins a journey in hope of finding him, but her journey in hope turns, literally, into a journey of despair when she must abandon finding him. The faithful Adam begins a quest to find her, but she is nowhere to be found. The next time the reader sees Hetty, she is in prison in Stoniton. She has been convicted of murdering her newborn baby!

Eliot renders Hetty in prison as speechless. She even writes of Hetty exclusively in the third person. Not only does Hetty say nothing about the crime and remain "sullen," but she is never even addressed, save when the judge sentences her to death. Even when the verdict is given, her scream is depicted by the narrator, not performed by Hetty. She faints.

As soon as Arthur returns, he opens a letter which informs him that the dairymaid he seduced has murdered the child he had fathered. He rushes off, apparently to Stoniton. But he does not return to the narrative until the last moment.

Dinah has also been traveling. As soon as she learns of the situation, she rushes to Hetty, begs admission to the gaol, and agrees to stay the night in the cell with Hetty.[4]

> "Hetty . . . Dinah is come to you." After a moment's pause, Hetty lifts her head slowly and timidly from her knees, and raises her eyes. The two pale faces were looking at each other,—one a wild, hard despair in it; the other full of sad, yearning love.

This is the key scene: a squalid cell, a hopeless and speechless infanticide, and a 'Methody' woman preacher.[5]

Dinah asks Hetty if she recognizes her or thought she would not come when Hetty was in trouble. Dinah says, "I'm come to be with you, Hetty—not to leave you—to stay with you—to be your sister to the last." They clasp, they do not speak. Eventually, Hetty responds:

> "Yes, . . . But you can do nothing for me. You can't make 'em do anything. They'll hang me o' Monday—it's Friday now." . . .
> "No, Hetty I can't save you from that death. But isn't the suffering less hard when you have somebody with you that feels for you,—that you can speak to, and say what's in your heart? . . . Yes, Hetty; you lean on me; you are glad to have me with you."
> "You won't leave me, Dinah? You'll keep close to me?"
> "No, Hetty, I won't leave you. I'll stay with you to the last . . . But, Hetty, there is someone else in this cell besides me, some one close to you."
> "Who?"

But when Dinah talks of God, Hetty changes the subject: "Oh, Dinah, won't nobody do anything for me? *Will* they hang me for certain? . . . I wouldn't mind if they'd let me live." Dinah acknowledges Hetty's dread and continues, "If you could believe [God] loved you and would help you, as you believe I love you and will help you, it wouldn't be so hard to die on Monday, would it?" But Hetty says she "can't know anything about it." Dinah says that Hetty is keeping God out, urges her to cast off her sin which is the block against God's healing, and concludes:

> "Let us kneel down together, for we are in the presence of God."
> Hetty obeyed Dinah's movement, and sank on her knees. They still held each other's hands, and there was a long silence. Then Dinah said, "Hetty, we are before God; he is waiting for you to tell the truth."
> Still there was silence. At last Hetty spoke, in a tone of beseeching,—
> "Dinah . . . help me . . . I can't feel anything like you . . . my heart is hard."
> Dinah held the clinging hand, and all her soul went forth in her voice. . . .

And Dinah prayed for Hetty, a prayer that God act to rescue her, if he would only move before it is too late, a prayer of her own deep faith, a prayer of her own inability to help. And Hetty then confesses her confusion, her despair, her fear, her weakness, her act of burying her newborn child, her return to the scene, and her continually hearing the ceaseless crying of the dead child, even after the body had been found and taken away.

Hetty was silent; but she shuddered again, as if there was still something behind; and Dinah waited, for her heart was so full that tears must come before words. At last Hetty burst out, with a sob,—"Dinah, do you think God will take away that crying and the place in the wood, now I've told everything?"

"Let us pray, poor sinner; let us fall on our knees again and pray to the God of all mercy."

Eventually, Hetty and Adam confront each other with Dinah present. Hetty requests Adam to forgive her for deceiving him. He responds that he forgave her long ago. He weeps.

Hetty made an involuntary movement towards him; some of the love that she had once lived in the midst of was come near her again. She kept hold of Dinah's hand; but she went up to Adam and said timidly,—"Will you kiss me again, Adam, for all I've been so wicked?"

Adam took the blanched wasted hand she put out to him, and they gave each other the solemn, unspeakable kiss of a lifelong parting.

"And tell him[Arthur]," Hetty said, in rather a stronger voice, "tell him . . . for there's nobody else to tell him . . . as I went after him and couldn't find him . . . and I hated him and cursed him once . . . but Dinah says I should forgive him . . . and I try . . . for else God won't forgive me."

And they go on praying until at the last moment Arthur arrives with a pardon from death, but at the price of Hetty's being transported. Dinah remains with Hetty until she leaves, but Hetty's story is apparently over. We only hear of her in the epilogue. By then Dinah is joyously married to Adam, and Seth appears as the happy bachelor uncle of their children. Dinah merely mentions in passing that Hetty died as she struggled to make her way back to Hayslope.

## Speaking to Give Voice to the Voiceless

The conversation in the prison between Dinah and Hetty is the centerpiece of *Adam Bede*. To account for it requires understanding the discourse practice which empowers the silenced to speak. To understand what Dinah does is not merely to analyze rules she implicitly or explicitly knows and applies. Dinah does not merely "apply rules" nor does she somehow dispose Hetty to act in accordance with rules. Rather, she engages in a creative communicative and emancipative praxis.

The scene of Dinah and Hetty's interactions may remind one of the interactions of the prisoner and Lady Philosophy in Boethius's

*Consolation*. Eliot and Boethius both create worlds in which the prison is central. Like Boethius's prisoner, Hetty was incarcerated and silent, but the similarity ends there. The prisoner portrays himself as innocent; Hetty is guilty. The prisoner, like Boethius himself, was a serious intellectual, a civil servant and scholar; Hetty a shallow dairymaid. Lady Philosophy could use the prisoner's memory, voice, and forgotten wisdom to resolve his basic problem (and Boethius's text can function as a script for others to resolve analogous problems). At the beginning of Eliot's prison scene, Hetty displays no memory, voice or wisdom for Dinah to educate. Boethius's prisoner was alone and needed only an allegorical figure to activate his memory and help him find his proper voice; Hetty badly needed a real flesh-and-blood friend, if she were to become human enough to *have* a life story. Like Lady Philosophy, Dinah had wisdom, diagnostic ability, and compassion. But Dinah had no poisonous voice to silence. She had to enable Hetty to remember so Hetty could speak. To do so, Dinah had to make the diagnosis and commit herself to participating in the therapy. Finally, Dinah's purposes were different from Lady Philosophy's: she did not need to bring her patient to contemplation, but to enable her to have a life by performing the act of confessing.[6] In short, the conditions and the personal qualities of Dinah and Hetty are such that they could not have interacted as the prisoner and Lady Philosophy did. Indeed, it is even difficult to imagine how they could have acted otherwise than they did if Hetty is to be enabled to speak.

Making explicit each specific speech act performed in the conversation between Dinah and Hetty brings out how these acts are chained together. Their interaction reveals the shape of a discourse practice of empowerment. When Dinah comes to the prison cell, she is not trying merely to inform or direct Hetty, but to enable Hetty to perform the complex assertive declaration of confession. Dinah begins by coming into the cell unexpectedly, announcing herself (hybrid assertive-directive) and asking Hetty leading questions (directive). Hetty remains silent, gazing on Dinah's face "like an animal that gazes, and gazes, and keeps aloof." To this point Dinah has done nothing that affects Hetty.

Dinah begins to shift their relationship by pledging (commissive) herself to "be your sister to the last." As noted in Part 1, a speaker must have specific position, ability, or relationship to perform some speech acts successfully. To make this sort of commitment, a commitment until death (or as it turns out, the social death of deportation), Dinah must have a quality that can be called the virtue of constancy.[7] The whole novel displays Dinah's constancy, a virtue so deep in her, that even when she turns down Seth Bede's marriage proposal, he is not hurt by it, for he sees Dinah's constancy in her fidelity to her vocation.

Dinah can recall in the gaol her earlier pledge to Hetty and show her that she has been constant. Of course, a chaplain might drop in and promise to stay with her to the end, but there is little possibility of Hetty seeing him as being able to make the same sort of commitment that Dinah made.[8] Being, and being perceived as, a person of constancy are necessary conditions for making such a commitment successfully. Without constancy, a person cannot make a commitment, but only a bargain. Without the speaker's appearing constant, the addressee cannot accept the commitment and act on it subsequently.

Dinah again asks Hetty if she recognizes her (directive) and recalls her promise (hybrid assertive-commissive) to Hetty. Dinah's initial actions set the tone for the scene. She both creates an atmosphere in which Hetty can respond to her by her initial recall of her earlier promise and directs Hetty to answer by asking her questions. In effect, her verbal and physical actions create conditions in which Hetty can also act.

Hetty finally speaks. She says (assertive) that Dinah is impotent to help her. Dinah acknowledges (assertive) the limits of her power, but also points out (hybrid assertive-commissive) that there is something else she could do for Hetty: to stay with her. Hetty must come to recognize Dinah's commitment to her, as Hetty's request for reassurance (directive) presumes Dinah's commitment. Dinah affirms her commitment (hybrid assertive-commissive) and asserts (assertive) that someone is present, an assertion seemingly false, as they are alone in the cell.

Most of Hetty's initial responses to Dinah seem "nonresponsive." But finally, Hetty does respond to this apparently false and surprising assertion by asking (directive) who is present, but when Dinah testifies to God's presence (assertive), Hetty changes the subject to her death and the fact that no one will help (assertive, and implied refusal to accept Dinah's testimony).

At this point Dinah has heard and seen enough, for she then diagnoses (assertive declaration) Hetty's problem as hardness of heart. A diagnosis is a declaration in that it labels a patient as having a disease. As with other declarations, giving a diagnosis ipso facto alters the subject of the declaration. The diagnosis makes the patient be treated as having the disease diagnosed. A diagnosis is flawed if what it asserts to be so is not so. A misdiagnosis results in mistreating the patient. To remedy a misdiagnosis and to counteract its consequences requires that a healer give a new, supervening diagnostic declaration.

To render a diagnosis requires not merely a skill of applying a rule to a situation nor a skill of inferring hidden causes from visible evidence. Diagnosis is neither deduction nor induction, but an exercise of practical wisdom, Aristotle's *phronesis*.[9] To diagnose also presumes that the relationship between the speaker and hearer is that (or is like that) of physician and patient. The diagnostician's relationship with the patient gives her a status that enables her to perform this declaration. As a physician of the soul, Dinah has exactly the abilities and status necessary to diagnose. Parson Irwine recognized it, Seth and Adam Bede recognized it, and the magistrate who admitted her to the jail recognized it: "I know you have a key to unlock hearts" (423). Presumably, her involvement in the intense interaction of late eighteenth century Wesleyan groups gave her the skills to engage in the practices of preaching and spiritual diagnosis and therapy. Thus, constancy and practical wisdom are virtues necessary for performing speech acts of commitment and diagnosis. Performing those two acts effectively is necessary for Dinah to perform her next acts properly.

Like the prisoner who could not utter his "self-diagnosis" in *The Consolation of Philosophy*, Hetty is not in position to utter her own diagnosis. Neither had the ability to speak at that point. The prisoner's diagnosis (I pr 2) is given by the narrator, Hetty's by Dinah. Unlike the prisoner, who had merely to remember his skill at the prompting of Lady Philosophy to resolve his problem, Hetty needed Dinah to empower her to overcome her disease.

Dinah then urges Hetty to confess (directive) and issues Hetty an invitation (hybrid commissive-directive) to kneel with her. This invitation cannot be fully understood either as an attempt to get Hetty to kneel or as committing Dinah to kneel. Dinah performed the act of kneeling—Eliot has Hetty respond to her movement. She was not directing Hetty to kneel alone. This invitation has the force of both a commissive and a directive. This hybrid illocutionary act includes in its contextual conditions the fully successful accomplishment of the previous two acts, those of commitment and diagnosis. Dinah's kneeling concretizes her commitment to be with Hetty and begins the 'therapy' based on her diagnosis, a therapy designed to enable Hetty to act.

Dinah must communicate to Hetty her understanding of Hetty's suffering and her own commitment to share in it as a presence if Hetty is to recognize Dinah's act. While a pious Ranter (or a prison chaplain or Pastor Irwine) could *direct* Hetty to confess, as Dinah also did earlier, it is not clear that they would be in position to *invite* Hetty as Dinah did. Their vision of her and their consequent commitments to her would be significantly different. Perhaps a Ranter would see an invisible soul to save, a chaplain yet another prisoner to be ministered to, and Irwine a baffling creature beyond his ability to help. Such people could issue directives, but not the powerful invitation Dinah gave.

Similarly, a person who had not succeeded in making a diagnosis could surely issue this commissive, offering to remain and pray. But it is just the weakness of such a "do-gooder" that he could not be in position vis-à-vis Hetty to give the correct complex directive-commissive that would begin to enable Hetty to resolve her problem of voicelessness. While a do-gooder might stumble by luck on to the right strategy, including a commitment to be present to Hetty in her suffering, she could not prescribe treatment of a disease, for she would not have diagnosed the disease, and to prescribe a remedy presumes the previous diagnosis of a disease. In short, the complex act of invitation Dinah performed, with its multiple illocutionary forces, presumes the success of the previous acts of diagnosis and commitment. And Hetty accepts the invitation by kneeling.

Dinah then exhorts Hetty to confess (hybrid assertive-directive). Hetty is now able to request (directive) Dinah's help to do something she cannot do by herself—to feel what Dinah can, to confess. Dinah's commitment and diagnosis make it possible for Hetty to request Dinah's help. Because Dinah has performed those actions, Dinah shows herself to Hetty as a person who can help her, a person wise and constant enough to be a person who can answer this request. A contextual condition for a speaker to make a request is a presumption that the hearer can fulfill the request (cf. p. 57 above and Searle 1969:66). Hence, Dinah's successful performance of the earlier speech acts and her fulfilling the commitments she made are necessary for the occurrence of Hetty's act that begins Hetty's empowerment: her request for help. And as Dinah had to have the virtues of practical wisdom and constancy to perform those speech acts effectively, it follows that Dinah had to have those virtues to enable Hetty to make her request.

Dinah then prays—a powerful prayer of demanding petition (Eliot renders it starkly) to an adored God who bears the marks of agony, encompasses the petitioners, and will rouse Hetty's dead soul so she can confess. Her prayer seems almost a command to God: "'thou wilt not let her perish forever.'" But her directive act also has multiple forces. Its ostensive addressee is God, but Hetty is also part of the intended audience. As with the act of confession (cf. pp. 76-77), to be effective, this prayer may require not only that God hear it, but that others also hear it. Dinah's prayer presumes both her religious commitment and her belief in the God she addresses. But she also must expect that Hetty will "overhear" the prayer.

Hence, the prayer is also a directive to Hetty, but has a different force for her because Dinah's relationship to her is different from Dinah's relationship to God. As shown in chapter 2, a directive intended to be heard by audiences in different relationships to the speaker can have multiple forces. And, indeed, it must have been effective, for as Dinah finishes, Hetty not only speaks, but acquires a narrative voice in performing her own confession. One may assume that God answered Dinah's prayer and moved Hetty's soul. Or one may attribute causal efficacy to Dinah. In either case, Dinah's prayer was an effective directive. Dinah's (not anybody's) successful acts of commitment, diagnosis, and prayer enable Hetty to perform the act that can resolve her situation: her confession.

Hetty confesses (assertive declaration). This is the key. All the other acts (and possibly the entire novel to this point) lead to it. As Carlisle puts it, "Hetty's confession is one of those rare experiences that Adam describes to the narrator in chapter 17. It is a time 'when feelings come into you like a rushing mighty wind, as the Scripture says, and part your life in two a'most, so as you look back on yourself as if you was somebody else'" (1981:212). In confessing before God, Hetty did what Augustine did in his *Confessions*. As Augustine surveyed his life and claimed both the good and the evil he had done as his own, so Hetty narrated her own story as her own. As chapter 3 showed, this act cannot be reduced to a historical report of what happened. It is an institutionally free assertive declaration. It both presumes that the content of the utterance is factually accurate and makes Hetty a new person. The fit between act and the rest of the world is bidirectional: Hetty becomes who she says she is.

As with Augustine's confession, the conditions for performing it are complex. Hetty must come to see things in such a way that she can "own" the acts she performed. She must abandon her vanities, her self-absorption, and the protection of her "little, silly imagination." She must go through what the gospels call metanoia (a reorientation of one's life away from self and to God). The results of performing it are also important. Hetty becomes a person able to ask forgiveness (of Adam, whom she had betrayed and abandoned, and by extension, perhaps, of her family). She can accept consolation from those who care for her even though they know her. She can try to forgive Arthur. However, this does not mean that she must lose her fear and become confident or become so equanimous that she no longer suffers. As William James observed, even the soul healed by conversion may often still bear the marks of its fractures (1901:158-59). Hetty's difficulty with forgiving Arthur attests that the healing is not perfect. Hetty's confession starts her on the road to becoming a new character.[10]

Having made her confession, which has sorted things out and made her hear—and tell—what had happened, the formerly silent and sullen Hetty can now finally express (expressive) her pain, grief, and remorse. She is in position, for the first time, to have feelings to express, rather than merely to remain sullen. Because she has put them into a narrative through her confession, she can identify acts and events. Only now can she respond expressively to them, for only now are they hers.

That "crying and the place in the woods" which evoke her feelings could be alluding to the deed she had owned up to. She could be recalling her haunted feeling. She could mean her own feeling of inability (part of her confession) to move physically or spiritually when she had returned to the scene of the crime. She could be recalling the baby she had abandoned to die. Perhaps it is all of these. But had she not come to own her life and deeds in confessing, it would have been impossible for Hetty to have had and express these—or any—feelings about things other than her small vanities and fantasies.

Dinah responds by renewing her invitation to pray—for now the answers to Hetty's questions can become clear. Dinah again invites (hybrid directive-commissive) Hetty to join her in prayer as the scene ends.

Later in the story, Hetty begs (hybrid directive-commissive) Adam's forgiveness, accepts his bittersweet forgiveness (declaration), and she tries to forgive (declaration) Arthur. Interestingly, forgiving is yet another institutionally free declarative: when the aggrieved party properly says that the offender is forgiven, that makes the offender forgiven. Hetty is now able to beg Adam to forgive her—she has become a person who can ask for forgiveness, who can allow someone to change her. Her confession has enabled her to want to be and to become a forgiving and forgiven person, a person who can act effectively.

In short, Hetty had been ground down by all the forces of evil. Her pettiness, Arthur's violation of her, the (self-imposed?) ostracism from the stable society of Hayslope, and her abandoning (or murdering) her baby had made her less than human. Her animal-like gaze on Dinah's face suggests that she had become "de-natured," as portrayed by Boethius (cf. pp. 155-57 above). Dinah had the virtues of courage and wisdom, and the established relationship with Hetty, to be able to engage in a discourse practice necessary and sufficient to allow Hetty to overcome her affliction and become human again. Dinah's speech acts were powerful enough to give voice to the voiceless. But what makes Eliot's work ring true is that this resolution does not mean that all the evils are redeemed or "undone."

## *"It Can Never Be Undone"*

When a sickened, weakened, distraught, and impotent Adam Bede is told that Hetty will not see him before the trial, Adam is angry: he looks for vengeance on Arthur from a just God. Adam accuses the Rev. Mr. Irwine of not minding that Arthur does not know of, and is not suffering because of, Hetty's disgrace. Irwine responds:

> "Adam, he *will* know—he *will* suffer, long and bitterly. He has a heart and a conscience: I can't be entirely deceived in his character. I am convinced—I am sure he didn't fall under temptation without a struggle. He may be weak, but he is not callous, not coldly selfish. I am persuaded that this will be a shock of which he will feel the effects all his life. Why do you crave vengeance in this way? No amount of torture that you could inflict on *him* could benefit *her*."
>
> "No—O God, no," Adam groaned out, sinking on his chair again; "but then, that's the deepest curse of all . . . that's what makes the blackness of it . . . *it can never be undone*. My poor Hetty . . . she can never be my sweet Hetty again . . . the prettiest thing God made—smiling up at me . . . I thought she loved me . . . and was good . . ." (401-2).

But *what* can never be undone? Adam, whose "voice had been gradually sinking into a hoarse undertone, as if he were only talking to himself" (402), is apparently referring to Hetty's seduction by Arthur, a rival he could never outshine in "sweet Hetty's" eyes.

But no act can ever be "undone." To assert that an act did not happen would be a lie. To declare it undone or not what it was is either an illocutionary impossibility or an effacement of the reality of the past. Performing such a declaration would be the creation of a falsehood, a maximally deceptive or self-deceptive act.

One of the acts that can never be undone is Hetty's act of confession. It made her a "new person." That person could never be Adam's "sweet Hetty." But Adam was not quite right in saying that Hetty "will never be his sweet Hetty *again*." Even before her infatuation with Arthur she was not his sweet Hetty. Adam didn't see her straight before or after her fall.

Later, Adam responds to a suggestion that good would come out of the evil and that he would rise above it all and be a man again:

"Good come out of it!" said Adam passionately. "That doesn't alter th' evil: *her* ruin can't be undone. I hate that talk o' people, as if there was a way o' making amends for everything. They'd more need be brought to see as the wrong they do can never be altered. When a man's spoiled his fellow-creatur's life, he's no right to comfort himself with thinking good may come out of it. Somebody else's good doesn't alter her shame and misery" (434).

Adam's point is well taken. Nonetheless, even if the act which ruined her cannot be undone, and even if nothing can mend it, it is not clear that her ruin is irredeemable. Even though no act, including speech acts, can be undone, acts can be atoned for, repaid in kind, reacted to, resisted, thwarted, counteracted, retracted, repented of, discounted, undermined, etc.

Although her ruin can neither be undone nor justified as bringing about some good, and her confession cannot undo the evil, Hetty's confession "does something" about the evil. This raises moral questions, for if it is an assertive declaration which denies the reality of evil, then it is a truly self-deceptive, and perhaps diabolically wicked, declaration.

Like every other human act, speech acts have moral weight. They may be sincere or deceptive, performed for virtuous or vicious purposes, and have good or bad results.[11] That it may be difficult to evaluate those acts or to agree on whether a given act is morally right does not remove speech acts from the moral realm. If Job's comforters tortured him with their words and if God shamed and silenced him with words from the whirlwind, these verbal acts may not be "lies," but are still morally wrong. If Lady Philosophy 'trained' the prisoner's voice for a good purpose and with good results, these acts are morally right. If an author of Job used a text to warn readers away from what is good for them, that would be wrong. If Boethius scripted a text sufficient for readers in foreseeable contexts to engage in a practice that demeans or destroys them, that would be wrong.

The point is that both speech acts *within* texts and texts *as* communicative acts are open to moral evaluation. If Dinah induced Hetty into a confession which constituted her as a necessarily self-deceived person, her action would be truly vicious. If Eliot's text advocates such action, her directive would also be vicious. What is the moral status of these actions?

First, speech acts are presumed to be "sincere" in that they express a disposition a speaker has (compare Searle and Vanderveken

1985:18-20 and note 9). A speaker is deceptive just in case he expresses a disposition (belief, attitude, intention, etc.) he does not
have; his speech act is deceptive. If a person promises what she
does not intend to do, asserts what she believes is not true, advises
what she believes is not in the hearer's interest, those acts are at
least prima facie morally wrong. A speech act is misleading (although
not necessarily intentionally so) just in case that its presumptions
can be shown to be incoherent. If a speaker advised a hearer in
saying "It would be right for you to murder your friend," that act
would be confused. It is implicitly self-contradictory in that
"murder" is "wrongful killing," and the speaker is in fact saying,
"It would be right for you to kill your friend wrongfully." If a
speaker attempts to perform a communicative act with incompatible
points, "I order you and forbid you to open the window," that act
misfires. If the speaker 'buries' two incompatible points in a speech
act, that act is confused or deceptive (Searle and Vanderveken
1985:143).

Dinah's commitment presumes that Dinah is a certain kind of
person, a person of constancy who keeps her commitments. It implies
that Hetty can trust her. It does not *assert* Dinah's virtue. Dinah
must also presume that Hetty does not expect Dinah to stay with
her. If she presumed otherwise, there would be no need to *act* to
commit herself. As a commissive, it also implies that she intends to
do what she promises. Given the text, Dinah's commissives are
morally correct.

Dinah's exhortation to Hetty ("Hetty, we are before God. He is
waiting for you to tell the truth.") not only directs Hetty to confess,
but also presumes that there is a God. As engaging in the practice
of confession presumes the reality of God, a directive to confess
shares that presumption. Dinah's invitation has both directive and
commissive force. The act presumes Dinah is the sort of person who
can give such an invitation, and that Hetty is in a position to accept
its direction. In all of these Dinah is not being deceptive. The question is whether her acts are confused because they have inconsistent
presumptions.

Dinah presumes that God is such that God is the proper audience
of prayer and confession.[12] Some of Hetty's acts also presume the
way things are. Her plea, for instance, presumes Dinah could answer
it. Hetty's expression of remorse presumes that she did what she has
remorse over. If she didn't do it, her remorse is deceptive, at best. If
she did not acknowledge that she did it, she could not express
remorse over it. In these cases, then, if the presumptions do not obtain
or are not presumed, Hetty's speech acts would be wrong or

misleading. Given the narrative, all these actions seem morally right, rather than deceptive or misleading or insincere.

Some of the actions performed do not presume, but assert, claims about the way the world is. These must "fit the world" in a more straightforward way to be epistemically proper. If a person performs an act with the assertive illocutionary point in certain situations, she may have to be able to justify not only holding her beliefs, but also performing her actions. She may have to be able to justify her claim. For instance, Dinah's first answer—that she cannot "save" Hetty, and her claim that knowing God's presence can make dying easier, are both simple straightforward assertives. Although a presumption of that action might not be fully justifiable—i.e., that there is a personal God—that would not render the assertions Dinah actually makes deceitful. Dinah asserts that she cannot save Hetty and that knowing God's presence (or believing in a saving God) can comfort some who are dying. These specific claims are surely not only justifiable, but empirically verifiable.

Dinah's diagnosis must also be accurate: Hetty must have "hardness of heart." Hetty must have been unable to feel or know God's presence. Hetty's request for Dinah's help implies that she accepted the diagnosis, as one cannot coherently ask for therapy for a disease one does not believe one has. Presumably, Dinah would have to be able to give her reasons for making the diagnosis she did, had she been challenged. But no one challenged her. Had Dinah intentionally misled Hetty as to her disease, her diagnosis would have been wicked since it would cause Hetty to be treated as, and to treat herself as, having a disease she did not have. Such a falsifying declaration would create a state of affairs which would change false claims into true ones, seemingly a remarkable sleight of hand trick, but actually a diabolical creation of falsehood. Dinah's diagnosis is not deceptive.

Hetty's most complex speech act is her confession. In uttering it she becomes what she describes. Even if she has gotten it wrong, she has declared who she is. Had Hetty, in her confession, denied what she had done or confessed "falsely," her confession would have been not only deceptive but self-deceptive, in that it would construct her "new self" in deception. Given the text, she has confessed truthfully.

Assertive declarations, if performed successfully, must be true. There can be no question of their truth or justifiability. Save where appeal to a higher authority results in a supervening declaration which undermines a questioned declaration, as a new diagnosis can undermine a previous one, a declarative makes itself true. Both

Dinah's diagnosis and Hetty's confession literally make truth: what–they–declare is what–is.

Dinah's exhortation initially was not successful. Hetty's request implies that she could not sense what Dinah exhorted her to sense: she couldn't sense God's presence, she couldn't do what Dinah directed her to do. Dinah's prayer would resolve her perplexity by making her aware of God's presence. Dinah's prayer would be effective even if it were deceptive. But is it deceptive? Clearly, Dinah was not attempting to deceive. She believed in God. Certainly, if God exists, one can be in God's presence and make oneself aware of that presence. But the fact that the presumption of God's existence is not proven does not make Dinah's communicative action deceptive. The problem—insoluble unless God's reality can be proven or disproven—is whether her successful and effective act was flawless. We cannot show either that all the conditions were met or that they were not. So we can't show that the act was misleading or that it was not. But further, unless Dinah had good reason to think that this condition was not met, Dinah is entitled to presume that it was met. Morally speaking, Dinah, and those in positions like hers, are in the clear.

It is important to note what Dinah and Hetty have not done. Neither ever *asserts* in this context any doctrine that promises "in the end, God will make it all well, so don't worry about the meantime." Neither Dinah nor Hetty ever *recommends* such a doctrine to others. Neither Dinah nor Hetty ever *promises* that such will be the case. As noted in the introduction, what is vicious about "pie in the sky by and by" doctrines is not their "content," but the acts performed in uttering such doctrines: Those in positions of institutional authority are able to take advantage of their positions to use doctrines of eschatological recompense for present suffering to maintain their power and control over a 'captive' audience, and even to silence the voice of the oppressed and afflicted by instilling a dubious hope for postmortem reward. In sum, although some acts performed in talking of God and the justification of suffering are immoral, there is no reason to think that either Dinah's or Hetty's actions are anything other than truly virtuous.

But even if their acts do not appear deceptive, their purposes may be vicious or virtuous. That Dinah's purpose in coming to Hetty was to enable or induce her to confess is clear. As she begs entry to the prison from the magistrate, she reveals it: "Oh sir, it may please God to open her heart still. Don't let us delay" (423). Her verbal and physical acts fit it: she prays that "the eyes of the blind be opened. Let her see that God encompasses her; let her tremble at nothing but at the sin that cuts her off from him. Melt the hard heart; unseal the closed lips. Make her cry with her whole soul, 'Father, I have sinned'" (428). Dinah's prayer is answered. Her acts achieve her purpose: Hetty confesses.

Moreover, Dinah bears a heavy burden of responsibility for Hetty's confession. At the beginning of the prison scene, Hetty could not have had *any* purposes at all before Dinah arrived. Eliot's rendering her voiceless and portraying her only in the third person show this. Yet once she speaks, she evidently wants Dinah to save her from death. That's not possible. Her subsequent request indicates she wants Dinah to support her. But Dinah believes her support insufficient and testifies to Someone who will support Hetty even through death. In response to Dinah's testimony, she changes the subject and refuses to accept it. Dinah then brings her to acknowledge God by portraying her own care and support as a sign of God's care. She tells Hetty she must confess to receive not the consolation she wants from Dinah, but the support she needs from God. Finally, Hetty comes to want to be saved not from the evil that is to be inflicted on her for her misdeeds, but the evil that threatens to be an unending torment to her: "Dinah, do you think God will take away that crying and the place in the wood, now I've told everything?" Dinah responds, "Let us pray, poor sinner. Let us fall on our knees again, and pray to the God of all mercy."

Dinah's purpose was not to silence Hetty's complaint or to force her to "repent" as Job "repented." Rather, she sought to give a voice to the voiceless, to empower a woman, whose terrible afflictions rendered her mute, to speak. Once Hetty declares her *self* and in so doing owns her deeds, she can face that evil, have and express feelings about it, live with it, and die with it. She does not efface it. Not even God can annihilate that evil. *"It can never be undone."* But Hetty can live with it and perhaps in some way God can counteract it. Ultimately, Hetty comes to have the purpose simply to be forgiven—indicated by her asking Adam's forgiveness and her trying to forgive Arthur.

Dinah enables Hetty not only to act so as to achieve the purpose she has for Hetty, but also to move Hetty from having inchoate 'desires' of escape and denial to wanting acceptance and forgiveness in solidarity with her Hayslope family and community. Dinah's purposes for Hetty are to enable Hetty to do the best she can imagine for her, given the situation. In sum, her purposes are virtuous: she acts to enable Hetty to do the best she can.

We also must consider the results of their actions. Given the situation, could Dinah have done better for Hetty? The results she sought and achieved were for Hetty to be able to claim herself in her irreparably miserable situation. What could she have done that would enable Hetty to come out better? Break her out of jail? What could Hetty have done better? Kill herself? She is able to "try" to forgive the man who dallied with her and to accept the death she expects to be imminently hers.

It is also important to note that neither narrator nor characters have sugar-coated the bitter pill the sufferer must swallow. The narrator (and author?) voices the following:

> That is a base and selfish, even a blasphemous spirit, which rejoices and is thankful over the past evil that has blighted or crushed another, because it has been made a source of unforeseen good to ourselves. Adam could never cease to mourn over that mystery of human sorrow which had been brought so close to him; he could never thank God for another's misery. And if I were capable of that narrow-sighted joy in Adam's behalf, I should still know he was not the man to feel it for himself; he would have shaken his head at a such a sentiment and said: "Evil's evil, and sorrow's sorrow; and you can't alter its natur' by wrapping it up in other words. . . ."
>
> But it is not ignoble to feel that the fuller life which a sad experience has brought us is worth our own personal share of pain. Surely it is not possible to feel otherwise, any more than it would be possible for a man with a cataract to regret the painful process by which his dim blurred sight of men as trees walking had been exchanged for clear outline and effulgent day. The growth of higher feeling within us is like the growth of a faculty, bringing with it a sense of added strength (498-99).

*Adam Bede* recognizes, then, that there is a sort of evil which cannot be made up for or undone (cf. 402, 434, 441). Clearly, the resolution proposed in Eliot's text is not a facile consolatory dream. The characters do not, as do some Christians, disguise real evils as hidden or partial goods. In short, Dinah acted as well as a person of practical wisdom could in that situation. Her actions are as epistemically justifiable as they need be and morally praiseworthy.[13]

"Evil's evil, and sorrow's sorrow; and you can't alter its natur' by wrapping it up in other words. . . ." Confession is the act that recognizes the truth in those words, words curiously given by Eliot not to the voice of Adam Bede, but to the narrator who then attributes them to Adam. Removing those words which would fit most naturally in Adam's mouth suggests that these are not merely Adam's view, nor the narrator's incidental view, but moved by the author from one voice to another for a purpose—in this case, why else than to suggest her own authorial view? But if that is so, then she also presents confession as a practice not merely enabling the evildoer to recognize the evil, to own it, and to grieve over it without denying its viciousness, but also to return to the human community again, to become human.

One form of appropriate consolation to a suffering person guilty of an act which results in genuine and irreversible evil, would be a friendship that enables the sinner to acknowledge the evil as her or his own. Nothing can reverse the evil. Nothing should efface it. But confession can arrest the rot which has infected and corrupted the "sinner's" humanity. And insofar as a friend provides the help necessary to enable the sinner to perform the assertive declaration that is a true confession, that action is morally praiseworthy.

But the curious placing of those words in the narrator's voice suggests that more is at issue than merely resolving Hetty's evil.

## On Writing for Victims

Hetty Sorrel is a victim. She is victimized at least by her own vain fantasies and by Arthur Donnithorne, who was "no doubt more guilty than Hetty for the child's existence" (Liddell 1977:48). She is victimized in a family and society powerless to enable her to become a self sufficiently developed to own up to what she has become. The novel's early "rhetoric forbids the reader to like Hetty" (Auerbach 1982:174). Hetty is too shallow a character to evoke a reader's initial sympathy. Yet she is ultimately "the character for whom [Eliot] would demand the reader's closest attention and most wide-ranging sympathy" (Carlisle 1981:211). Indeed, close attention reveals that Hetty did not so much murder her child "as abandon it to nature. Without human care, without society, the child will die, as we say, 'of exposure'" (Fisher 1981:49). Hetty also suffers from exposure on her journey and from the isolation that living in fantasy creates. Eliot's rhetoric invalidates "any conventional response to Hetty and her actions. As she is reduced to the level of her physical reality—no more a responsible agent than a child or an animal—the reader is invited to see her plight primarily in its physical terms" (Carlisle 1981:208). Even Hetty's abandoning her child is an act of one so victimized and abject as to be "de-natured," no longer humanly able to be responsible for her life or act.

Hetty seems to fill the role of a surrogate victim, a scapegoat (compare Girard 1986), especially if her suffering is seen as key to the novel. For instance, Liddell suggests this when he writes that "Hetty's suffering has gone for very little, if a softening of Adam is all that is to come out of it" (1977:48). But this won't do, for her suffering does not resolve the problems of Hayslope.

Yet Hetty does carry the marks of a scapegoat in being a victim, not quite innocent, not fully a member of the society, physically marked as different from the others (by her beauty). She could carry all the evil of Hayslope society because she is declared guilty of crimes of sex and infanticide, crimes which undermine the basic stability of society. Executing her as a scapegoat (*pharmakos*) seems to be the medicine (*pharmakon*) which is the antidote for the poison (*pharmakon*) destroying society. The society, unbalanced by her crime, can be rebalanced by her death. Indeed, one might read the final book of *Adam Bede* as Eliot's portraying not merely the softening of Adam Bede, but just that rebalancing of society, the return to stability and order which the vicious scapegoating process is deceptively designed to ensure.

Yet this victim can confess her guilt and forgive her victimizer. No scapegoat either confesses or forgives. Hetty may be a sinner, but Eliot draws her as a person seduced into sin. Even if Hetty is legally guilty of infanticide, her moral guilt is hardly more than that of a child or animal. The incongruity of the *victim's* confession and forgiveness is too often overlooked. Ignoring it leads Carlisle to think that by "manipulating Hetty's fate, Arthur and his creator are given the sense that they can erase the consequences of events they have initiated." Eliot's ending the novel with the tranquility of Hayslope restored "casts doubt on the very perspectives she has so carefully developed" (1981:210), in which suffering is permanent, obscure, and dark (1981:209). Ignoring that a *victim* confesses leads Liddell to think Eliot has gotten herself into an impasse in which she cannot allow Hetty to die and must resort to a *deus ex machina* reprieve from Arthur (1977:42).

They miss the point. Eliot's novel subverts and rejects the myth of the scapegoat. Acts of violence against Hetty for her "unforgivable" crime do not "save" Hayslope from evil or its effects. It is not her "suffering" which is the medicine which cures. Rather, declarations of confession (which ipso facto remake the self) and forgiveness (which ipso facto restore relationships) are counteractions to evil. These do not declare undone an evil which can't be undone, but can redeem people from the destructive effects of that evil, insofar as those effects can be counteracted. It is not the victimized scapegoat which saves, but the declarations of confession and forgiveness which, if an agent performs them properly, deconstruct structures of victimization and reconstruct relationships and the selves who have performed those actions.

Hetty confesses, begs forgiveness, and at least tries to forgive even Arthur, who has primary responsibility for her fall. Chapter 48 narrates another scene in the same forest in which Adam beat Arthur into unconsciousness. Here Arthur confesses to Adam and reveals that he has become a new self unwilling to inflict more destruction on Hayslope by his presence. Adam, having forgiven Hetty, now can forgive Arthur not only in word, but in the deed of remaining in Hayslope to benefit that society. Adam confesses that he has been hard and reveals a new self: "God forbid I should make things worse for you. I used to wish I could do it. . . . I'll stay sir. I'll do the best I can. It's all I've got to think of now—to do my work well and make the world a bit better place for them as can enjoy it" (446). Arthur forgives Adam with a handclasp and Adam feels "that sorrow was more bearable now hatred was gone" (446).

If society is reconstructed, it is not through the magic potion of slaying scapegoat Hetty. Violent acts cannot reconcile. Effacing evils cannot reconcile. Declarations of confession and forgiveness which reinscribe the self and relationships among people can reconcile them. Eliot's story rejects scapegoating by showing that the suffering and death of scapegoats is not sufficient for reconciliation. Hetty is not alone. All are guilty. All must reinscribe their lives through confession. All are victims. All must forgive. "The time has come for us to forgive one another. If we wait any longer there will not be time enough" (Girard 1986:212). Dinah's enabling Hetty to confess and be forgiven is the communicative and emancipative praxis which starts the chain of social reconciliation in Hayslope.

Eliot's text does portray "the regeneration that is constant in social life" (Fisher 1981:63). But it demonstrates that the process of regeneration cannot be violent. It does teach the "'art of vision'" (Carlisle 1981:195). It shows the reader how to move beyond her initial perceptual limitations to a richer view. Not only does the text enlarge the readers' limits, but within the text, Adam, Arthur, and Hetty provide examples of transcending limits.

But it is also a deliberately ambivalent text which reveals the terrible depth of scapegoating. *Pace* Carlisle, Eliot does subtly and surely portray the permanency, obscurity, and darkness of suffering. For also at issue is an act which remains unowned, effaced, unconfessed, unforgiven, unreconciled. It is an action whose evil also can never be undone. It is an act which effaces the virtues and the practice of giving voice to the voiceless. It is the scapegoating perpetrated within the Christian communities. It is the continuing evil of silencing women, an evil which cannot be altered by wrapping it up in words. It is the social sin which disables a voice which brings reconciliation to a community.

Dinah is the agent who enables Adam, Arthur, and Hetty to move beyond their original limitations to their new vision. But Eliot also shows that Dinah is a victim in and of the Christian society which silences her powerful and regenerating voice, a voice which enabled the voiceless to speak. The ending of the novel may be "disfigured," but it is not a "happy ending." The ending makes the novel a high tragedy, a tragedy subtly woven through the surface happiness of the ending. It is a necessity to complete the novel, to portray the permanence of evil, for the ending which appears happy displays an unhealed and fatal wound in the society.

Dinah's marriage to Adam is not a failure of Eliot's artistry or merely an unhappy acceptance of her lover Lewes's suggestion for a 'happy ending.' Rather, its literary ugliness displays the evil of the convention which silenced women in the churches. Dinah is a victim of those who silence her. In a novel "centered so completely on the public spaces of society as *Adam Bede*" (Fisher 1981:39), Dinah is permitted after her marriage to act only in the private space of the home. Carpenter (1986) claims that Eliot portrays her as a prophet stripped of her proper role by the institutional powers. Another way to put it, more clearly licensed by the text, is to notice that Adam's mother on one Sabbath morning (cf. Chopp 1989:49) has envisioned her as just like the angel outside Jesus' tomb (470), who speaks in public to women of the greatest mystery of the resurrection, the ultimate symbol of reconciliation even in death. Adam's mother recognizes the power of Dinah's voice.

Yet the Methodist conference abrogates Dinah's power to announce the Good News in public. They reduce her to public silence. They take away her voice. In the epilogue, strategically deferred by Eliot to take place after the silencing of women preachers by the Methodists, Seth continues to advocate that they all leave the Wesleyans to join a church "that 'ud put no bonds on Christian liberty" (506). Adam says that Dinah was right to decide to stay, and Seth wrong. Even Adam now believes that "Most o' the women do more harm nor good with their preaching—they've not got Dinah's gift nor her sperrit." Like all those who would silence women in general, Adam neglects the fact that the same is true of men who are *not* silenced in general. And when Adam says that Dinah "thought it right to set th' example o' submitting," *Dinah says nothing*. "This was a standing subject of difference rarely alluded to, and Dinah, wishing to quit it at once," changed the subject. This recalls Hetty's changing the subject in response to Dinah's initial testimony in the gaol. Dinah's private home is now her gaol.

Hetty refused to accept Dinah's testimony then. This change of subject indicates that Dinah refuses to accept Seth's and Adam's words now. Carpenter has ingeniously pointed out parallels between Hetty's silencing and Dinah's: "we discover that women's prophecy is a black, silent pool, a moving emptiness, a lasting bitterness" (1986:52). As Hetty was the silenced victim, so Dinah is the victim of silencing. But Hetty had Dinah to speak powerfully to her. Dinah's speech enabled Hetty to confess and to forgive. That started a chain of reconciliation. But Dinah was the only character in the novel with the constancy and wisdom to speak with a voice which gives voice to the voiceless. Who can teach the silent to speak when the agent of reconciliation is forbidden to act? The enduring evil is not erased in the "happy ending," but remains in the silencing of the only agent who can engage in the creative discourse praxis necessary to regenerate society.

In the gaol, Dinah enabled Hetty to speak, to forgive. But now, in her happy gaol, no one enables Dinah to speak. She has been disabled by an act of the church. Dinah never even speaks of her silencing within her prison. Her silence is reflexive. She is a messenger of God, whether prophet or angel, silenced by those men and women who are inspired by Paul's silencing of women (1 Cor. 14:34). The church has made women scapegoats, imprisoning their voices in their homes, thinking that rendering them voiceless will remove evils from the public realm of the church. The denouement of *Adam Bede* is so dissatisfying not because Eliot's artistry failed, but because it has brilliantly succeeded: She shows Adam wrapping other words around that silencing. But his words can't alter the nature of that act. Its evil disfigures not only the story of *Adam Bede*, but the history of the Christian traditions. The obviousness of the "joy" in both conceals the enduring wickedness that undermines the possibility of making that divine joy a reality.

Both the form and the content of *Adam Bede* display not merely the re-creative power of confession and forgiveness, but also the destructive power of scapegoating, and the poison of victimization and its antidote. What makes it a classic is not merely that it discloses "a reality we cannot but name truth" (Tracy 1981:108), but, in speech act terms, it declares the truth. If readers recognize Eliot's power to make such a declaration,[14] that recognition empowers them to see the world anew and to hear new directions for acting in that world. The denouement to *Adam Bede* makes it clear that the churches have participated in scapegoating by silencing women, but had not then—and in many ways have not yet—begun the process of reconciliation by confessing such silencing and owning it as their own sinful practice. Until the churches change, the "happy ending" which "redeems" evil will be as phony and as ugly as the "happy ending" which "redeems" *Adam Bede*.

*Adam Bede* empowers its readers to recognize the evil of victimization and shows how to remedy it. All are victims. All are victimizers. All must confess victimization to stop it. All must forgive victimization to counteract it. But Eliot is not advocating the masochism of unconditional forgiveness or making victims take the blame for their victimization. Forgiveness and confession are necessarily correlated as the medicine for victimization, for forgiveness without confession endorses the unconfessed victimization; and confession without forgiveness recreates the conditions which begin the process of victimization. As the second meeting in the woods between Adam and Arthur illustrates, forgiveness and confession are mutual and correlative. Eliot's depiction of Dinah's silence even within her home suggests that Dinah is not yet able to forgive. And she neither can nor should forgive because the church has not confessed its act and owned the evil of silencing women.

But like all classics, *Adam Bede* is open to multiple readings, for it can be taken as a declaration in any "world" with structures or practices of victimization. It enables readers to recognize their own roles as victimizing victims by sympathizing with hardhearted Adam, frivolous Hetty, or weak-willed Arthur. But Eliot's text properly has different specific illocutionary forces depending on the context in which it is read, the purposes for which it is read, and the relationship the reader has with the author. As it has different forces, and illocutionary force is a constituent of meaning, the text not surprisingly has multiple meanings.

But all those forces can be brought together if one recognizes its central force as a declaration. As a declaration, it diagnoses and displays the varied poisons of victimization. It prescribes an antidote to the venomous practice of silencing the uncomfortably powerful voices of those messengers who would empower us to abandon those practices which make us victimizing victims and which promise relief from evils by creating scapegoats, victims whom we kill to efface the evils we have done. And it shows that evil's evil, and sorrow's sorrow, and you can't alter its nature by wrapping it up in other words. To wrap evils in good words is to hide their viciousness, to disguise their poison, to refuse to acknowledge the rot that eats at our humanity—in short, to engage in practices which reproduce evils. But recognizing such practices is difficult when voices like George Eliot's are silenced by those who construct theodicies. Voices like Eliot's remain unheard by those authors and cannot echo when they declare what is good and evil. The result is that the theodicists' declarations obscure the practices which can truly overcome evil and the social evils which need to be overcome. Having explored classic biblical, theological, philosophical, dialogical, and literary texts relating God and evils, we are now in position to display most clearly the evils of theodicy.

# NOTES

1.  Some might balk at identifying *Adam Bede* as a "classic." One recent critic has read *Adam Bede* as merely a few good scenes and inventions artificially pumped up into a novel (Liddell 1977:49-50). Its denouement is often said to be at least problematical, if not completely unsatisfactory (cf., inter alia, Fisher 1981:56), and its literary repute is inferior to *Middlemarch*. However, as *Adam Bede* at least arguably does disclose "a reality we cannot but name truth" (Tracy 1981:108), it is at least arguably a classic text.

The interpretations of *Adam Bede* have been varied. Fisher has taken it to construct a specific society and portray "the regeneration that is constant in social life" (1981:63). Carlisle sees it as teaching the "'art of vision'" (1981:195), enabling the reader to move beyond her initial perceptual limitations to a richer view. Carpenter uses the hermeneutical strategy of taking *Adam Bede* as a deliberately ambivalent text with a determinative chronology which can be 'interleaved' with readings from the Anglican lectionary to provide not only "keys to a scheme of 'hidden' hermeneutics that turns the narrative from a conventional historian's account of the silencing of Methodist women preachers to a ghostly interpretation of female prophecy as the 'voice of one crying in the wilderness'," but also to school "the reader in the duplicity of any story" (1986:31-32). The present chapter learns from all of them and extends Carpenter's view by arguing for the necessity of the denouement to disfigure the text.

2.  Only immediately relevant characters and their relationships are sketched in order to show the relationships, practices, and institutions necessary for these speech acts to be performed.

3.  Carpenter sees this as the key turning point in Adam Bede's story, when he turns away from his "hardness" and begins the process of softening him that will make him human (1986:38-39). However, this is not the crux of the novel.

4.  The ellipsis marks in quotations from Eliot do not mark elisions from her texts, but are her punctuation. The quotations in this and the next paragraph are all from pp. 422-31.

5.  Eliot's brief history of the inspiration for and composition of *Adam Bede* in her journal shows the centrality of chapter 45, when Dinah Morris visits Hetty Sorrel "In the Prison." This scene is based on an autobiographical story her "Methodist Aunt Samuel" had told her nearly two decades before (Haight 1955:2/502). Most readers recognize this chapter as the crux of the novel, but rarely probe the dynamics of the scene (as shown, for instance, in the offhanded comments in Liddell 1977:41).

6.  Kristeva's remarks on the discourse practice of confession which "does nothing else but weigh down discourse with sin" (1982:130), unhappily conflate confession as an assertive declaration of one's self with confession as a listing of sins addressed to another which "ushers in judgment, shame, and fear" (130). Abject confession which she properly excoriates is not the proper practice of confession, but

a disfigured form of an ancient ascetic practice, imposed upon people who neither sought ascetic perfection nor were thought capable of it by the ecclesiastical authorities who imposed the practice.

7. At this point, issues surrounding Dinah's "sincerity" must be raised. Previous chapters simply assumed the honesty of a speaker or writer. The problem was to discern the force of their actions. However, even if they were in some sense dissembling, most of their speech acts could still be successful, if not fully effective. In contrast, it is hard to see how Dinah's commitment could be effective if she were insincere or if Hetty saw her as dissembling.

Speech act theorists disagree about the necessity of "sincerity." On the one hand, Bach and Harnish find that "illocutionary or communicative success does not require sincerity" (1979:39). In their view, a person can perform a speech act even if s/he is insincere and even if the hearer takes her or him to be insincere. On the other hand, Searle claims that "the conditions of satisfaction of the speech act and the conditions of satisfaction of the sincerity condition are identical" (1983a:165). Searle has said that sincerity in a narrow sense (i.e., not fooling, not duplicitous, not dissembling, not lying, etc.) is required for every speech act's successful performance, although the precise form that sincerity takes differs from act to act as the speaker's purposes in performing the act differ. But the addressee must accept the "sincerity" of the speaker.

Analyzing this specific speech act shows that both accounts are overextended. *Pace* Searle, some speech acts, especially institutionally bound ones, may not require *personal* "sincerity" to be successful. For instance, a counterfeit judge may successfully bind over a person for trial even though she sincerely thinks the defendant innocent. *Pace* Bach and Harnish, it is hard to imagine how Dinah could be insincere and her commitment be successful. Her main purpose is to enable Hetty to confess and to sustain her as she confesses herself to be. To do this for Hetty (as opposed to some abstract person to be covered by *ceteris paribus* conventions) requires Dinah to continue to support her. If Dinah does so, how could she be insincere?

Each view applies to some cases, but not to all. And those which have what Searle calls "sincerity conditions" for their success must construe those conditions not in a narrow sense that all one needs to be able to perform some speech acts is to be "sincere," but in a broader sense that a person must have the position, virtues, abilities, etc., appropriate to the speech act being performed if it is to be successful (which is why I could not simply adopt Searle and Vanderveken's seven components of illocutionary force [1985:12-20] for the analysis in Part 1).

In the present instance, any "sincerity conditions" or "contextual conditions" require that Dinah have the virtue of constancy. Without it, she might utter the words, but has little, if any, chance of achieving her purposes.

8. Neither the prison chaplain nor Parson Irwine could move Hetty to speak. Irwine also failed to diagnose Arthur Donnithorne's problem with Hetty earlier, apparently before their sexual encounter. Arthur came to talk with him, but distractions intervened. Had Irwine been a doctor of the soul, perhaps he could have helped Arthur channel his passions.

9. To be a good diagnostician requires learning a practice through apprenticeship—it is this practice that medical school graduates need to acquire in residency programs. A person without this ability may perform an act that simulates diagnosis and may often do so without rendering any harm, at least in simple cases. But when the disease is complex or the evidence unclear, the difference between someone with the skill and someone without it is obvious.

MacIntyre's (1981:170-71, 222-26) discussion of "constancy" interestingly aligns constancy (in Jane Austen) with *phronesis* in Aristotle. Nonetheless, his account is misleading in that it claims that Jane Austen offers the last "classic" portrayal of constancy as a virtue. Constancy is also a crucial theme in Eliot's portrayal of Dinah, and it appears not only in their relationship, but in Dinah's ability to diagnose.

10.    If a narrative can exemplify Aquinas's notion of infused virtue, perhaps this one does, as Hetty seems suddenly to acquire the theological virtues (cf. *ST* Ia, IIae, 62, art. 1, *ad cor*) that had been notably absent from her life.

11.    These points are applicable in this context independently of the status a moral theory attributes to them. A deontological moral theorist can see these points as symptoms for discerning whether a concrete act was intrinsically right or wrong. A teleological moral theorist can see these points as criteria for determining right or wrong acts. A virtue theorist can take these as marks indicating whether the persons performing the actions are *phronimoi* (cf. Aristotle, *NE* 1140a25-30).

12.    At this point, some philosophers' discussions of the problem of evil are relevant. At first glance, Hetty's problem and Dinah's helping her to resolve it seem to have no connection with the logical problem of evil and the resolutions proposed for it. Hetty's problem is not a philosophical one. Hetty is caught in a web of evil and has no way out. Dinah comes along and frees her from the trap. This practical problem seems to have little to do with philosophical gymnastics.

However, defenses show that the presumptions of Dinah's acts are defensible. They show the compatibility of the presumptions of her acts. They suggest that her practice is not confused. Indeed, Augustine, Boethius, and Demea have shown that asserting belief in a God who can answer Dinah's prayers and hear Hetty's confession is compatible with asserting that there is evil in the world. Insofar as these beliefs, or beliefs that entail them, function as presumptions of these practices, a defense of these beliefs defends the practices from a charge of being incoherent.

13.    I discuss these issues in more general terms in Tilley 1990 with reference to Alston 1985 and 1986 and Plantinga 1983, which make even stronger claims about epistemic entitlement than I find warranted.

14.    The desultory debate about the logical status and illocutionary force of fictional discourse (summarized in Lanser 1981:283-94) can be resolved by construing fictional narratives as candidates for declarations. As shown in Part 1, not all attempted declarations work, and whether or not they work is not within the author's control. They must be received by their hearers. For institutionally bound declarations, this is automatic, *if* the audience recognizes the institutional authority of their speakers to make the declaration (debates about rebaptism in the Christian communities show the relevance of this condition). However, authors of fiction issue institutionally free declaratives. Whether they have the status of a declarative with regard to the audience depends entirely on whether the audience accepts them as declarations. Texts could be accounted classics to the extent that they have declarative status for all the readers in a culture or tradition.

# PART THREE

# THE DISCOURSE OF THEODICY

# Introduction to Part Three

Iris Murdoch raised the question which no one discussing any resolution to a problem of evil dares ignore:

> How is one to connect the realism which must involve a clear-eyed contemplation of the misery and evil of the world with a sense of an uncorrupted good without the latter idea becoming the merest consolatory dream? (I think this puts a central problem in moral philosophy.) (1971:61)

Murdoch also noted the problems to which theorists (whether philosophers or theologians) are prone when they attend to sin and suffering:

> It is very difficult to concentrate attention upon suffering and sin, in others or in oneself, without falsifying the picture in some way while making it bearable. . . . Only the greatest art can manage it, and that is the only public evidence that it can be done at all. (73)

Part 3 mobilizes the discussions of Part 2 to show that theodicies do falsify the picture and construct consoling dreams to distract our gaze from real evils. To counteract that falsification requires not merely academic argument and refutation, but the interruption of their speech acts, a counteraction to their actions. The action undertaken here is necessary to counteract the practice of theodicy. After analyzing theodicy as a discourse practice, I deploy the texts interpreted in Part 2 to counteract the misdeclarations of evil performed by theodicists. My conclusion is that theodicy is a discourse practice which ought to be abandoned.

*Chapter 9*

# THE EVILS OF THEODICY

*A monstrous generalization, like a staggering lie,*
*may sometimes pass,*
*where a more restricted claim would be challenged.*
*The vast assertion, the mighty lie,*
*overwhelms our faculties*
*and puts our art of criticism out of action.*
—Austin Farrer (1962:17)

## Constructing Theodicies

The practice of constructing theodicies only became possible in the context of the Enlightenment.[1] It is not merely that the term gained currency when Leibniz used the term "theodicy" as a title in 1710. Rather, the profound shifts in the intellectual and social world of Europe created the conditions in which theodicy can become a discourse practice. Both the status of the churches and the shape of the intellectual debate are especially relevant conditions.

First, the churches had lost credibility. As Buckley put it, the "Western conscience found itself deeply scandalized and disgusted by confessional religions" (1987:39). The churches in the sixteenth and seventeenth centuries supported wars and revolutions in the name of 'true' religion. In England, on the Continent, and in America, protectors, governors, princes, and kings waged war in the name of God. The secular authorities engaged in practices of persecuting, ghettoizing, and massacring religiously identified opponents both in Europe and in the American colonies on a scale unknown before the Reformation. Theologians debated incessantly over predestinarian doctrines which many read as demeaning human efforts, destroying human initiative, and inculcating religious sadomasochism. Such political practices and theological contentions contributed to a context in which the scholars who erected the edifices of modern thought could plausibly question, and find wanting, both the practices and dogmas of particular churches. The issue is how to describe this situation properly.

Stout has viewed the emergence of modern thought in the early seventeenth century as a flight from authority and a quest for autonomy. The merit of Stout's work is that it shows that, when authorities are fragmented, appeals to authority are dialectically useless. He found that the question which acquired real force is "what might be said in favor of God's *existence* if we do not assume from the beginning that certain documents and persons possess divine authority" (1981:169). But is this the *only* central religious question? Stout's focus on modern philosophical and theological thought tends to downplay the cultural and religious determinants for this sort of question (cf. Stout 1981:126-27). The issue of God's existence is a philosophical face of the multifaceted question of plausibility in a general cultural crisis of authority in which the locus of authority shifted.

The cultural and religious facet was the issue of the nature of God. This is reflected in the agreement of Philo and Demea in Part II of Hume's *Dialogues* that the issue is not the being, but the nature, of the deity. Their agreement may be ironic, and Cleanthes may not have been party to it. To some, this "irony" suggests the possibility that Hume's having his characters voice the problem as God's nature means he may have been dissembling about the real issue, the existence of God, so as not to give offense to pious ears. If he were not dissembling, then the issue addressed in the *Dialogues* is the nature of God. If he were dissembling, to be able to dissemble thus presumes that a philosophical dispute about the nature of God was less likely to offend his late eighteenth century readers than an argument about God's existence. No one could have successfully 'dissembled' as Hume may have, if 'pious ears' were not ready to hear without scandal a discussion of God's nature. But what sort of debate is the Enlightenment debate about God?

Buckley has shown that the debate about the nature of God is a burning religious as well as philosophical issue. He cites a letter written in 1823 by Thomas Jefferson to John Adams which illustrates this:

"I can never join Calvin in addressing *his* god. He was indeed an atheist, which I can never be; or rather his religion was daemonism. If ever man worshipped a false god, he did. The being described in his five points, is not the god whom you and I acknowledge and adore, the creator and benevolent governor of the world; but a daemon or malignant spirit. It would be more pardonable to believe in no god at all, than to blaspheme him by the atrocious attributes of Calvin." The value of deism, in its last and American ambit, was that it prevented confessional religion from driving human beings into atheism as the only alternative! (1987:39)

Because of the crisis of "many authorities," many rejected the authority of the churches. But some did so in the name of religion. The churches ceased being effective witnesses to a god worth worshipping. The crisis of authority which gives birth to modern thought is not merely a crisis which provokes a turn to autonomous reason to settle philosophical issues. It is also a crisis which provokes a turn to reason for religious reasons because the lack of credibility of religious authorities and of their churches was undercutting religious belief.

Second, in the context of a cultural crisis of authorities and authority, philosophical providential theism becomes a dominant discourse pattern in religious thought. Although such theism may not be logically incompatible with trinitarianism, theism's image of God is basically unipersonal. For better or worse, the particularity of Christianity, in which the figure of Christ and the doctrine of the Trinity are essential, is ignored. Buckley evidently regrets the fact that from the beginning of the seventeenth century, Catholic theologians set the terms of a debate with burgeoning atheism in which in "the absence of a rich and comprehensive Christology and a Pneumatology of religious experience Christianity entered into the defense of the existence of the Christian God without appeal to anything Christian" (1987:67). Yet given the lack of cultural credibility of particular Christian authorities and authority, it is hard to imagine how debate and discussion could have gone otherwise.

Third, as Surin notes, the revolutions in accepted scientific theory undermine the authority of both Scripture and the Aristotelian-Thomistic synthesis in portraying the world (1986:40-46). Galileo argued against scriptural authority in matters of fact. Newton portrayed the universe as a self-contained mechanical system for which God was practically irrelevant. Surin summarizes the consequences nicely:

The problem for the person who accepted Newtonian mechanics was this: if the nature of the world, as represented by this cosmological synthesis, was so precisely ordered, so (seemingly) flawlessly proportioned, then why were there evil and disharmony in the world? The 'problem of evil' still existed, but given this new synthesis, with its deistic, and ultimately even atheistic, implications, it was now difficult to reconcile the existence of evil with the workings of divine providence. This, of course, was one particular aspect of a more general problem posed for philosophy and theology by the thinkers of the Enlightenment, namely, how are morality and faith to be accommodated in a world governed by the laws of a rigidly mechanistic, and ultimately godless, system? (1986:42)

The acceptance of the Newtonian synthesis occasions the "disenchantment" of the world.

In this context, argument from design becomes a central and necessary strategy in theological debate. In the absence of the authority of the religious authorities, the authority of evidence and inference becomes central, and the burden of proof shifts away from those who would argue *against* the existence of God. The burden of proof is now on the theologians who would argue *for* God's existence. God's design of the world, no longer evident to all, must be demonstrated. It must be the foundation on which religious thought can be erected. However, when God is seen as the "creator and benevolent governor of the world," and when the world God created seems hardly benevolent or well governed, the supporter of the design argument must address challenges about the adequacy of this foundation for religious thought. Specific theoretical issues become pressing, especially those concerning the meaning of divine providence, and the 'enlightenment' problem of evil, as sketched in the epigraph to chapter 7, p. 165.

In the context of the design argument, "evil" becomes a theoretical term abstracted from specific instances of sin, suffering, and violence. Archbishop King, in *An Essay on the Origin of Evil* (written in 1697; published in Latin in 1702; ET, 1731), is the author of the classic fully developed Enlightenment theodicy.[2] Although philosophers, theologians, and poets had been attempting to deal with concrete evils in God's world, King now drives home the use of "evil" as an abstraction from any particular evils. King typically divides evil into moral evils brought about by wrong elections, natural evil, and the imperfection of being (72). King states, in evident dependence on Augustine, what has become a standard categorization. Yet in a book written by the Anglican Archbishop of Dublin, less than a decade after the Glorious Revolution, there is no reference to the previous century of religious wars or the evils in and of those wars. Even martial metaphors are remarkably rare in King's text. There is no mention of the fact that King himself was imprisoned during the struggle less than a decade earlier. Nor is the redistribution of land from the Irish peasant to the English landowner, which began with settling of the English into Ireland on the plantations created in the sixteenth century and was decisively ratified by the victory of King William III at the battle of Boyne in 1690, an issue. Specific events, e.g., the Lisbon earthquake of 1755, would later vivify the rhetorical force of the theoretical "problem of evil," and give its challenge a bite which went beyond the sphere of theoretical debates. Nonetheless, "evil" would remain an abstract theoretical term in the discourse of philosophical theism.

Moreover, it is only in the Enlightenment context that the abstract problem of evil becomes a central issue. Surin put the issue elegantly: "Pre-seventeenth century Christian thinkers were certainly not unaware of the conceptual difficulties that these antinomies [between divine omnipotence and worldly evils] generated; but, unlike their post-seventeenth century counterparts, they did not regard these problems as constituting *any* sort of ground for jettisoning their faith" (1986:9). For Augustine, Boethius, Aquinas, and the great reformers, the conceptual problems of evil were small anomalies in intellectual systems of great strength. "Evil" was not a single problem to be solved, but an aspect of various issues.

For Aquinas, for instance, there is no single problem of evil. In the *Summa*, evil is an objection to the existence of God (*ST*, I,q2,art 3, obj 1 and reply) and is a problem for the theology of the creation (*ST*, I,qq47-49). Other problems are sprinkled throughout the *Summa*. Aquinas does divide evil affecting creatures with volition into two types, *poena* and *culpa* (roughly, injury/pain and fault/sin; *ST*, I,q48,art 5), but this has the purpose of showing that temptation is not evil. He explicitly does not reduce all evil to these, but recognizes that corruption and defect are also evils. Certainly one can construct a Thomistic resolution to the problem of evil (cf. Journet 1963, E. E. Harris 1977), but "the problem of evil" was not Thomas's problem.

Theodicy proper, as a resolution to the problem of evil, is a discourse practice, then, which emerges in the Enlightenment. Within this realm of discourse, two different shapes of "the problem of evil," and of responses to it, can be discerned in the eighteenth-century debates. In the first part of the century, discussions of worldly evil presumed the reality of an all-good, all-benevolent God. Leibniz' *Theodicy* (1710) presumes that God has these attributes. The issue is to understand how it is possible that there is evil in the world God created (123-29). King set up the problematic explicitly:

> [T]o point out a Method of reconciling these Things [evils] with the Government of an absolutely perfect Agent, and make them not only consistent with Infinite Wisdom, Goodness and Power, but necessarily resulting from them . . . then we may be supposed to have . . . answered all the Difficulties that are brought on this Head, against the Goodness, Wisdom, Power and Unity of God (1731:80).

Even Kant's negative evaluation of theoretical theodicy (1791:284) near the end of the century showed that the task was not demonstrating the existence of God, but showing how worldly evil is consistent with the reality of the god of providential theism—presumed to be an appropriate representation of the Christian god.

However, as the century progressed, the problem acquired an important new shape and significance. The design argument was becoming, at best, a dubious foundation even for deism. Authorities no longer had the authority to render basic religious beliefs plausible, even as "mysteries." Evidence was required to give them any probability. In this context, a new problematic emerges. As Stout put it:

> The problem of evil is no longer a problem of figuring out what God is up to, given all the theology we already believe. In a context shaped by the new probability, it is a problem of figuring out what kind of God—if any—is plausible as an explanation of the origins of the universe as we find it. Given the existence of earthquakes, plagues, and the suffering of innocent children, the existence of a supremely perfect personal God seems unlikely (1981:123).

The theodicist must then bear the burden of proof to show that it is *not* improbable that God exists.

Hence, the discourse practice of theodicy, responding to the "problem of evil," generates two different forms of argument in the context of Enlightenment theism. One is the problem of explaining how the evil in the world is consistent with an accepted belief in God, and the other is one of the plausibility of belief in God, given the evidence of the world, including its sufferings (*poenae*) and individuals' sins (*culpae*).

Interestingly, the work of a preeminent contemporary theodicist shows itself as shaped by both these problems. In material composed for the first edition of *Evil and the God of Love*, John Hick wrote:

> For us today the live question is whether this [evil] renders impossible a rational belief in God: meaning by this, not a belief in God that has been arrived at by rational argument (for it is doubtful whether a religious faith is ever attained in this way), but one that has arisen in a rational individual in response to some compelling element in his experience, and decisively illuminates and is illuminated by his experience as a whole. The aim of a Christian theodicy must thus be the relatively modest and defensive one of showing that the mystery of evil, largely incomprehensible though it remains, does not render irrational a faith that has arisen, not from the inferences of natural theology, but from participation in a stream of religious experience which is continuous with that recorded in the Bible (Hick 1978:244-45).

This conception of the project of theodicy is in the tradition of the projects of Leibniz and King, demonstrating how evil can be shown to be coherent with and incorporated into an accepted theistic faith. Yet in the same book, in material added for the revised edition, the same author also wrote:

> In other words, the facts which give rise to the 'problem of evil', if taken by themselves, point away from rather than towards the existence of God. Accordingly, theodicies proceed by bringing other facts and theories into account so as to build up a wider picture which includes the fact of evil but which is such that it is no longer more natural to infer from it that there is no God than that there is. But this very procedure acknowledges that evil, by itself, *does* count against there being an infinitely good and powerful creator (Hick 1978:371).

This second conception of the project of theodicy responds to the problem of the plausibility of theism. It seeks not to answer difficulties *believers* have with their faith, but to show to *anyone* that belief in God is plausible despite the "natural inference" from the reality of evil to the nonexistence of God.

I have argued elsewhere (1984) that Hick's account is inconsistent. The two conceptions of theodicy have different presuppositions, argument structures, and goals. The former presupposes religious faith in the god of theism, must respond to challenges to its consistency, and is directed to believers. The latter presupposes epistemic neutrality about God, must bear a heavier burden of proof against challengers, and is directed to any readers, whether they presume the reality of God or not. But even if Hick's account were consistent, the key point is that it, like the theodicies of Leibniz, King, Journet, Griffin, and Farrer, is structured by the discourse practice of theodicy which presumes the task is either to understand the attributes of, or to argue for the reality of, a 'unipersonal' god of

Enlightenment theism despite the abstractly conceived moral and natural evils of the world. The task is not to enable folk to believe in the trinitarian god of Christianity.

Even if one of these projects were successful, it would only render plausible belief in a creator and designer of the universe. It is not at all clear that this is sufficient to overcome the implausibility of faith in the triune God worshiped in the Christian churches (cf. Buckley 1987: passim and Surin 1986:3-7). These theodicy projects make sense only on the presumption that Enlightenment theism is the expression of belief in God proper to Christianity. But this presumption has increasingly been called into doubt by those contemporary theologians who do not construe doctrines of the Trinity, Christology, and soteriology as auxiliary to basic theism, but as constitutive of Christian belief in God (compare Swinburne 1979:221-22).

A corollary of this view is that the 'classic theodicists' of the Christian tradition cannot have been doing theodicy—in the sense of responding to the 'Enlightenment' problematics. Chapter 5 has already argued that understanding Augustine as a theodicist is mistaken. One of his discourse practices is a defense (*Enchiridion*). Another is confession. And even in the *City of God*, the problematic is not the plausibility of theism, but a hermeneutic of history. Surin puts it bluntly: "Augustine's treatment of this 'problem' has as its proper locus a *theology of history* which views history as both a work and a sign of God's providence" (1986:12). Augustine did not write a theodicy, although theodicies can be constructed from his writings.

Similar claims can be made about other major Christian authors. Chapter 6 has argued that Boethius was also not doing theodicy, but therapy for the misfortunate. Aquinas did not write a treatise on theodicy (although he did address a *quaestionem disputatem*, *De Malo*, to evil) but treated evil in the contexts of other problems, as noted above (compare Journet 1963:13,17). Theodicists typically extract Luther's and Calvin's "discussions" of evils from texts written for purposes other than to resolve the problem of evil, and apply them an Enlightenment problematic (compare Griffin 1976:101-30). Moreover, the inspiration for the "Irenaean theodicy," supposedly opposed to the Augustinian themes of the mainstream traditions, comes from an author who was not doing theodicy at all, but also proposing a theology of history and arguing against gnostic dualism. The problematic for Irenaeus was not a "kind of 'soul-making' or anything resembling a theodicy . . . . The real problem of evil, for Irenaeus, arises in connection with the struggle to love God truly in Christ . . ." (Surin 1986:18-19). Irenaeus's project is to inoculate Christians against what he saw as the comforting, but delusive, intellectual illness of gnosticism. In short, constructing theodicies is not a Christian discourse practice before the Enlightenment.

## Theodicy as a Discourse Practice

Theodicy is a discourse practice which is "impractical."[3] That is, it is a purely theoretical practice responding to theoretical problems, not a practical theory responding to actual problems in religious practice. Theodicies do not respond to complaints or laments. They are not addressed to people who sin and suffer. They are addressed to abstract individual intellects which have purely theoretical problems of understanding evil. Given the intellectual contexts as sketched above, the purpose of constructing a theodicy seems purely theoretical.

But in their interminable pursuit of theory, theodicists devalue the practical issues. Numerous examples of the neglect of the practical litter theodicies, but consider how even a religiously sensitive writer of our era, Austin Farrer, sets up the problem of theodicy by marginalizing suffering:

> The practical problem is pastoral, medical, or psychological, and differs from case to case too widely to allow of much useful generalization. We are concerned with the theoretical problem only. If what we say is neither comforting nor tactful, we need not mind. Our business is to say, if we can, what is true. So far from beginning with the sufferer and his personal distresses, we will attempt to get the issue into perspective, and sketch the widest possible view (1962:7).

Farrer addresses an appendix on "imperfect lives," to the "death of speechless infants" and "the survival of imbeciles" (189-91), but offers no answers to people baffled by any actual and seemingly unlimited ills.

Journet also refuses to approach "the concrete, existential and specifically religious aspect of the problem of evil, or to listen to the cry of man afflicted by pain, the supplication of a Job or Jeremiah, overwhelmed by unbearable trials who calls upon God to come out of his silence . . ." in favor of the "metaphysical difficulty which no one can elude" (1963:59,60). He finishes his neo-Thomist approach with a chapter on the right attitude to evil in which he cites numerous spiritual writers. Journet concludes his book with the truly comforting final words that "if ever evil, at any time in history, should threaten to surpass the good, God would annihilate the world and all its workings" (289). At this high level of abstraction, not only are practical concerns which generate problems for religious believers ignored, but so marginalized and distorted that the possibility of God's destruction of the whole world God created is rendered a good thing!

David Griffin presents his work as different from this tradition of "impractical" theodicy. As part of his opposition to those who eschew theodicy in favor of practical and existential approaches to practical evils, he claims that the theoretical issues at least partially constitute the practical problems of evil because "the questions people raise about evil always contain theoretical dimensions" (1976:16). Indeed, the expectation of comfort, safety, and divine care that belief in the doctrine of divine providence creates in people is a result of theological renderings of providence. The theoretical problem is part of the existential problem, and "a theoretical problem can only be met with a theoretical solution" (16). So Griffin introduces his theodicy project.

Yet the main 'practical' application of his theodicy seems to be the removal of "the basis for that sense of moral outrage which would be directed toward an impassive spectator deity who took great risks with the creation" (309). The God Griffin portrays took great risks in creating, but is not merely a spectator. So Griffin's God not only risks what is created, but God also risks God's self. Because God shares the risks inherent in the development of higher intensity and deeper feeling, that somehow removes the cause of moral outrage. But is this so? Why does sharing a risk with others make it moral to induce the risk? Does this alleviate our moral outrage at some drunken driver who "shares the risk" of getting home safely with others in the car? God has also risked those I love. If they turn out to be some of the "losers" in the great divine wager, whatever the cause of their destruction, if they are the victims of the process, then that's just the way the dice of creation rolled. The real practical problem for me, then, would be how to forgive God for playing dice with the lives not only of those dearest to me, but also of all the life in the universe (not to mention my own life).

The practical issue relevant to Griffin's theodicy is how we can come to forgive God for taking the risks that have destroyed so many so miserably. Yet Griffin offers no suggestions on how we might be able to do so. Griffin's conclusion simply puts God on the risky hook with creation. If we're all on the hook, and God put us there, then God is not a spectator. But God, then, cannot do what is necessary to resolve the destruction which can emerge from this risk. If God could save those marginalized, betrayed, destroyed, or crushed by the practically perpetual process, God might be forgiven for initiating it. But Griffin's God cannot. Griffin's impracticality finally undermines his initial linkage of practical and theoretical problems.

In writing theodicies, individuals detach themselves from the realities of sin and suffering. The purpose of most theodicies is to show why the sufferings which people endure and the sins which they commit do not count against belief in God. Yet can any writer get into position to be so detached? And who is their audience? No one is without some sin. No one lives without some suffering. Yet theodicies are not only produced by, but also directed to, people detached from sin and suffering. Theodicists even encourage the reader to "try to be the most dispassionate" (Griffin 1976:16). Can and should anyone be so dispassionate, so detached from the realities of evil? If *Adam Bede*, for example, portrays what is required to overcome the real evil of human "denaturing," accepting the recommendation of detachment when considering evils may render one oblivious to the commitment, practical wisdon and constancy needed to counteract some evils.

Thus, theodicists' very attempts to be detached are not the ways to solve the problem, but are part of the problem:

> A theodicist who, intentionally or inadvertently, formulates doctrines which occlude the radical and ruthless particularity of human evil is, by implication, mediating a social and political practice which averts its gaze from the cruelties that exist in the world. The theodicist . . . cannot propound views that promote serenity in a heartless world (Surin 1986:51).

The theodicist encourages readers to "distance" themselves from the evils of the world to "understand" them. Yet should readers distance themselves from their own sins, and refuse to own them? If the points made in chapter 8 are correct, it is just those who can't or don't own their lives—including their sins—who are fated to continue the process of dehumanizing victimization without reconciliation. Should readers distance themselves and be serene in the face of all their suffering, including their victimizing victimization? Perhaps so—but such attitudes must be differentiated from the advocacy of quietistic fatalism, the inculcation of masochism, or the promotion of escapism so often the upshot of prescribing serene distantiation from real evils.

Theodicies are part of the Enlightenment obsession with reducing the muddy and mixed to the clear and distinct. But in doing so, the theodicist idealizes the reality of evils. No theodicist claims to have explained fully how God allows evil in the world or eliminated the mystery of evil by such distancing. For all theodicists, the practical problems remain. Indeed, they are exacerbated by the practice of distancing oneself from the reality of evils to understand how evil does not count against belief in God. The practice of theodicy valorizes the spotless hands which write about evils without being sullied by them.

Some theodicists do not even claim to solve the theoretical problem. In the face of evils they give only a theoretical possibility (cf. Hick 1978:386). This theory is supposed to give readers grounds for hope. Even if theodicies did give warranted answers to the theoretical problems, the *real* problem is not theoretical. Theoretical hopes ought not to be raised lest they be shattered when those encouraged to hope confront the realities of massive destruction alone while the theodicists keep cerebrally beyond the fray.

If theodicy is "impractical" discourse, what speech act is it?

At first glance, theodicy seems to have the assertive illocutionary point. Although theodicists carefully cultivate a style which requires the reader to pay homage to the fear and trembling with which theodicists approach their work, they see their task as representing with sufficient accuracy the way things are. Some are more modest than others, but none denies that his purpose is to get matters straight, to show how things really are (despite appearances), to tell the truth. Swinburne provides a clear example by first formulating a question and then supplying a (presumably true) answer:

> What then is wrong with the world? First, there are painful sensations, felt both by men, and, to a lesser extent, by animals. Second, there are painful emotions, which do not involve pain in the literal sense of the word—for example, feelings of loss and failure and frustration. Such suffering exists mainly among men, but also, I suppose, to some small extent among animals too. Third, there are evil and undesirable states of affairs, mainly states of men's minds, which do not involve suffering. For example, there are states of mind of hatred and envy; and such states of the world as rubbish tipped over a beauty spot. And fourth, there are the evil actions of men, mainly actions having as foreseeable consequences evils of the first three types, but perhaps other actions as well—such as lying and promise breaking with no such foreseeable consequences. As before, I include among actions, omissions to perform some actions. If there are rational agents other than men and God (if he exists), such as angels or devils or strange beings on distant planets, who suffer and perform evil actions, then their evil feelings, states, and actions must be added to the list of evils (1977a:83; compare Swinburne 1979:180-224; compare King 1731:iii).

While Swinburne seems more reticent, or perhaps more abstract, when he writes of the God who made this world, his communicative actions at least have an assertive illocutionary point. His assertions about God seem to have a weaker specific illocutionary force than his assertions about evils, but nonetheless, he does not promise or command or merely express feelings in his writings. His discourse—and the discourse of all theodicists—is basically assertive, for all theodicists' purpose is to portray what is true with the force appropriate to the reliability or warrantability of their claims.

Moreover, theodicies seem to be institutionally free discourse practices. No theodicist invokes a "privileged institutional position" which gives her discourse a validity because she has the office of bishop or priest, etc. Although most theodicists are religious believers of various stripes, and many are also ordained to an institutional status in a church, their theodicies as communicative actions do not presume that they have any specific status in a religious community.

Nonetheless, there are peculiarities about theodicy as a discourse practice. One has been noted: it is an impractical practice. A second is that theodicy has become a discourse with a home more in the academy than in the churches. It is not institutionally bound; theodicy, like prayer, does not require that the speaker have a specific role within the institution. Nonetheless, those participating in that practice now usually have *some* role—critic, student, researcher, teacher—in (or toward) one of the institutions of academia—college, university, seminary. People in pastoral work are notoriously absent from the discourse practice of theodicy, unless they write what is clearly derivative (as Kushner does).

Contemporary academic theodicy has also come to construe certain approaches and certain texts as its tradition. Farrer mentions the tradition, and even feels comfortable within the constraints it imposes: "There is nothing new to say on the subject. Only the fashions of speech alter, and ancient argument is freshly phrased" (1962:16-17). Surin describes part of this tradition in more lucid terms:

> There is a sense in which scholarly reflection on the 'problem of evil' is a highly ritualistic activity, which requires the theodicist to focus her attention on a number of canonical or 'sacred' texts (Leibniz's *Theodicy*, Tennant's *Philosophical Theology*, Journet's *Le Mal*, and so forth), and to engage in certain professional rituals (writing doctoral theses, submitting articles to learned journals, and producing books!) (1986:49).

Yet rarely, if ever, are "practical" or "spiritual" texts on God and suffering admitted to this tradition (Job, Boethius, Julian of Norwich, Simone Weil). Nor do literary texts, texts of protest, or even biblical texts contribute substantially to the tradition of theodicy. Theodicy is a practice of the detached. It is now at home in the academy, where detached, "value-free" research is still valorized. And the practice constrains its practitioners to retrace the paths marked out in the past.

Beyond this academic focus, a third peculiarity of contemporary theodicy is that theodicists also rewrite the past as if all writings on suffering and sin were not only commensurable, but also contributions to the conversation constituted in the Enlightenment. Hume and Augustine—to note two of the 'canonical' authors considered in the present book—are often taken, respectively, to be asserting the Enlightenment problematic and answering it. Alternatively, Augustine is taken to have embedded answers in his texts which would have been answers to Enlightenment problems, if only he had been able to read Leibniz, Hume, Kant, et al. Theodicists, as discussed at length in chapter 5 and noted briefly in the previous section, 'mine' an earlier author to 'find' his answer—and then often displace the 'theodicies' they 'find.' Contemporary theodicists work hard to create a commensurability, to make a tradition by construing pre-Enlightenment authors as participants in the discourse practice of theodicy, whatever the illocutionary force and purposes of their writings may have been.

A fourth and most telling peculiarity is the way theodicists talk of evil. More than other critics, Surin has brought out the fact that theodicies render "evil" an abstraction. But the language he uses to reveal this is strained to the breaking point. He has claimed that theodicies obscure "the radical and ruthless particularity of human evil" and are a "practice which averts its gaze from the cruelties that exist in the world" (1986:51). But how is this possible? How can theodicies' talk and writing avert "its" gaze from cruelties in the world? How can theodicy "provide—albeit unwittingly—a tacit sanction of the myriad evils that exist on this planet" (50)? How can a form of writing be unwitting? How can theodicy silence "the screams of our society" (52)? Does it "outshout" them? The strain of Surin's syntax, his personification of theodicy as an agent, and his invocation of a moral judgment that these sorts of theodicies are "not worth heeding" (52) suggest that theodicies may have a power that is practically demonic and which should be fought. But just as the oddities in Peter Brown's portrayal of Augustine's *Confessions* fall into place if one recognizes that Augustine is performing an assertive declaration when he performs the speech act of confession, so the strains in Kenneth Surin's portrayal of the power of theodicies make sense if one recognizes that to do theodicy is not to participate in merely an assertive discourse practice, but to perform an assertive declaration. In short, theodicy is a speech act in which theodicists do not describe, but declare, what is evil.

However, if they fail to declare "evil" what is truly evil, their declarations create a reality in which what is truly evil is not evil. If theodicists misdeclare evil, they create an inconsistent and finally destructive discourse.[4] What follows argues that they all do so, because to write a theodicy is to perform an assertive declaration that is a falsifying declaration which effaces genuine evils.

## Theodicy as Assertive Declaration

For a speech act to be a declarative, it must meet a number of conditions.[5] The first condition is that the context must be such that declarers' utterances are necessary and sufficient, given the context, to create a fact or state of affairs. Indeed, in the context of the Enlightenment, as sketched above, the ways in which God and evil were discussed in philosophical theology shifted dramatically. Perhaps no single individual is fully responsible for originating the discourse practice of theodicy any more than any individual is fully responsible for making up the possibility of a sacramental declaration or the possibility of confession. But just as Augustine's *Confessions* and John's baptism of Jesus in the Jordan become models for similar confessional and sacramental declarations, so the theodicies of King and Leibniz become paradigms for subsequent theodicists. Although it sounds odd, once theodicy was successfully performed as a speech act in the culture, a new state of affairs was created: the discourse practice of theodicy became real.

One way to explain the possibility of creating novel speech acts or discourse practices would be to follow Jameson's Marxist approach and construe texts in theodicy as symbolic acts:

> When we . . . find that the semantic horizon within which we grasp a cultural object has widened to include the social order, we will find that the very object of our analysis has itself been thereby dialectically transformed, and that it is no longer construed as an individual "text" or work in the narrow sense, but has been reconstituted in the form of the great collective and class discourses of which a text is little more than an individual *parole* or utterance. Within this new horizon, then, our object of study will prove to be the *ideologeme*, that is the smallest unit of the essentially antagonistic discourse of social classes (1981:76).

Theodicy would then be a possible (and perhaps inevitable) discourse practice (in the *langue* of a specific society or social class) which individual theodicies instantiate. The issue of "who" created it would be unimportant, or rather the real issue would be the power of the discourse created. Even if Jameson has overstated the case, at least the Enlightenment was a time "ripe" for the emergence of the practice of theodicy. Further, if Jameson is correct in claiming "We can think abstractly about the world only to the degree to which the world itself has already become abstract" (66), then "evil" has become an abstract, unreal entity in the theodicists' world (and rendering evil abstractly is both ideologizing and utopian, as will be shown below).

The discourse practice has a basic shape. Theodicists cite external challenges like Bayle's or Hume's, declare what evil is, cite "relevant" themes from the tradition as evidence, show how the challenges are met, and snipe at other theodicists in order to show how their own theories are more intellectually reliable than those of their "worthy opponents" in finding God justified for creating the world by defeating the challenges. For instance, for all his concerns with the pre-Enlightenment Christian tradition, Hick's two purposes for his theodicy are structured neither by Irenaeus's nor Augustine's purposes, but by those common to the Enlightenment practice (1978:3-14); Griffin's work details biblical and ancient philosophical issues, but his purpose is to offer a more credible doctrine of God than his predecessors' doctrines (1976:11-12). These texts also replicate the other constituents of the practice of theodicy, save at the end they declare, in a modest way, that hope is possible (Griffin 1976:313; Hick 1978:386).

Each theodicist mimics (with individual variations) the key declaration that evil (other than metaphysical evil) *is* the acts individuals commit and the sufferings each undergoes (a declaration Aquinas, for instance, did not make). Those who write theodicies declare what evil is. And this consistent declaration makes theodicy a practice of falsifying declaration. For instance, when Swinburne confidently answers the question, "What's wrong with the world?" he is not merely describing evils. Rather, he is but participating in a discourse practice which declares what is to count as evil (also see King 1731:72; Griffin 1976:22-23; Hick 1978:12-14). Painful sensations and emotions, undesirable attitudes, ugly states of affairs are "passive evils," evils which individuals suffer. Actions (or omissions), which bring about those sensations, emotions, states of affairs, or attitudes, are evil actions. "Now much of the evil in the world consists of the evil actions of men and the passive evils brought about by those actions" (Swinburne 1977:84). Of course, what other evil might exist is never mentioned (save as the abstraction of "metaphysical evil" or the evil of imperfection—an Augustinian concept easily liable to misconstrual). So, if there are other evils neither ascribable to the forces of nature nor to the individual acts of humans and if Swinburne ignores them, then he has misdeclared what is evil.

Hume's Philo recognized other forms of evil. When he identified "man" as "the greatest enemy of man," he did not so much mention individual sins as cite social practices and conditions: "Oppression, injustice, contempt, contumely, violence, sedition, war, calumny, treachery, fraud; by these they mutually torment each other . . ." (Hume 1779:195). Are these passive evils or active evils? If any of them are neither, then they are not evil in the theodicist's world.

Some are not passive evils. They involve actions, but cannot be reduced to actions alone. For instance, one act alone does not necessarily constitute oppression. Nor does any definite number of individual evil acts constitute "oppression" or any other social practice. Swinburne suggests that the sum of such actions and omissions ("long years of slackness by many generations of men"; 1977:84) may create many contemporary evil states of affairs or passive evils. But Swinburne's account (quoted on p. 232 above) which attributes such evils to a combination of individual omissions and commissions obscures the power of evil practices, a power often identified in early Christianity as demonic.

For instance, one might say that a long history of noninclusive language in theological writing is the sort of slackness that creates the conditions under which Swinburne's writing appears unrelievedly, even intentionally, sexist. He, however, could maintain that he had no intention to write sexist prose nor to cause the pain I (and others) suffer on reading his texts because of his unregenerately noninclusive language. Nonetheless, his prose is sexist. It marginalizes half the human race. Females are either not subjects in Swinburne's discourse or are construed as men. Is it merely that the sum of noninclusive theological writings creates this pain we feel? To claim so would be rather odd. Or does Swinburne's writing style create it, especially in the context of a discourse practice in which almost no women participate? That seems more likely. But if Swinburne had no intention to write a sexist theology, what made him so insensitive to the contemporary context in which his work would be easily perceived that way? I would claim that he participates in a practice of sexist writing which marginalizes and effaces women. Such a practice cannot be attributed merely to the slackness of the past or to the sum of noninclusive writings. Rather, a practice of sexist writing has the power to twist and warp even the best-intended human acts. It is thus an evil practice, and one for which theodicists do not account.

In general, a society, a social practice, or social situation can be recognized as oppressive if it is structured so that good people ordinarily perform acts they think good, but which ordinarily and unwittingly injure others. A society or social situation is unjust if it is structured so that good people ordinarily perform acts they think good, but which unwittingly deprive others of what they are due. These are structures or practices of evil, visible to Hume and to contemporary feminists, Marxists, and poststructuralist literary critics, but invisible to the practitioners of theodicy because the practice of theodicy necessarily effaces them as evils.

Perhaps the most conspicuous effacement of or blindness to the structures of evil is Hick's effacement of Hume's view of social evil. At one point Hick writes that what Hume made clear in the *Dialogues* "is precisely the fact of evil in its many forms" (1978:244). Yet when he responds to Hume's challenges, he centers on Part XI, where social evils are absent (1978:257, 302-9, 324-29). His only reference to Part X, where Philo catalogs social ills and vices (1978:321), is taken from Demea's speech about mental disorders which immediately follows Philo's list. When Hick acknowledges that much human misery results not from "material lack but from a morally paralyzing sense of meaninglessness of life as a whole" (1978:320-21), he never considers the social structures which contribute to or bring about such meaninglessness as part of the problem of evil. Elie Wiesel's *Night* portrays the way social structures of destruction can destroy a sense of meaning and faith. But Hick doesn't notice the power of those structures which Wiesel's narrative reveals all too clearly. The general point is this: engaging in the practice of theodicy makes one read texts, even texts dealing with evils and attempting to undermine theodicy, so as to valorize certain evils as significant and to efface the evil of other forms of evil.

Theodicists fail to recognize that some practices or structures bring evil out of good acts. But on the theodicist's account, they are neither passive nor active evils. Therefore, they are not evils. To account for the repeated effacement of social evils, theodicies cannot be construed as mere assertions. Assertive speech acts alone, unless they are institutionally bound and authoritative (as theodicy is not), cannot have the power required. Assertives cannot represent and present a world where social evil is absent. The only discourse practice, in speech act terms, which can present and change the world in the required way is a declaration. Hence, to explain the absence of social evil as a category, despite its traces in theodicists' writings, the practitioners of theodicy cannot be construed as performing assertive speech acts, but must be performing assertive declarations.

Moreover, the purpose of theodicists' declarations is to find God not responsible for, not guilty of, what they declare evil. But this sort of declaration evokes judicial contexts, as if the theodicist were rendering a verdict on God. Indeed, theodicists tacitly (Griffin 1976:310) or, rarely, explicitly (McCabe 1987:26,37) assume the roles of defense counsel and judge in a trial of God (cf. Kant 1791:283-84; *sed contra*, Farrer 1962:16). If such a declaration is effective, then the theodicist has gotten God off the hook for the evils in the world. While theodicists might claim that they are simply trying to show how belief in God is consistent with recognition that there is genuine evil in the actual world, that wouldn't change the status of their speech act any more than if judges claimed that their verdicts were simply trying to show how belief in the guilt or innocence of a defendant was consistent with the evidence in the case. Given the contexts of both, the appropriate speech actions are declarative in both cases.

For a theodicy to be a declaration, the second type of condition which must obtain is that the declarer and the audience must recognize the speech act as having the illocutionary point of an assertive declaration. This requirement may seem, on the surface, not to have been met. However, it is clear that theodicies are assertive speech acts and that the audiences for them take them as such. But it is also clear that readers often take the declaration of evil as sin and suffering in theodicy to be sufficient without giving it a second thought. Indeed, that seems to be part of the academic and theological practices in which theodicies flourish. But it is just that lack of resistance to the declaration among those who accept theodicy that shows it is accepted as a declaration.

The significance of resistance to declarations is rarely, if ever, discussed in speech act theory. Someone who resists being baptized cannot be baptized. She refuses the declaration. A thief who outruns an arresting cop is not arrested. He resists the declaration. A senator who declines to be appointed to a committee is not appointed. She aborts a declaration. A person who reveals that he went through a wedding service under severe duress may not be entitled to a divorce from the person he married, but to an annulment of the declaration. What differentiates opposition to assertives and declaratives is that refusals to accept assertives do not rob assertives of any assertive illocutionary point, but may change the strength of the assertion; however, successful resistance to declarations renders those declarations forceless, because declaratives have only one possible force—either they work or they fail (cf. Searle and Vandervecken 1985:174). Declarers who encounter resistance to their declarations may argue with (perform acts with assertive and/or directive force) those who resist their declarations. But if their arguments fail, they may resort to performing other declarative acts, e.g., excommunicating the resisting parties, or to performing other acts with similar import, e.g., ignoring them.

Those who do challenge the practice of theodicy do not merely refuse to accept a theodicist's assertion, but "resist" a declaration. They resist the declaration of what is evil. They do not merely argue with theodicists about the proper way to declare what evil is. They refuse to make or accept the theodicists' declaration. That they resist a declaration is indicated by the theodicists' response to their resistance. Theodicists do not so much argue against them, as they do against other theodicists who make similar declarations of evil as sin and suffering. Rather, theodicists write those who resist such declarations out of the community in which theodicy is a discourse practice (as some reviewers of this book will do). They declare their opposition to be "outside the camp." This is the verbal abuse which the practice of theodicy makes possible and real.

For instance, D. Z. Phillips refuses to accept Swinburne's declaration of what evil is. Philips finds him making a self-contradictory attempt to make sense out of senseless evil or to claim that God has a point for pointless evils. Hick then accuses Phillips of having no use for theodicy not because he rejects Swinburne's theodicy, but because, according to Hick, Phillips believes that "there is no theos" (S. C. Brown 1977:122). Hick attempts to declare Phillips out of the community which talks of God and evil by calling him an atheist, a declaration which Phillips shows to be totally inappropriate in the context (S. C. Brown 1977:134). The phenomenon of resistance to declarations, and the fact that controversies between theodicists and antitheodicists are instances of declaration and resistance as much as argument and counterargument, suggests that theodicy is implicitly recognized as an assertive declaration. Once one recognizes the abuse of theodicy, this implicit recognition can become patent.

For a theodicy to be an assertive declaration, the third set of conditions which must obtain is perlocutionary. Theodicy must not only reflect, but also effect, a state of affairs. The points made in exploring the contextual and illocutionary conditions for theodicy support the actuality of the perlocutionary results of theodicy. Indeed, theodicy is not the only literary practice which both reflects and effects a world. As Dowling writes, "every narrative simultaneously *presents* and *represents* a world, that is, simultaneously creates or makes up a reality and asserts that it stands independent of that same reality" (1984:98). In that sense, like other effective narratives, theodicy is "both a symbolic *act* and a *symbolic* act" (122).

Dowling construes the fact that narratives effect and reflect a world as an ambiguity: "it is a genuine act in that it tries to do something to the world, and yet it is 'merely' symbolic in the sense that it leaves the world untouched" (122). However, this is a mistake. These "symbolic acts" are not ambig*uous* but ambi*valent*. They are hybrid speech acts, assertive declarations. Chapter 1 showed that actions can have multiple forces, depending upon their content, context, purpose, etc. The ambivalence of narratives which "create" worlds (cf. Tilley 1985:40-46) is merely one instance of the multiplicity of forces any action can have.

A key problem in Dowling's account of fictional narratives as symbolic acts is that his use of "world," if applied to a "nonfictional" declaration, becomes ambiguous. The world that it leaves untouched, and 'merely' represents, is the actual world prior to the point of the action. Its assertive force represents the world prior to the action. The world that it does something to is the actual world including the action. Its declarative force affects a "different world" (or a different world segment) than its assertive force represents. To the extent that a declaration is effective, it makes its representation of the actual world to the point of the declaration true—unless an effective supervening declaration, which counteracts the assertive declaration, is performed. The emergence of a tradition of theodicy with both standard rhetorical shape and a standard canon fits as an effect of a successful declaration: one recognizes a successful declaration by its success: the world with which we have to do is/becomes what the declarer says it is.

Theodicies have definite effects. The most obvious is that they limit moral evil (and hence our perception of it) to individual acts and ignore evil practices and structures. Yet the literature studied in previous chapters suggests that constructing theodicies has other, similar effects. Was the silencing of Dinah Morris (or her "real-world" analogues) by the Wesleyans evil? If it did not produce very painful emotions, nor undesirable attitudes nor ugly states of affairs, to use Swinburne's criteria, it was not evil—or only minimally so. Yet silencing her silenced not only a powerful preaching voice, but also a voice which enabled confession, forgiveness, and reconciliation to occur. Silencing her made Dinah a victim of the church's own destructive practices.

On the theodicists' grounds, the ecclesiastical practice of silencing a reconciling voice simply because the voice is female is in itself not declared evil. It is or can be seen as evil only if it results in bad attitudes or emotions. This is because theodicists cannot construe performing actions which are distorted by social practices as evil.[6] "'There's no rules so wise but what it's a pity for somebody or other. Most o' the women do more harm nor good with their preaching'" says Adam Bede (Eliot 1859:506). The social practice of silencing women is acceptable in Hayslope even though it's a pity for Dinah. Yet theodicists cannot identify the practice as an evil because it is neither a passive evil nor an active evil attributable to individuals' "elections." The disabling of the able is merely an unfortunate byproduct of a rule. One result of theodicy, then, is that it makes it impossible for those who inhabit the theodicists' world to construe that, or any other, rule as a powerful practice or structure of evil. And insofar as theodicists often have ordained status in churches which repress voices of reconciliation, it becomes rather suspicious that their theodicies obliterate the evil that their institutions perform.

Is the "denaturing" of people that Boethius identifies in the *Consolation* evil? Those people who become animals as a result of their brutish behavior may not have very painful emotions. Indeed, Hetty Sorrel, an exemplar of such denaturing, had apparently no human emotions at all. Is it merely that their attitudes are "undesirable"? On Swinburne's grounds, the denaturing of human beings is or can be seen as evil only if it results in bad attitudes. It is not in itself declared evil. This is because Swinburne, like other theodicists, never identifies the practices of vice as evil. Individual sins committed by individual people at specific times and in particular places are evil—but the power of those practices and social structures that make viciousness attractive or tolerable or the "only alternative" for the oppressed and marginalized is ignored.

Certainly, it is possible that bad characters may be constituted by acquiring bad habits developed through repeatedly performing bad actions. But theodicists cannot construe "He's a pig" or "She's a vulture" or "He's a devil" as anything more than insult or metaphor. Yet it is possible that these "metaphors" might be the revelatory key to understanding a practice or set of practices which are destructive of human natures. Peck has described some of those practices at length and identified the characters which result from those practices. These people are practically centers of destruction.

"Strangely enough, evil people are often destructive because they are attempting to destroy evil. The problem is that they misplace the locus of the evil. Instead of destroying others they should be destroying the sickness within themselves" (1983:74). Thus, another perlocutionary result of theodicy is that it makes it impossible for those who inhabit the theodicists' world to consider the possibility that a person might be so twisted and distorted as to destroy her or his own nature (compare Peck 1983:120-27).

There is also a distinction between goods of nature and goods of fortune in Boethius. Theodicists fail to recognize that difference. The destruction of a person's fortune is one sort of evil. Boethius provides a therapy that helps the unfortunate to see misfortune in perspective. But the possibility of engaging in Boethian therapy presumes that a person's basic or natural needs are met. Without natural goods, therapy is useless. But another result of theodicy is that it blinds those who inhabit the theodicists' world to the evil of "unconscious" social and economic mechanisms and relationships which destroy the possibility of the unfortunate being consoled because they have no basic goods.

Are the *mala* of misplacement and intrinsic defect in Augustine evil? These are often taken to be simply aesthetic evil or the evil of metaphysical imperfection, that no being is perfect compared to Being. Yet can the evil of misplacement ever be merely "aesthetic"? To use examples from chapter 5, are misplacements of flowers in gardens or miscasting athletic teams merely aesthetic evils? Or are these indicators of those deeper structures which produce our perceptions of what gardens should be and how teams or athletes should play? While the *malum* of a thing may consist in its being less than it should be, it may be deprived of its full measure of goodness by something other than its "natural defect" or the entity's "sin." Is it not possible that there are social structures which disable entities from being what they could be? Is it not also the case that our language sometimes hides the evils from us or makes it possible to talk about evil in ways that obscure the evil?[7] Another result of theodicy, then, is to blind those who inhabit the theodicists' world to theodicists' "*structures of containment*," whereby theodicists are able to "project the illusion" that their readings of aesthetic evil are "somehow complete and self-sufficient" (cf. Jameson 1981:10), that they are simply "objective" and "true." The illusion—or inconsistency—they create is the fact that once an evil is labeled as "aesthetic" or "moral" or "natural," no other categories are relevant or even possible. Yet it is possible that there are other dimensions to *mala* in Augustine.

Theodicists rarely, if ever, write of the evil done by and in religious contexts. They tend to ignore the possibility that even the Christian communities incorporate structures of evil as part of their own structures. They tend to whitewash religious practices by neglecting to notice the evils done within religious communities and institutions. Religious beliefs and practices seem a blindspot for theodicists—perhaps because the structures they construct for containing evil necessarily distance evil from religion, and render them blind to evil done within their own religious traditions.

The problem is that theodicists construe all evils as either resulting from human acts (whether sinful or not) or resulting from events beyond individuals' control. In so doing, the theodicist declares those evils not resulting from human acts to be "natural" or "passive." Where is social evil in theodicy? Are all moral evils attributable only to individuals—or is theodicy constrained by its "cognitional individualism" (Surin 1986:21-23) to an individualistic morality? Where are the practices of denigration and destruction, of oppression and despoliation, of environmental destruction and maldistribution of the basic goods of life, of conspicuous consumption and unrelieved sexism, which blind us to the real evil some of our acts create and which can twist and warp even our best-intended acts? These forces are absent not only from the tradition (in the theodicists' reading of it), but also from the assertive declarations that are the central constituent of the discourse practice of theodicy. Since they are not due to individual humans, are they on God's account? Is the real purpose of theodicy not to justify God but to justify the established social structures and practices as so "natural" as to be divinely given and part of the "natural" world God created?

In the world theodicists declare to be real, the screams of the marginalized and oppressed, the cruelties people suffer, the unwitting perpetuation of evils in the attempts to overcome them (see Noddings 1989:226-27), and the silencing of the voices of forgiveness and reconciliation cannot be morally evil unless they are the result of individuals' acts. Therefore, any protest against the causes of oppression, cruelty, marginalization, and silencing must be protest against the other sort of evil, natural evil. But natural evil is what individuals can do nothing about. Hence, such protests should either be silenced or ignored since they are illegitimate. They are protests against what is, by definition, beyond human control.

If there are forces of evil, theodicists must construe these structural, social evils as natural. But this effaces the moral status of social evils. In effect, theodicists do declare that the world is such that God, who is responsible for the natural world, is responsible for the natural evil of oppression. In so doing, theodicists disable hearers from considering social evils as genuine moral evils, amenable to change. Theodicists declare real a world in which vicious and destructive practices cannot be identified as moral evils, for those practices are God-given. They provide readings of the tradition which efface the social dimensions of evil as various as Augustine's descriptions of *mala*, Boethius's discriminations of denaturings and misfortunes, Hume's catalog of social vices, and Eliot's revelation of oppressive scapegoating. Theodicists declare what evil is, and in the theodicists' world, none of these is morally evil.

But perhaps the most shocking of all the results of the practices of theodicists for those whose religion is centered on the Bible is the effacement of Job.[8] McCabe sees Job as offering us an alternative to thinking of God as infantile by teaching us to find, "as Job did, that it was our own view of God that was infantile" (1987:25). Journet presents Job as merely an example of a person lamenting and tried by God and Satan (1963:59, 256), but never mentions Job in his discussion of "the right attitude" toward evil. Griffin uses a number of out-of-context quotations from the Book of Job in portraying biblical views of God's power and immutability (1976:32-35). I found the Book of Job mentioned only once in Leibniz (1710:296), and not at all in Swinburne (1977a, 1977b, 1979, 1981). Hick doesn't refer to Job in his constructive work, although he mentions the Book of Job in his discussion of the way evil appears in the Bible (1978:353-54). Farrer recognizes Job's problematic, but prefers another (1962:17, 186). Farrer's real worry is with being identified with the comforters (16-17, 158), so he vilifies those defenders of the Deuteronomic tradition as "liars." Rather than taking the warning of the Book of Job never to write theodicies, Farrer refuses to heed the warning—and recognizes how he might join with the comforters' chorus of oppression, naturally thinking that he avoids singing their tune. Kant takes the Job story seriously and recognizes that "some tribunal of dogmatic theologians, some worthy presbytery or some high consistory of today," would have found Job less worthy than those "pious flatterers" who tried to comfort him (1791:293). But Kant also accuses the comforters of "dishonesty" (292). He then finds a startling ancient confirmation of his own philosophy: "Job proved that he did not base his morality on his faith but his faith upon his morality" (293). Chapter 4 noted that contemporary interpreters of Job joined God-as-portrayed-in-the-Book-of-Job in silencing Job's voice. Contemporary theodicists join the chorus which drowns him out; the points I made in chapter 4 can also be applied to theodicists.

One consequence of theodicists' declarations is their disabling Christian theology from exploring the new phenomena of evil. For instance, Christian theodicists never, and Christian theologians rarely, even ask questions like Tiger asks:

> Herein lies one of the implicit obsessions of this book: when the industrial system produces undesirable consequences, who or what is responsible? How can we locate the culprit? Is someone in particular responsible for pollution, urban noise, traffic jams, birth defects, unemployment? Who? The bosses, the workers, the government, engineers, cooks?
>
> This book is part of an effort at secular theodicy: to identify the source of evil but without recourse to the supernatural (1987:71).

Theodicists cannot undertake anthropological explorations of social evils, but must leave it to the secularists, because, for theodicists, social evils are obliterated. Theodicy literally blinds us to the social evils of our day, except as they affect the life of individuals, just as King was blind to the evils of forcing Scottish and English colonizers on Ireland and to the evils of the battle waged to preserve and extend the plantation system which was the economic side of the English hegemony over the Irish people and their countryside.

Theodicy also contributes to blinding theologians to the possibility that Noddings' findings about torture might be true:

> In discussing torture, we saw that it is both normal and pathological; that is, that tendencies to inflict pain are in all of us and that different [human, structural, and ideological] agents in the environment trigger the illness in different human beings. . . . The belief that justifies us in inflicting pain parallels the belief in the male God who inflicts or allows pain to accomplish his ends. . . .
>
> In discussing the rise of sadism during the Enlightenment, we saw what might be called the logical conclusion of theodicy. Cruel acts must be good. The capacity for cruelty is godlike and the acts pleasurable (1989:227-28).

Noddings seeks to write a phenomenology of evil from a "feminine" perspective. She advocates educating people to recognize structural and relational evils. Yet theodicists simply erase the horrifying concrete realities Noddings names by only seeing evil in the abstract as relevant to their projects. The possible connections between theodicy and sadism cannot be explored because theodicists cannot recognize them even as possibilities.

In sum, those who accept the theodicists' declarations can and do report that the evils in the world are sins and sufferings. That is the way the world is, for that is how the discourse of theodicy renders it. Structures of evil are either divinely sanctioned or tolerated (because they are natural) or merely the sorts of "passive evils" which are the result of "long years of slackness by many generations of men [sic]" (Swinburne 1977:84). And those who thus construe evil cannot hear the warning Noddings draws from the Marquis de Sade which intensifies the warning from Job: "Believe your fairy tales, fabricate your elaborate rationalizations, repress what you know to be true, de Sade suggests, and eventually the monster will burst forth, and that monster will be you in the image of God" (1989:220).

This leaves only one perlocutionary condition to be met if theodicy is to fit in the class of declarations. It must not be obvious to declarers or audiences that the declared state of affairs would have obtained if the declaration had not been issued. Perhaps even without the performance of a speech act of theodicy, or the initiation of the practice, the "declared state of affairs," the declaration of God's innocence of responsibility for what theodicists declare to be evils would still obtain. Perhaps it was obvious to the audiences of theodicies that social evil is and was a natural state of affairs. Perhaps no such strategies of the effacement and containment of evil were and are needed as part of a declaration. But these are counterfactuals, and there is no way to show whether counterfactuals of the past are true. I have tried to show it possible, if not obvious, that the discourse practice of theodicy was and is a practice which created and sustains the continued misdeclaration of evil. If one could demonstrate historically that only King or Leibniz or another Enlightenment theodicist could have made such a declaration to start the tradition with the effects as shown, then one would be able to identify an "originating event" for the practice. But such a demonstration seems impossible. Hence, it seems plausible to construe theodicy to be a declarative discourse practice whose origins developed in the seventeenth century. Although the "first engagement" in the practice is not clear, the emergence and continuing existence of the practice is sufficient to raise the question of the morality of those speech acts which instantiate the practice of theodicy.

## On Counteracting Theodicy

If theodicists misdeclare evil, they create a destructive discourse. Either they must engage in the continued practical and theoretical strategies which contain and efface the evils they miss, or the "traces" of the evils they exclude from the world which they declare to be real will cry out from oppression to show the incoherence of their declared world. Their exoneration of God cannot be sustained when evils are effaced or the world is incoherent. In the end, theodicy is a declaration which cannot but be a falsifying declaration which is either destructive or incoherent.

In the world theodicy declares to be real, the poison of an opiate becomes useful medicine for victims of oppression. The Marxian critique of religion as the opiate of the people, then, is correct for the world which theodicy declares real. The opium of religion treats the symptoms and leaves the structures of oppression intact. But it is far from clear that all religious traditions opiate people. Forms of religion other than those which valorize Enlightenment theism are stimulants to counteracting evils and to undermining structures of evil.

Yet even if the practice of theodicy is so destructive that its continuation perpetrates further evils, it is not possible to judge the practitioners of theodicy immoral. How could I—or anyone—have the unobstructed vision needed to be their judge, to declare them guilty? While one of the virtues of speech act theory is to reveal the moral component in writing and speaking in ways far beyond the desultory discussions of the possibility of justifiable deception, it does not offer an Archimedean perspective from which theodicists can be declared evil. Such a declaration would be as contextually determined and as perspectivally limited as those of the theodicists. It would be especially susceptible to ideological taint. It would attempt to efface their labor. It would presume that I, as the declarer of their guilt, could contain evil in my own discourse practices. Such a declaration would at best replicate the structures of the theodicists' own practices. Unless someone had achieved an Archimedean position or God's-eye view from which to make such a declaration, one could have an opinion about the morality of theodicy, one could argue against the discourse practice, but one could not make a declaration of individual theodicists' guilt.

Moreover, alongside the effacement and containment strategies for dealing with evil in theodical discourse, there is also a vision of a world that theodicists wish would be. Theodicy is not merely ideological; it is also utopian. It offers a vision of a world in which all evils would be effaced, in which all could live in peace. The reason that a monstrous generalization, or a staggering lie, can pass where a more restricted claim would be challenged is not only that it stabilizes an inherently unstable world by declaring it stable, but that it displays a world which we wished existed, a world in which evil was manageable, if not by us, at least by God. This is why the vast assertion, the mighty lie, overwhelms our faculties and puts our art of criticism out of action (cf. Farrer 1962:17): it holds out the boon of stability and fulfills our wishes.

But to write a theodicy is not merely to express a wish. Such writing is an illocutionary act which is not merely an expressive act, but a declarative act which makes 'true' what is only a wish. One of the evils of theodicy is that it effaces the difference between the world that theodicists wish to be (a world wherein God reigns) and the world that is.

It is not possible to write an "untainted" theodicy. This is not because one cannot have, and represent, a perspective on the whole. One can have a utopian vision, whether utopia is imagined as the reality of the kingdom of God or of the classless society or of some other construct. But to declare what the whole is presumes that there could be what Jameson calls "the vision of a moment in which the individual subject would be somehow fully conscious of his or her determination by class and would be able to square the circle of ideological conditioning by sheer lucidity and the taking of thought" (1981:283), or a moment when the individual could transcend her or his historical particularity. In Christian terms, only divine intervention could reveal a vision of the totality. And even if such transcendent vision could be achieved, it is not clear that any representation of it could ever be immune, or properly be thought to be immune, from the taint(s) of ideology or "original sin." A declaration of what History or Creation is truly, is beyond the capability of agents determined by History or Creation.

Moreover, the necessarily partial visions of the totality can provide no final criteria for the praxis which will bring a wished-for utopia into being. Utopian ideologies may motivate those who work for a reform of the present in a direction determined by a vision of utopia. That is their limit. The discrimination among praxes by global visions of the unreal (or the not yet realized) is inherently ideological. Praxis cannot be legitimated by utopian theory alone, but only by reflection on praxes and on what those who engage in those praxes create.

Yet even if no human can properly declare how everything really is, or infallibly warrant the claim that theodicies are destructive and distorting, we can use texts to interrupt the declarative process of theodicy, to reveal the true dimensions of the world it declares, to reconstruct the traditions it effaces, and to counteract its force. Examining the texts of Job, of Augustine, of Boethius, of Hume, of Eliot, serves these purposes. Noddings, Soelle, and Tiger reveal how other texts can resist the declaration of the way the world is by theodicy. In our era, most importantly, narratives of the Holocaust also must be deployed to counteract theodicy (cf. Surin 1986:146-51, 160-63).

One must write or read and remember such texts not merely to provoke "epistemological crises." One must deploy them so they can throw the declarative process itself into crisis. The "symbolic acts" of theodicy are hybrid speech acts, assertive declarations. They represent that segment of the actual world up to the point of the declarative action, and effect the segments of the actual world which include the action. But one key way to counteract theodicists' declarations is to confront them with interruptive texts. To the extent that we can marshal texts to resist theodicists' declarations, their distortions can be exposed, the aporias in their representations can be revealed, and their strategies of containment and effacement of evil can be aborted. In sum, these strategies provide ways to counteract theodicies, and thus to undermine their declarative force.

If theodicy is a destructive practice, and if declaring theodicists immoral is quixotic and hypocritical, then the task before us is to engage in counteractive interruptive actions to undermine theodicists' old strategies and make room for new strategies. Our own symbolic acts must not efface evils, but identify their multiple forms, understand the processes which produce them, retrieve discourses which reveal them, and empower the praxes of reconciliation which will overcome them. We must never forget that Victory over Evil may be impossible for us. The practices of discerning specific evils and counteracting them may seem pale and trivial in contrast to the glorious promise of devising totalizing final solutions to 'the problem of evil.' But final solutions, whether bloody or benign, are never final.

Theodicy accepts "both the rule of non-contradiction and that of systematic totalization" (Ricoeur 1985:635) and seeks to be a self-sufficient discourse practice. But confrontation with genuine evils shows that theodicies cannot be self-sufficient, noncontradictory, and total. They can be noncontradictory and total only if they are sustained by repression. This is possible only if theodicies are not successfully interrupted. They can be self-sufficient and total only at the cost of being self-contradictory; that is the real challenge of the Enlightenment problem of evil. Or they can be noncontradictory and self-sufficient if they give up being totalizing, that is, if they give up attempting to declare the Whole; they can become defenses (which are not solutions) or they can retreat more directly into declaring evil a "mystery of God."

Theodicy is truly an "impractical" practice. While it should never be forgotten, it must be counteracted and finally abandoned. To attempt to redeem it, for instance, by writing a new 'theodicy' which included social and structural evil, would be to engage in a new discourse practice, perhaps one in which the power of God was radically reconceived (cf. Suchocki 1988:passim). A traditional theodicy which dealt with social evil would be a justification of the human status quo, not of God. But such 'justifications' of structural evils litter the political ideologies of East and West, ideologies which legitimate the need for such structural evils 'for the good of all.' The self-deception of such an "anthropodicy" would not 'redeem' the discourse of theodicy, but magnify the evils of its declarations.

Within the Western traditions, the warning against theodicy sounded by the Book of Job is a warning all too often ignored. In the past, theodicists have declared what the evil in the world is. The point now, however, is to change the world by learning anew how to recognize the many forms and forces of evil and to counteract them, especially to counteract those discourse practices which perpetuate the power of evil practices by declaring them part of the natural process of the world or the divine plan for the world and thus efface them as actual evils in the real world.

## NOTES

1.    What follows in this section is especially indebted to Buckley, who has shown the historical circumstances in which the design argument became central, and to Surin, who has explored the emergence of theodicy. I tend to disagree with their analyses only in nuances. I would include more social and political determinants of discourse practices than Buckley sometimes does and find more continuities than Surin sometimes does. Stout's later text is more attuned to historical particulars than his earlier one, but still tends to abstract changes in discourse practices from their actual and historical material conditions.

2.    I see no way to show that one text is the "originating event," a communicative action which is the "first theodicy." One could dub one of a number of specific texts as the "first theodicy," but I am unable to see how such a determination would not be arbitrary. Buckley has shown the key intellectual event that makes theodicy possible: the shift of the arguments of natural theology out of theology proper and into scientific, common-sense, and philosophical discourse near the beginning of the seventeenth century. Moreover, the issue of relating evil and God is a concern of much of seventeenth century European letters. In this context, it seems practically impossible to designate a first actual theodicy. One could posit as an origin the 1622 publication of *Les Quatrains de Déistes ou l'Antibigot* and Marin Mersenne's 1624 response *L'Impiété des Déistes, Athées, et Libertines de ce temps* (Buckley 1987:56-58), which includes theodical themes. One could posit one of the numerous treatises and

tracts produced in the Puritan controversies in mid-century England as the origin, e.g., *The Originall Cause of Temporall Evils* published in 1645 by Meric Casaubon (Danielson 1982:32-34). One could also posit influential works by Leibniz or Samuel Clarke's Boyle Lectures of 1704 and 1705. Each of these has atheists or deists as its main polemical opponent; each debates on philosophical grounds; each seems concerned to establish the truth; and each uses a form of the design argument. Any one might be a candidate for being "first," depending on how one reads the text and context. King's text, however, is fully developed enough and so influential on both Bayle and Leibniz that it represents an early and classic example of the genre, even if it is not the "first" one.

One might argue that the real originating event was the publication of *Paradise Lost* in 1667 by John Milton. Yet despite its prayer to the spirit: "what is in me dark/Illumine, what is low raise and support;/That to the highth of this great argument/I may assert Eternal Providence,/And justify the ways of God to men" (I/23-26), and despite the fact that it contains argument about and explanation of the origin of evil, it is not an Enlightenment theodicy. First, its form is obviously not that of a treatise. Second, its portrayal of evils is quite "thick," not abstract. Third, the entity with the responsibility for moral evils is apparently Satan (Danielson 1982:102, citing III/129ff), a move not typical of theodicy. Indeed, the power of Satan is rarely invoked by theodicists. Fourth, the poem "entangles" the reader in a way in which philosophical texts simply do not (Danielson:10). Fifth, it is explicitly theological in that it portrays the hope of redemption by the Son, which Enlightenment theodicies typically do not. Sixth, it is rarely cited in any substantive manner in theodicists' writings.

While Danielson, strongly influenced by the philosophical tradition in theodicy, is surely illuminating in labelling *Paradise Lost* a "literary theodicy," that is an example of the extended use of the term "theodicy" (see p. 2 above). We are clearly in Danielson's debt for showing conclusively how deeply the theodical debates of his time influenced Milton. But *Paradise Lost* is not a theodicy.

3. *Pace* Surin, defenses are not a kind of theodicy. Surin does not distinguish the illocutionary forces of the problems and responses which structure the discourse practices of theodicy from those which structure the discourse practices of defense (cf. chapter 5). To use his terms, a defense is not a "signifying practice" (1986:50), but a repudiation of opponents' material significations. Defenses or defense-like practices do not necessarily carry the same presuppositions as Enlightenment-generated theodicies. Plantinga, whom Surin labels a theodicist, unfortunately follows the Enlightenment practice of separating theoretical from practical issues (1974a:29) and may accept the same vision of God as classical theodicists do. Nonetheless, "defenses" or "defensive strategies" like his are both abstractable from his material presuppositions and can be clearly appropriate practical therapy for those who have a "storm in the soul" generated primarily by attacks from academic challengers who claim that Christian beliefs are incoherent (see p. 216, note 12).

4. This possibility is at least prima facie inconsistent with Searle and Vanderveken's illocutionary logic. They postulate that one form of self-defeating illocutionary act is one in which the "illocutionary point cannot be achieved with the required mode of achievement of [the illocutionary force] on the propositional content" (1985:151). Their example is, "I order you to disobey all orders." To declare what is evil not to be evil would also seem to be self-defeating. However, to find an innocent person guilty of a crime in a court situation is not self-defeating. Rather, that speech act creates a new state of affairs, but one which falsifies facts. To perform successfully an assertive declaration incorporating a false assertion is to falsify (make false) the world. If neither speaker nor audience realizes the speaker's illocutionary

inconsistency (161), then the act is an effective falsification. That such is possible may be a symptom of what Marxists identify as alienation.

5.   For charts of the conditions for assertive declaration see pages 48-49 and 74. Although the conditions can be considered sequentially, they cannot be separated. Hence, to show that theodicy is a declarative practice requires assembling a cumulative case rather than simply charting conditions and showing how a typical act would meet them. Obviously, evidence adduced in the discussion of one condition is relevant to the discussion of the others.

6.   The same point could be made using the writings of other theodicists who also declare what is evil in as abstract a manner as Swinburne does. Cf. Hick 1978:262-64, 292-93, 318-19; Farrer 1962:21; Journet 1963:27-28, 50-57; Griffin 1976:252-56, 282-85, 292. The apparent exception is Suchocki, who is profoundly conscious of concrete social evils, but attributes them to the power of freedom in the contexts of finitude and community, especially when ideals are "born out of season" (1988:66). The responsibility of dealing with such evils, e.g., the exclusion of women from ministry, is the community's (73); but is it not also the case that the community (and not only the freedom in it) as it structures itself is also, at least in part, the cause of such evils? Suchocki seems to downplay this.

Suchocki, following Whitehead, also apparently denies that the dehumanization of humans is in any profound way evil. Such denaturing is said to be "self-imposed" (72), but that is not evident in all cases. If Boethian insights are correct, then Suchocki has profoundly underestimated the malignancy of the destruction of entities' potential to realize their nature.

Like Hick's Irenaean theodicy, Suchocki's process eschatology centers on the end rather than the origin of evil. Yet if "the end of evil is its continuous transformation in God beyond all history, which then provides possibilities of particular transformations in time" (155), then is not all evil merely prima-facie evil? Is there no genuine, irredeemable, concrete evil in Suchocki's world? Although Suchocki has begun to move beyond the individualism that afflicts the practice of theodicy, it is not clear that her vision can coherently include the reality of concrete evils as evil.

7.   In chapter 5, I used Griffin's distinction between prima facie and genuine evils as a way of retrieving what remains important in distinguishing these two sorts of *mala*. Although such a distinction as Griffin's seems formally legitimate, its use in material application is amenable to ideological distortion. Moreover, ideological distortion is so prevalent that constant vigilance is necessary. Feminists have worked to expose the ways the distorted language we use structures our perceptions. For instance, Mary Daly has shown how our use of "redundancy and contradiction" can disable us from perceiving evils:

> An especially important example of reversal by redundancy and contradiction is the elementary phrase *forcible rape*. This fallacious extension of the genus *rape* to include the redundant subcategory *forcible rape* opens the way for the absurdly contradictory subcategory *benign rape*. Indeed, re-searchers have actually referred to a pornographic depiction of rape that results in orgasm for the woman as a "benign rape." This phrase, of course, is a woman-battering device which invites and legitimates exploitation of women who cannot prove that their rapes were "forcible." The usage of this particular reversal paves the way for the legitimation of all sorts of woman-victimizing behaviors (1987:257).

The existence of the redundant linguistic usage "forcible rape" makes it possible to render some rapes only prima facie evil—a horrid state of affairs.

Hence, if one accepts the distinction, anyone arguing that a prima facie evil is not genuine must bear a heavy burden of proof, for a prima facie evil is one that is recognized by its causing someone distress. Alternatively, one could refuse to accept the distinction as having any nondistorting practical application, but that would seem to preclude any argument against painful practices which enable a person or society to move beyond present comfortable limits. Accepting the distinction and acknowledging its capacity for distortion seem to me preferable to rejecting it (cf. Farrer 1962:16).

8.   Those who find the Crucifixion the absolute center of Christian faith might find this claim overstated. Theodicists' ignoring the passion and death of Jesus would seem even more shocking from their perspective. At this point I can only state my view of the matter; I hope to explore it more fully in the future.

Those who do focus on the Crucifixion tend to concentrate on the suffering of Jesus on the cross and the suffering in which Christians must participate. They sometimes write as if Jesus' suffering alone saves (cf. Surin's discussions of Soelle, Moltmann and Forsyth [1986:112-36]). In doing so, they tend to ignore Jesus' healing practices (cf. Tilley 1985:101-15) and the other praxes of salvation in the Christian traditions. The strengths of the cross-centered approaches are that they avoid the strategies of containment and effacement typical of Enlightenment theodicy and the heavenly escapism too often part of 'spiritual' religion.

Yet some theologies of the cross seem to accept the suffering of Jesus as an instance of salvation through scapegoating. Others never connect the theological *doctrine* of atonement with the religious *practice* of atonement in any concrete way, especially the practice of the actual church (see D. J. Hall 1986:123-47). Others partake of a Christomonism which sounds at best like Orwellian doublespeak ("suffering is joy," "death is victory," "loss is gain") and at worst like religious sadomasochism (Soelle 1975:13-28). But the horrors of scapegoating are well described (Girard 1986). The separation of practice from doctrine simply undermines the credibility of the doctrine. And such Christomonism is escapist not because it advocates the 'paradoxes' of Christianity, but because it avoids providing even a notional understanding of how the Christian vision or myth dethrones the 'normal' meaning of such terms.

The narrative of the cross, like any story or experience of suffering or oppression, must interrupt 'normal' discourse (compare Surin 1986:159, 162-63) and reveal its strategies of containment. Yet the history of the Christian traditions shows how these same narratives can also be twisted to serve as foundations for even further oppression and effacement ("cheap grace" is the code often used to identify the belief in extrinsic redemption which contributes to oppression and effacement). But no narrative, even that of the suffering of God, can guarantee either that the cross will never be twisted again or that the praxis of atonement has a divine guarantee of certain success. The cross alone is not sufficient as a basis for Christian thought and reflection.

Rather, Christians collectively and individually must become agents of salvation, agents empowered to act to overcome the causes and effects of concrete evils in the world. Although many urge that Christians must realize the praxis of overcoming the social conditions which lead to suffering, no matter what the danger and cost, so far as I know only McClendon (1974) has tried to make the connection between doctrine and praxis by showing how the conviction of the atonement has structured the praxis of actual Christians in their "life-work." McClendon notes the constant presence of death and suffering in the praxis of reconciliation. But as the contexts in which the reconciliation of at-one-ment need to be actualized vary radically, so vary the praxes of Christians who participate in the divine praxis of atonement. Suffering is never sufficient for reconciliation nor ever to be sought. Yet agents of reconciliation (or participants in, not mere receivers of, grace, as D. J. Hall

1986:139 put it) must accept it for themselves as part of the praxis of atonement which aims at the overcoming of suffering and the conditions which bring it about.

Christians must neither efface the cross nor be exclusively cruciformed. While theodicists efface the scandal of the cross, their doing so is nothing new in Christianity.

# Works Consulted

The following list includes a few items not cited in the text, but which provided important background for the work. Save for the use of standard abbreviations as indicated for some classic texts, I use a standard social sciences referencing format.

Ackermann, Robert
  1982    "An Alternative Free Will Defense." *Religious Studies* 18(3): 365-72.
Adams, Marilyn McCord
  1986    "Redemptive Suffering." In *Rationality, Religious Belief and Moral Commitment*, edited by Robert Audi. Ithaca: Cornell University Press.
Alston, William P.
  1964    *The Philosophy of Language*. Englewood Cliffs, N.J.: Prentice-Hall.
  1981    "The Christian Language-Game." In *The Autonomy of Religious Belief*, edited by Frederick Crosson. Notre Dame, Ind.: University of Notre Dame Press.
  1985    "Plantinga's Epistemology of Religious Belief." In *Alvin Plantinga*, edited by J. E. Tomberlin and P. van Inwagen. Dordrecht: Reidel.
  1986    "Religious Experience as a Ground of Religious Belief." In *Religious Experience and Religious Belief*, edited by J. Runzo and C. K. Ihara. Lanham, Md.: University Press of America.
Alter, Robert
  1981    *The Art of Biblical Narrative*. New York: Basic Books.
  1985    *The Art of Biblical Poetry*. New York: Basic Books.
Amnesty International
  1984    *Torture in the Eighties*. London: Amnesty International.
Anscombe, G. E. M.
  1957    *Intention*. Oxford: Clarendon Press.
Ante-Nicene Fathers (cited by abbreviation)
  ANF:I   *The Ante-Nicene Fathers*, Vol. 1: *The Apostolic Fathers-Justin Martyr-Irenaeus*. Grand Rapids, Mich.: Eerdmans.
Aquinas, St. Thomas (cited by standard abbreviations)
  ST      *Summa Theologica*.
Arendt, Hannah
  1965    *Eichmann in Jerusalem. A Report on the Banality of Evil*. Revised and enlarged edition. New York: Viking.

Aristotle (cited by standard abbreviations)
  NE    *Nichomachean Ethics*. Translated by H. Rackham. Loeb Classical
        Library. Cambridge, Mass: Harvard University Press.
Audi, Robert, ed.
  1986    *Rationality, Religious Belief and Moral Commitment*. Ithaca: Cornell
          University Press.
Auerbach, Nina
  1982    *Woman and the Demon: The Life of a Victorian Myth*. Cambridge,
          Mass: Harvard University Press.
Augustine of Hippo (cited by title or abbreviation given)
  *Enchiridion*; see Barbel and Ernest Evans.
  *Confessions*. Translated and introduced by R. Pine-Coffin. New York:
    Penguin, 1984. Citations are to Book/Section.
  (Civ. Dei)*The City of God*. Translated by Henry Bettenson. New York:
    Penguin, 1984. Citations are to Book/Section.
  *Retractations*. Translated by Sister May Inez Bogan. The Fathers of the
    Church, vol. 60. Washington, D.C.: Catholic University of America
    Press, 1968.
  (*Ep.*)   *Saint Augustine: Letters*, vol. 3. Translated by Sr. Wilfrid Parsons,
            S.N.D. The Fathers of the Church, vol. 20. New York: Fathers of
            the Church, Inc., 1953.
  (Lib. Arb.) "The Free Choice of the Will." In *Saint Augustine: The Teacher,
            The Free Choice of the Will, Grace and Free Will*. Translated by Robert P.
            Russell, O.S.A. The Fathers of the Church, vol. 59. Washington, D.C.:
            Catholic University of America Press, 1967.
Austin, John L.
  1962    *How To Do Things With Words*. Reconstructed by J. G. Warnock.
          Cambridge, Mass.: Harvard University Press.
Bach, Kent, and Robert M. Harnish
  1979    *Linguistic Communication and Speech Acts*. Cambridge, Mass.: MIT
          Press.
Barbel, Joseph, translator and commentator.
  1960    *Aurelius Augustinus: Enchiridion de Fide Spe et Caritate; Hand-
          büchlein über Glaube Hoffnung und Liebe*. Testimonia: Schriften der
          altchristlichen Zeit, Band I. Dusseldorf: Patmos-Verlag.
Battersby, Christine
  1979    "The *Dialogues* as Original Imitation: Cicero and the Nature of
          Hume's Skepticism." In *McGill Hume Studies*, edited by David
          Fate Norton, Nicholas Capaldi, and Wade L. Robison. San
          Diego: Austin Hill.
Berger, Peter
  1969    *The Sacred Canopy: Elements of a Sociological Theory of Religion*.
          Garden City, N.Y.: Doubleday Anchor Books (first published,
          1967).
Berthold, Fred
  1981    "Free Will and Theodicy in Augustine: An Exposition and
          Critique." *Religious Studies* 17:525-35.

Blair, Alexander
  1984    "Christian Ambivalence toward the Old Testament. A Correla-
          tion among Some Issues in Philosophy, Theology and Biblical
          Studies." Unpublished Ph.D. dissertation. Graduate Theological
          Union, Berkeley.
Bok, Sissela
  1983    *Secrets: On the Ethics of Concealment and Revelation.* New York:
          Pantheon.
Boethius, Anicius Severinus Manlius
  1973    *Tractates, De Consolatione Philosophiae.* Translated by H. F.
          Stewart, E. K. Rand, S. J. Tester. Loeb Classical Library.
          Cambridge, Mass.: Harvard University Press.
  523     *The Consolation of Philosophy.* Translated with introduction and
          notes by Richard Green. Indianapolis: Library of Liberal Arts,
          1962.
Boone, Kathleen C.
  1989    *The Bible Tells Them So: The Discourse of Protestant Fundamen-
          talism.* Albany: SUNY Press.
Bowker, John
  1970    *Problems of Suffering in Religions of the World.* Cambridge:
          Cambridge University Press.
Brown, Peter
  1967    *Augustine of Hippo: A Biography.* Berkeley: University of Califor-
          nia Press.
Brown, Stuart C., ed.
  1977    *Reason and Religion.* Ithaca: Cornell University Press.
Brümmer, Vincent C.
  1982    *Theology and Philosophical Analysis: An Introduction.* Philadelphia:
          Westminster.
Buckley, Michael, S.J.
  1987    *At the Origins of Modern Atheism.* New Haven: Yale University
          Press.
Burns, J. Patout
  1988    "Augustine on the Origin and Progress of Evil." *Journal of
          Religious Ethics* 16/1 (Spring):9-27.
Carlisle, Janice
  1981    *The Sense of an Audience: Dickens, Thackeray and George Eliot at
          Mid-Century.* Athens: University of Georgia Press.
Carpenter, Mary Wilson
  1986    *George Eliot and the Landscape of Time: Narrative Form and Protes-
          tant Apocalyptic History.* Chapel Hill: University of North Caro-
          lina Press.
Cavell, Stanley
  1976    *Must We Mean What We Say?* Cambridge, Mass.: Harvard
          University Press.
  1982    "Politics as Opposed to What?" *Critical Inquiry* 9(1):157-78.
Childs, Brevard S.

1979    *Introduction to the Old Testament as Scripture.* Philadelphia: Fortress.
1985    *The New Testament as Canon: An Introduction.* Philadelphia: Fortress.
Chopp, Rebecca S.
1989    *The Power to Speak: Feminism, Language and God.* New York: Crossroad.
Clarke, Samuel
1964    *Demonstration of the Being and Attributes of God.* 1705. *A Discourse Concerning the Unchangeable Obligations of Natural Religion.* 1706. Facsimile reprint of the London edition. Stuttgart-Bad Cannstatt: F. Frommann.
Clebsch, William A.
1979    *Christianity in European History.* New York: Oxford University Press.
Cobb, John B.
1969    *God and the World.* Philadelphia: Westminster.
1981    "'The Problem of Evil' and the Task of Ministry." In *Encountering Evil*, edited by Steven T. Davis. Atlanta: John Knox.
Crenshaw, James L.
1981    *Old Testament Wisdom: An Introduction.* Atlanta: John Knox.
1984    *A Whirlpool of Torment: Israelite Traditions of God as an Oppressive Presence.* Overtures to Biblical Theology Series no. 12. Philadelphia: Fortress.
Crenshaw, James L., ed.
1983    *Theodicy in the Old Testament.* Issues in Religion and Theology Series no. 4. Philadelphia: Fortress.
Culler, Jonathan
1982    *On Deconstruction: Theory and Criticism after Structuralism.* Ithaca: Cornell University Press.
Curley, Thomas F., III
1986    "How to Read the *Consolation of Philosophy.*" *Interpretation: A Journal of Political Philosophy* 14(2 and 3):211-63.
Daly, Mary, and Jane Caputi
1987    *Websters' First New Intergalactic Wickedary of the English Language.* Boston: Beacon.
Danielson, Dennis Richard
1982    *Milton's Good God: A Study in Literary Theodicy.* Cambridge: Cambridge University Press.
Davidson, Donald
1973    "On the Very Idea of a Conceptual Scheme." *Proceedings of the American Philosophical Association* 17:5-20.
Davis, Steven T., ed.
1981    *Encountering Evil.* Atlanta: John Knox.
Denzinger, H., and A. Schönmetzer
DS      *Enchiridion Symbolorum, definitionum et declarationum de rebus fide et morum.* 35th ed. New York: Kenedy.

Derrida, Jacques
  1977    "Signature, Event, Context." *Glyph* 1. Baltimore: Johns Hopkins
          University Press.
  1978    "Limited, Inc." *Glyph* 2. Baltimore: Johns Hopkins University
          Press.
  1981    *Dissemination*. Translated by Barbara Johnson. Chicago: Univer-
          sity of Chicago Press.
Dowling, William C.
  1984    *Jameson, Althusser, Marx: An Introduction to the Political Uncon-
          scious*. Ithaca: Cornell University Press.
Duquoc, Christian, and Casiano Floristan, eds.
  1983    *Job and the Silence of God*. Concilium 169. New York: Seabury.
Eemeren, F. H van, and Rob Grootendorst
  1984    *Speech Acts in Argumentative Discussion*. Dordrecht, Holland and
          Cinnaminson, U.S.A.: Foris Publications.
Eissfeldt, Otto
  1965    *The Old Testament: An Introduction*. Translated by Peter R.
          Ackroyd. Oxford: Basil Blackwell; reprint edition, New York:
          Harper and Row, 1976.
Eliot, George
  1859    *Adam Bede* (citations to the New American Library edition, 1981).
Evans, Donald D.
  1963    *The Logic of Self-Involvement*. London: SCM Press.
Evans, Ernest, translator and commentator
  1953    *Saint Augustine's Enchiridion, or Manual to Laurentius Concerning
          Faith, Hope and Charity*. London: S.P.C.K.
Evans, Gillian R.
  1982    *Augustine on Evil*. Cambridge: Cambridge University Press.
Farrer, Austin
  1962    *Love Almighty and Ills Unlimited*. London: Collins (citations to the
          1966 Fontana Library edition).
Fish, Stanley
  1979    "Normal Circumstances, Literal Language, Direct Speech Acts,
          the Ordinary, the Everyday, the Obvious, What Goes without
          Saying and Other Special Cases." In *Interpretive Social Science: A
          Reader*, edited by P. Rabinow and W. M. Sullivan. Berkeley:
          University of California Press (also in Fish 1980).
  1980    *Is There a Text in This Class? The Authority of Interpretive
          Communities*. Cambridge, Mass.: Harvard University Press.
  1982    "With the Compliments of the Author: Reflections on Austin
          and Derrida." *Critical Inquiry* 8(4):693-721 (also in Fish 1989).
  1989    *Doing What Comes Naturally: Language, Rhetoric and the Practice of
          Theory in Literary and Legal Studies*. Durham, N.C.: Duke Univer-
          sity Press.
Fisher, Philip
  1981    *Making Up Society: The Novels of George Eliot*. Pittsburgh: Univer-
          sity of Pittsburgh Press.

Flew, Antony
1976    *The Presumption of Atheism*. New York: Harper and Row.
Frankenberry, Nancy K.
1981    "Some Problems in Process Theodicy," *Religious Studies* 18(2):179-97.
Frei, Hans
1974    *The Eclipse of the Biblical Narrative: A Study in Eighteenth and Nineteenth Century Hermeneutics*. New Haven: Yale University Press.
Furhmann, Manfred, and Joachim Gruber, eds.
1984    *Boethius*. Wege der Forschung, Band 483. Darmstadt: Wissenschaftliche Buchgesellschaft.
Gaskin, J. C. A.
1978    *Hume's Philosophy of Religion*. London: Macmillan and New York: Barnes and Noble.
Geuss, Raymond
1981    *The Idea of Critical Theory: Habermas and the Frankfurt School*. Cambridge: Cambridge University Press.
Girard, René
1985    *La Route Antique des Hommes Pervers*. Paris: Bernard Grasset.
1986    *The Scapegoat*. Translated by Yvonne Freccero. Baltimore: Johns Hopkins University Press.
1987    *Violent Origins*. Edited by Robert G. Hamerton-Kelly. Stanford: Stanford University Press.
Gordis, Robert
1965    *The Book of God and Man: A Study of Job*. Chicago: University of Chicago Press.
Green, Richard
1962    "Introduction." *Boethius: The Consolation of Philosophy*. Translated by Richard Green. Indianapolis: Library of Liberal Arts.
Grice, H. P.
1968    "Utterer's Meaning, Sentence-Meaning and Word Meaning." *Foundations of Language*, vol. 3. Dordrecht, Holland: D. Reidel Publishing Co.
Griffin, David
1976    *God, Power, and Evil: A Process Theodicy*. Philadelphia: Westminster.
Gutierrez, Gustavo
1973    *A Theology of Liberation*. Translated and edited by Sister Caridad Inda and John Eagleson. Maryknoll, N.Y.: Orbis.
1987    *On Job: God-Talk and the Suffering of the Innocent*. Translated by Matthew J. O'Connell. Maryknoll, N.Y.: Orbis.
Gutting, Gary
1982    *Religious Belief and Religious Skepticism*. Notre Dame, Ind.: University of Notre Dame Press.
Habel, Norman C.
1985    *The Book of Job: A Commentary*. The Old Testament Library.

Philadelphia: Westminster.

Habermas, Jürgen
1979 *Communication and the Evolution of Society*. Translated by Thomas McCarthy. Boston: Beacon.

Haight, Gordon S.
1968 *George Eliot: A Biography*. New York: Oxford University Press.

Haight, Gordon S., ed.
1955 *The Letters of George Eliot*, vol. 2. New Haven: Yale University Press.

Hall, Douglas John
1986 *God and Human Suffering: An Exercise in the Theology of the Cross*. Minneapolis: Augsburg.

Hall, Roland
1967 "Dialectic." In *The Encyclopedia of Philosophy*, edited by Paul Edwards, 2:385-89. New York: Macmillan and Free Press.

Hallie, Philip P.
1967 "Stoicism." In *The Encyclopedia of Philosophy*, edited by Paul Edwards, 8:22. New York: Macmillan and Free Press.
1985 "The Evil That Men Think—and Do." *Hastings Center Report* (December):42-45.

Hamerton-Kelly, Robert G., ed.
1987 *Violent Origins: Walter Burkert, René Girard and Jonathan Z. Smith on Ritual Killing and Cultural Formation*. Stanford: Stanford University Press.

Harré, Rom B.
1987 "The Displacement of Truth." In *The Rationality of Religious Belief: Essays in Honour of Basil Mitchell*, edited by William J. Abraham and Steven W. Holtzer. Oxford: Clarendon Press.

Harris, Errol E.
1977 *The Problem of Evil*. Milwaukee: Marquette University.

Harris, S. H.
1987 "The 'Naturalness' of Natural Religion." *Hume Studies* 13/1 (April):1-29.

Hauerwas, Stanley, and David Burrell
1977 "Self-Deception and Autobiography: Reflections on Speer's *Inside the Third Reich*." In *Truthfulness and Tragedy*. Notre Dame, Ind.: University of Notre Dame Press.

Henze, Donald F.
1970 "On Some Alleged Humean Insights and Oversights." *Religious Studies* 6(3):369-77.

Hick, John H.
1976 *Death and Eternal Life*. San Francisco: Harper and Row.
1977 "Remarks [on Phillips 1977 and Swinburne 1977]." In *Reason and Religion*, edited by Stuart C. Brown. Ithaca: Cornell University Press.
1978 *Evil and the God of Love*. Revised ed. San Francisco: Harper and Row.

Hoffman, Joshua
  1985    "On Petitionary Prayer" and "Reply to Eleonore Stump." *Faith and Philosophy* 2(1):21-29, 38-42.
Hume, David
  1777    *My Own Life.* In David Hume, *Dialogues Concerning Natural Religion,* edited with an introduction by Norman Kemp Smith. Indianapolis: Bobbs Merrill, 1947.
  1779    *Dialogues Concerning Natural Religion.* Citations to the Norman Kemp Smith edition. Indianapolis: Bobbs Merrill, 1947.
James, William
  1901    *The Varieties of Religious Experience.* Citations to the paperback edition: New York: Collier Books, 1961.
Jameson, Fredric
  1981    *The Political Unconscious: Narrative as a Socially Symbolic Act.* Ithaca: Cornell University Press.
Journet, Charles
  1963    *The Meaning of Evil.* Translated by Michael Barry. New York: P. J. Kenedy & Sons.
Kant, Immanuel
  1791    "On the Failure of All Attempted Philosophical Theodicies." Translated by Michel Despland in *Kant on History and Religion.* Montreal: McGill-Queen's University Press, 1973, 283-97.
Katz, Steven T., ed.
  1978    *Mysticism and Philosophical Analysis.* New York: Oxford University Press.
Kaufman, Gordon D.
  1987    "Mystery, Critical Consciousness, and Faith." In *The Justification of Religious Belief: Essays in Honour of Basil Mitchell,* edited by William J. Abraham and Steve W. Holtzer. Oxford: Clarendon Press.
Kearns, John T.
  1984    *Using Language: The Structures of Speech Acts.* Albany: SUNY Press.
Kemp Smith, Norman
  1947    "Introduction." In David Hume, *Dialogues Concerning Natural Religion.* Indianapolis: Bobbs Merrill. First published, 1935.
King, William
  1731    *An Essay on the Origin of Evil.* Translated by Edmund Law. London: W. Thurlbourn.
Kristeva, Julia
  1982    *Powers of Horror: An Essay in Abjection.* Translated by Leon S. Roudiez. New York: Columbia University Press.
Kropf, Richard W.
  1984    *Evil and Evolution: A Theodicy.* Cranbury, N.J.: Fairleigh Dickinson University Press.
Kushner, Harold
  1981    *When Bad Things Happen to Good People.* New York: Schocken.

Lanser, Susan S.
   1981    *The Narrative Act: Point of View in Prose Fiction.* Princeton: Princeton University Press.
Leibniz, G. W.
   1710    *Theodicy. Essays on the Goodness of God, the Freedom of Man and the Origin of Evil.* Translated by E. M. Huggard. Citations to the edition edited by Austin Farrer. London: Routledge and Kegan Paul, 1952.
Lerer, Seth
   1985    *Boethius and Dialogue: Literary Method in The Consolation of Philosophy.* Princeton: Princeton University Press.
Liddell, Robert
   1977    *The Novels of George Eliot.* New York: St. Martin's.
Lindbeck, George
   1984    *The Nature of Doctrine.* New Haven: Yale University Press.
Livingston, Donald W.
   1984    *Hume's Philosophy of Common Life.* Chicago: The University of Chicago Press.
MacIntyre, Alasdair
   1981    *After Virtue.* Notre Dame, Ind.: University of Notre Dame Press.
   1984    *After Virtue.* Revised and enlarged edition. Notre Dame, Ind.: University of Notre Dame Press.
Mackie, John L.
   1955    "Evil and Omnipotence." *Mind* 64:200-12.
   1982    *The Miracle of Theism: Arguments for and against the Existence of God.* Oxford: Clarendon Press.
MacLeish, Archibald
   1958    *J.B.: A Play in Verse.* Boston: Houghton Mifflin.
Maker, William A.
   1984    "Augustine on Evil: The Dilemma of the Philosophers." *International Journal for Philosophy of Religion* 15:149-60.
Martinich, A. P.
   1975    "Sacraments and Speech Acts." *Heythrop Journal* 16:289-303, 405-17.
McCabe, Herbert, O.P.
   1987    *God Matters.* London: Chapman.
McCarthy, Gerald, ed.
   1986    *The Ethics of Belief Debate.* Atlanta: Scholars Press.
McClendon, James W., Jr.
   1966    "Baptism as a Performative Sign." *Theology Today* 23(3):403-16.
   1974    *Biography as Theology.* Nashville: Abingdon.
   1986    *Ethics: Systematic Theology I.* Nashville: Abingdon.
McClendon, James W., Jr., and James M. Smith
   1975    *Understanding Religious Convictions.* Notre Dame, Ind.: University of Notre Dame Press.
McGill, Arthur C.
   1982    *Suffering: A Test of Theological Method.* Philadelphia: Westminster.

First published, 1968.

Milton, John
   1667    *Paradise Lost.* Citations are to Book/line as in *The Portable Milton.*
            Edited by Douglas Bush. Harmondsworth, England: Penguin.

Mitchell, Stephen
   1987    *The Book of Job.* San Francisco: North Point.

Morrisroe, Michael, Jr.
   1969a   "Rhetorical Methods in Hume's Works on Religion." *Philosophy
            and Rhetoric* 2:121-38.
   1969b   "Hume's Rhetorical Strategy: A Solution to the *Dialogues
            Concerning Natural Religion.*" *Texas Studies in Language and
            Literature* 11:963-74.
   1970    "Characterization as a Rhetorical Device in *Hume's Dialogues
            Concerning Natural Religion.*" *Enlightenment Essays* 1:95-107.
   1974    "Linguistic Analysis as Rhetorical Pattern in David Hume." In
            *Hume and the Enlightenment: Essays Presented to Ernest Campbell
            Mossner,* edited by William B. Todd. Edinburgh: Edinburgh
            University Press and Austin: University of Texas Humanities
            Research Center.

Mossner, Ernest C.
   1977    "Hume and the Legacy of the *Dialogues.*" In *David Hume: Bicen-
            tenary Papers,* edited by G. P. Morice. Austin: University of
            Texas Press.

Moule, Charles Francis Digby
   1982    *The Birth of the New Testament.* 3d ed. San Francisco: Harper and
            Row.

Muenchow, Charles
   1989    "Dust and Dirt in Job 42:6." *Journal of Biblical Literature* 103/4
            (Winter):597-611.

Murdoch, Iris
   1971    *The Sovereignty of Good.* New York: Schocken Books.

National Conference of Catholic Bishops (U.S.)
   1983    *The Challenge of Peace.* Washington, D.C.: United States Catholic
            Conference.

Noddings, Nel
   1989    *Women and Evil.* Berkeley and Los Angeles: University of Cali-
            fornia Press.

Noxon, James
   1966    "Hume's Agnosticism." In *Hume,* edited by V. C. Chappell.
            Garden City, N.Y.: Doubleday.

Nussbaum, Martha Craven
   1986    *The Fragility of Goodness: Luck and Ethics in Greek Tragedy and
            Philosophy.* Cambridge: Cambridge University Press.

O'Connor, David
   1983    "Swinburne on Natural Evil." *Religious Studies* 19: 65-74.

Ogden, Schubert M.
   1966    *The Reality of God.* New York: Harper and Row.

1978 "Evil and Belief in God: The Distinctive Relevance of a 'Process Theology'." *Perkins School of Theology Journal* 30:29-34.

Pagels, Elaine
1988 *Adam, Eve, and the Serpent*. New York: Random House.

Parkin, David, ed.
1985 *The Anthropology of Evil*. Oxford: Basil Blackwell.

Peake, A. S.
1905 "Job: The Problem of the Book." In *Theodicy in the Old Testament*. *Issues in Religion and Theology* no. 4, edited by James L. Crenshaw. Philadelphia: Fortress, 1983.

Peck, M. Scott
1983 *People of the Lie*. New York: Simon and Schuster.

Penelhum, Terence
1979 "Hume's Skepticism and the *Dialogues*." In *McGill Hume Studies*, edited by David Fate Norton, Nicholas Capaldi, and Wade L. Robison. San Diego: Austin Hill.
1983a *God and Skepticism*. Boston: Reidel.
1983b "Natural Belief and Religious Belief in Hume's Philosophy." *Philosophical Quarterly* 33:166-81.

Phillips, Dewi Z.
1965 *The Concept of Prayer*. London: Routledge and Kegan Paul.
1976 *Religion without Explanation*. Oxford: Basil Blackwell.
1977 "The Problem of Evil." In *Reason and Religion*, edited by S. C. Brown. Ithaca: Cornell University Press.
1981 "Belief, Change, and Forms of Life: The Confusions of Externalism and Internalism." In *The Autonomy of Religious Belief*, edited by Frederick Crosson. Notre Dame, Ind.: University of Notre Dame Press.
1985 "The Friends of Cleanthes." *Modern Theology* 1:91-104.

Pike, Nelson
1964 "Hume on Evil." In *God and Evil: Readings on the Theological Problem of Evil*, edited by Nelson Pike. Contemporary Perspectives in Philosophy Series. Englewood Cliffs, N.J.: Prentice-Hall.
1979 "Plantinga on Free Will and Evil." *Religious Studies* 15(4):449-73.

Plantinga, Alvin
1974a *The Nature of Necessity*. Ithaca: Cornell University Press.
1974b *God, Freedom and Evil*. New York: Harper and Row.
1979 "The Probabilistic Argument from Evil." *Philosophical Studies* 26(1):1-53.
1981a "Reply to the Basingers on Divine Omnipotence." *Process Studies* 11(1):25-29.
1981b "Is Belief in God Properly Basic?" *Nous* 15(1):41-52.
1983 "Reason and Belief in God." In *Faith and Rationality*, edited by A. Plantinga and N. Wolterstorff. Notre Dame, Ind.: University of Notre Dame Press.

Pojman, Louis
1986 "Faith without Belief?" *Faith and Philosophy* 3(2):157-76.

Pope, Marvin H.
1973     *Job*. The Anchor Bible, vol. 15. 3d ed. Garden City, N.Y.: Doubleday.

Pratt, Mary Louise
1977     *Toward a Speech Act Theory of Discourse*. Bloomington: Indiana University Press.

Priest, John
1985     "Job and J.B.: The Goodness of God or the Godness of Good." *Horizons* 12/2 (Fall):265-83.

Proudfoot, Wayne
1985     *Religious Experience*. Berkeley: University of California Press.

Quaesten, Johannes
1950     *Patrology*, vol 1. Utrecht: Spectrum; citations to the reprint edition, Westminster, Md.: Christian Classics, Inc., 1984.

Ramsey, Ian T.
1957     *Religious Language: An Empirical Placing of Theological Phrases*. London: SCM Press.
1968     "Polanyi and J. L. Austin." In *Intellect and Hope*, edited by T. A. Langford and W. Poteat. Durham, N.C.: Duke University Press.

Reiss, Edmund
1982     *Boethius*. Boston: Twayne.

Ricoeur, Paul
1967     *The Symbolism of Evil*. Translated by Emerson Buchanan. Citations to the paperback edition. Boston: Beacon, 1969.
1985     "Evil, A Challenge to Philosophy and Theology." *Journal of the American Academy of Religion* 53(4):635-48.

Rorty, Richard
1982     *Consequences of Pragmatism*. Minneapolis: University of Minnesota Press.

Roth, John K.
1981     "A Theodicy of Protest." In *Encountering Evil: Live Options in Theodicy*, edited by Stephen T. Davis. Atlanta: John Knox.

Roth, Leon
1969     "Job and Jonah." In *The Dimensions of Job: A Study and Selected Readings*, edited by Nahum Glatzer. New York: Schocken.

Rouillard, Phillippe
1983     "The Figure of Job in the Liturgy: Indignation, Resignation or Silence?" In *Job and the Silence of God. Concilium* 169, edited by Christian Duquoc and Casiano Floristan. New York: Seabury.

Rubenstein, Richard L.
1966     *After Auschwitz*. Indianapolis: Bobbs Merrill.

Rurak, James
1981     "Hume's Dialogues as a Drama: Some Implications for the Argument from Design." *Perkins Journal of Theology* 34 (Summer):16-33.

Russell, Bertrand
1957     *Why I Am Not a Christian*. New York: Simon and Schuster.

Sanders, Paul S., ed.
  1968    *Twentieth Century Interpretations of the Book of Job.* Englewood
          Cliffs, N.J.: Prentice Hall.
Scarry, Elaine
  1985    *The Body in Pain: The Making and Unmaking of the World.* New
          York: Oxford University Press.
Schoedel, William R.
  1985    *Ignatius of Antioch.* Hermeneia—A Critical and Historical
          Commentary on the Bible. Philadelphia: Fortress.
Schweiker, William
  1988    "Beyond Imitation: Mimetic Praxis in Gadamer, Ricoeur and
          Derrida." *The Journal of Religion* 68(1):21-38.
Searle, John R.
  1969    *Speech Acts.* New York: Cambridge University Press.
  1973    "Austin on Locutionary and Illocutionary Acts." In *Essays on J.
          L. Austin.* Oxford: Clarendon.
  1975    "Indirect Speech Acts." In *Speech Acts: Syntax and Semantics,* vol.
          3, edited by R. Cole. New York: Academic Press.
  1977    "Reiterating the Differences: A Reply to Derrida." *Glyph 1.* Balti-
          more: Johns Hopkins University Press.
  1979    *Expression and Meaning.* Cambridge: Cambridge University
          Press.
  1983a   *Intentionality.* Cambridge: Cambridge University Press.
  1983b   *Meaning.* Protocol of the 44th Colloquy, 3 October 1982. Berke-
          ley: Center for Hermeneutical Studies in Hellenistic and Modern
          Culture.
  1983c   "The Word Turned Upside Down." *New York Review of Books* (27
          October):74-79.
Searle, John R., and Daniel Vanderveken
  1985    *Foundations of Illocutionary Logic.* Cambridge: Cambridge Univer-
          sity Press.
Soelle, Dorothee
  1975    *Suffering.* Translated by Everett R. Kalin. Philadelphia: Fortress.
Stewart, Melville
  1986    "'O Felix Culpa,' Redemption and the Greater Good Defense."
          *Sophia* 25 (October):18-31.
Stout, Jeffrey
  1981    *The Flight from Authority: Religion, Morality and the Quest for
          Autonomy.* Notre Dame, Ind.: University of Notre Dame Press.
  1988    *Ethics after Babel.* Boston: Beacon.
Stove, D. C.
  1979    "The Nature of Hume's Skepticism." In *McGill Hume Studies,*
          edited by David Fate Norton, Nicholas Capaldi, and Wade L.
          Robison. San Diego: Austin Hill.
Strawson, P. F.
  1964    "Intention and Convention in Speech Acts." *Philosophical Review*
          73:439-60.

1973     "Austin and Locutionary Meaning." In *Essays on J. L. Austin.* Oxford: Clarendon.

Stroud, Barry

1977     *Hume.* The Arguments of the Philosophers Series. London: Routledge & Kegan Paul.

Stump, Eleonore

1979     "Petitionary Prayer." *American Philosophical Quarterly* 16(2):81-91.

1985a    "Hoffman on Petitionary Prayer." *Faith and Philosophy* 2(1):30-37.

1985b    "The Problem of Evil." *Faith and Philosophy* 2(4):392-423, 430-35.

Suchocki, Marjorie Hewitt

1988     *The End of Evil: Process Eschatology in Historical Context.* Albany: SUNY Press.

Surin, Kenneth

1986     *Theology and the Problem of Evil.* Oxford: Basil Blackwell.

Swinburne, Richard

1977a    "The Problem of Evil." In *Reason and Religion,* edited by S. C. Brown. Ithaca: Cornell University.

1977b    *The Coherence of Theism.* Oxford: Clarendon Press.

1979     *The Existence of God.* Oxford: Clarendon Press.

1981     *Faith and Reason.* Oxford: Clarendon Press.

1983     "A Theodicy of Heaven and Hell." In *The Existence and Nature of God,* edited by Alfred J. Freddoso. Notre Dame, Ind.: University of Notre Dame Press.

Taylor, Mark C.

1986     *Erring.* Atlanta: Scholars Press.

Tiger, Lionel

1987     *The Manufacture of Evil: Ethics, Evolution and the Industrial System.* New York: Harper and Row.

Tilley, Terrence W.

1978     *Talking of God: An Introduction to Philosophical Analysis of Religious Language.* New York: Paulist.

1984     "The Use and Abuse of Theodicy." *Horizons* 11(2):304-19.

1985     *Story Theology.* Wilmington, Del:: Michael Glazier, Inc.

1988     "The Principle of Innocents' Immunity." *Horizons* 15(1):43-63.

1989     "Intratextuality, Incommensurability and Fideism." *Modern Theology* 5(2):87-111.

1990     "Reformed Epistemology and Religious Fundamentalism." *Modern Theology* 6(3):237-57; also in *The Struggle over the Past: Fundamentalism in the Modern World,* the annual volume of the College Theology Society, edited by William M. Shea. Washington, D.C.: University Press of America.

Tracy, David

1981     *The Analogical Imagination.* New York: Crossroad.

1987     *Plurality and Ambiguity: Hermeneutics, Religion and Hope.* San Francisco: Harper and Row.

Tweyman, Stanley

1986     *Skepticism and Belief in Hume's Dialogues Concerning Natural*

*Religion*. Dordrecht: Martinus Nijhoff.

1987 "Hume's Dialogues on Evil." *Hume Studies* 13/1 (April):74-85.

Vink, A. G.
1986 "The Literary and Dramatic Character of Hume's *Dialogues Concerning Natural Religion*." *Religious Studies* 22:387-96.

Wadia, Pheroze
1979 "Philo Confounded." In *McGill Hume Studies*, edited by David Fate Norton, Nicholas Capaldi, and Wade L. Robison. San Diego: Austin Hill.

Watts, V. E.
1969 "Introduction." *Boethius: The Consolation of Philosophy*. Translated by V. E. Watts. Harmondsworth, England: Penguin.

White, Hugh C., ed.
1988 *Speech Act Theory and Biblical Criticism*. Semeia 41. Decatur, Ga.: Scholars Press.

Whitman, Jon
1987 *Allegory: The Dynamics of an Ancient and Medieval Technique*. Cambridge, Mass.: Harvard University Press.

Wiesel, Elie
1960 *Night*. Translated by Stella Rodway. New York: Hill and Wang.

Williams, B. A. O.
1963 "Hume on Religion." In *Hume: A Symposium*, edited by D. F. Pears. London and New York: Macmillan.

Wittgenstein, Ludwig
1958 *Philosophical Investigations*. 3d ed. Translated by G. E. M. Anscombe. New York: Macmillan.

Wright, James R. G.
1967 "Seneca." In *The Encyclopedia of Philosophy*, edited by Paul Edwards, 8:406-7. New York: Macmillan and Free Press.

Yandell, Keith E.
1979 "Hume's Explanation of Religious Belief." *Hume Studies* 5/2 (November):94-107.

# Index